SAS²

A Guide to Collaborative Inquiry and Social Engagement

Jacques M. Chevalier
Daniel J. Buckles

International Development Research Centre
Ottawa Cairo • Dakar • Montevideo • Nairobi • New Delhi • Singapore

 Los Angeles • London • New Delhi • Singapore
www.sagepublications.com

Jointly published in 2008 by

SAGE Publications India Pvt Ltd
B1/I-1 Mohan Cooperative Industrial Area
Mathura Road, New Delhi 110 044, India
www.sagepub.in

SAGE Publications Inc
2455 Teller Road
Thousand Oaks, California 91320, USA

SAGE Publications Ltd
1 Oliver's Yard, 55 City Road
London EC1Y 1SP, United Kingdom

SAGE Publications Asia-Pacific Pte Ltd
33 Pekin Street
#02-01 Far East Square
Singapore 048763

**International Development
Research Centre**
P.O. Box 8500
Ottawa, ON, Canada KIG 3H9
info@idrc.ca/www.idrc.ca
ISBN (e-book) 978-1-55250-418-5

Second Printing 2009

Published by Vivek Mehra for SAGE Publications India Pvt Ltd, Phototypeset in 10/12 pt Adobe Caslon Pro by Star Compugraphics Private Limited, New Delhi and printed at Artxel, New Delhi.

Library of Congress Cataloging-in-Publication Data

Chevalier, Jacques M., 1949–
    SAS² : a guide to collaborative inquiry and social engagement / Jacques M. Chevalier, Daniel J. Buckles.
        p. cm.
    Includes bibliographical references.
    1. Social sciences—Research.   2. Sociology—Research.   3. Social sciences—Methodology.
    I. Buckles, Daniel, 1955–   II. Title

| H62.C376 | 300.72—dc22 | 2008 | 2008039452 |

ISBN: 978-81-7829-890-0 (PB)

The SAGE Team: Sugata Ghosh, Richa Raj, Rajib Chatterjee, and Trinankur Banerjee

Contents

Foreword

As a grassroots development worker, nothing could be a greater treasure to me than this book. I have been engaged in the use of participatory methodologies for three decades with some of the most marginalized communities in India. As a filmmaker, I have also documented and observed participatory practices in many parts of the world. It is through these lenses that I clearly see the invaluable insights this Guide brings to participatory thinking and action.

The family of approaches that make up PRA (Participatory Rural Appraisal) is deeply rooted in grassroots practice and liberatory thinking. SAS² extends PRA's boundaries by adding concepts and techniques adapted from economics, psychology, and anthropology. While these are scholarly efforts in their own right, the authors' constant emphasis on the co-generation of knowledge marks the philosophy outlined in this book. This is critical for our times, an era that parades itself as the Knowledge Society. Never before in human history has the exclusion and marginalization of people's knowledge been so upfront and brazen. In the guise of creating "knowledge societies" we have brushed aside longstanding traditions of knowledge generation and sharing and turned control over to big corporations and the mass media, the true picture of an Orwellian Society in action.

It is in this context that I gladly welcome SAS² as a quest for a *"living knowledge that has the potential to advance the common good on a global scale"* (see the Introduction). In this search, I believe SAS² offers invaluable conceptual and practical tools for reclaiming a vast knowledge base within marginalized communities. I am someone who squirms at the phrase Knowledge Management—the term widely used in information and academic circles without a second thought to the manipulative connotations it contains. Contrasted with such an understanding, SAS² offers "Social Grounding" and "Mediation" through an *"act of interpretation [that] concludes a thinking process applied with skill through the efforts of all the parties involved"* (see the Foundations and Skillful Means). Interpretation acquires a far more powerful and democratic soul—communities make sense of reality, liberating the task of interpretation from the subjectivity and biases of the individual researcher and authoritarian expert.

While these principles form the foundation of this book, *SAS²: A Guide to Collaborative Inquiry and Social Engagement*, also does exactly what it says in its title. It actually guides us through various processes and techniques, lovingly explaining and concretizing for us the skills involved. This is readers' time well spent. The Guide will help even the uninitiated clearly understand the continuum of the five skills it proposes: mediating, grounding, navigating, scaling, and interpreting (sensemaking). The great strength of this book is that it expertly balances conceptual propositions with practical skills.

The processes and techniques of PRA introduced development practitioners to the extraordinary capacities of people to be collaborators in development research, opening up a wonderful world of participatory research with ordinary people. SAS² elevates this endeavor to a much higher level by showing how people in all parts of the world can competently engage in very sophisticated analyses of their own situations. This contribution to higher learning of the inclusive kind includes new ways of looking at social relations. The SAS[2] approach to stakeholder analysis explores *legitimacy* as a factor, alongside power and interests, thus moving beyond the "upper" and "lower" class thinking of PRA methods. SAS[2] also helps us think beyond restricted notions of community as either geography, or simply "communities of interests", encompassing instead a much broader and nuanced definition of community life. It shows how to achieve a better understanding of complex relationships in traditional community structures where multiple bonds of kinship, culture, and livelihoods adapt to specific environments and broader societies. This I see as a very positive contribution.

The fascinating multi-country examples in the Guide illustrate how SAS[2] principles apply in the real world. For me, the Guide explores the multiple layers of different realities. Whether in Bolivia, or Bangladesh, Navliwadi (India), or Nepal, the issues and tensions among stakeholders have the same complexities. The creative application of SAS[2] to such situations has had a profound influence on the analysis by the actors involved and on the decisions they have made. The examples in this Guide enrich the book as nothing else could have.

Three decades after the groundbreaking advent of PRA in International Development, and following serious criticisms raised in books such as *Participation: The New Tyranny?*, SAS[2] infuses fresh life and energy into participatory thinking and practice. The timing of this book could not have been better.

I have seen both Drs Daniel Buckles and Jacques Chevalier at work in different contexts, in Canada, in Bangladesh, in Kenya, and in India. The deep conviction they bring to their work combines in this book with a great scholarship and makes this a must read for everyone interested in development studies and participatory practices.

P.V. Satheesh
Deccan Development Society

Introduction

The Earth and its varied human and ecological communities are now facing large-scale problems, from global warming and reduced biodiversity to more inequality between the poor and rich. Violence and fears of escalation are rampant. These are major challenges that require a wholesale shift in how we inquire into real life problems and mobilize, or create knowledge to address them. To survive and flourish in a world fraught with uncertainty, we must learn to think and learn differently. What is at stake is nothing less than the practice of democratic engagement in the sphere of knowledge, and its application to all levels of our 'glocal' world, from a village engaged in planning sustainable development to regional, national, or international bodies involved in health, education, governance, or peace.

The need for a new approach to knowledge is clear. Knowledge can no longer be generated, accredited or communicated only in scientific, corporate and university-based settings that exclude and ignore many segments of society. There is a need, more pressing than ever, to engage all human beings, without exception, in the application and co-generation of knowledge. We must draw on the information, imagination, skills, meaning, and reasoning of many people, seeing their different views and the methods they use as "living knowledge" that has the potential to advance the common good on a global scale. The challenge is to raise all forms of inquiry to the power of two: making the inquiry both socially relevant and doing it collaboratively or socially.

Social Analysis Systems (SAS²) is an international initiative responding to this challenge (www.sas2.net). It offers a new approach to creating and using knowledge for the common good. The purpose is to broaden and deepen the range of concepts, tools, and transferable skills we can use to mobilize the power of human intelligence and creativity, and to act on our world.

SAS² is coordinated by Carleton University (Canada) in collaboration with a number of institutional partners around the world. Since 2001, the International Development Research Centre (Canada) provided several grants to support collaboration between Carleton University and institutions in Asia, Latin America and Africa, including the Academy of Development Science (India), the Bolivian Centre for Multidisciplinary Studies (Bolivia), Local Initiatives for Biodiversity, Research and Development (Nepal), the National Agriculture University (Honduras), the National Autonomous University of Honduras, UBINIG-Policy Research for Development Alternatives (Bangladesh), and the Conflict and Collaboration Program of the University for Peace (Costa Rica). As the initiative has become more public, many other people and institutions from around the world have joined in, applying SAS² to wider sets of circumstances. Communities of practice have emerged in fields ranging from natural resource management to public sector planning, organizational development, education, governance, conflict management, and project, or program monitoring and evaluation.

Part 1 of this Guide outlines the concepts that form the basis for the SAS^2 approach to collaborative inquiry and social engagement. It introduces the social analysis and all-purpose techniques as well as the Process Management (PMt) approach embedded in SAS^2. PMt promotes continuous planning and inquiry in the middle of uncertain and complex situations where multi-stakeholder collaboration is needed. This approach goes beyond conventional models of expert inquiry and linear approaches to planning such as Result-Based Management. General explanations about SAS^2 tools are followed by more detailed instructions on Process Manager (PMr), a step-by-step technique for integrating collaborative inquiry into project plans and activities. Part 1 also provides guidelines on how to design and facilitate SAS^2 events and processes and reports on the results. The instructions show how to select, sequence and scale techniques to meet a group's specific needs and how to integrate the techniques into project plans and ongoing activities.

Part 2 of the Guide presents a selection of techniques included in training towards Professional Certification in SAS^2, drawn from the collection of more than 50 tools and software on the SAS^2 website (www.sas2.net). The techniques are theoretically informed, rigorous and fully participatory. Their descriptions are sometimes highly technical, a feature that may mask the dynamic and collaborative nature of the processes they support. In real-life settings, they can be used in groups of various sizes and adapted to the needs of both literate and non-literate participants. The techniques are especially relevant for multiple stakeholder settings where social engagement and dialogue across differences is critical. Our approach builds on diverse contributions to participatory action research and at the same time challenges the naïve assumption that equality and empowerment can be achieved through quick-and-easy participation. The materials presented in the Guide support a shift towards flexibly-structured processes that bridge the gap between conventional inquiry based on "hard evidence" and participatory methods that emphasize "building consensus" as the principal goal.

This section also contains reports on real-life applications of techniques in South Asia and Latin America, with a focus on land issues, local economic development, and natural resource management. The examples point to the myriad ways people mobilize and create practical, authentic knowledge through interaction with the material world and with each other. A database of reports showing how SAS^2 is being applied in different settings is available on the SAS^2 website (www.sas2.net). Publications that enter more deeply into the conceptual foundations of SAS^2 and provide examples from other fields such as education, organizational development, and the public sector will follow.

In this Guide we use the word "you" to guide our readers in applying SAS^2 to concrete situations. This form of address can be ambiguous. In English "you" can be either singular or plural. Instructions in this form can also give the impression that we are speaking to the expert researcher or facilitator rather than the participants working in groups. Given these ambiguities, we ask readers to keep in mind that "you" can mean all people actually engaged in the process of inquiry, with or without expert facilitation, or third party support.

PART 1
SAS^2 Concepts and Process

Foundations and Skillful Means

You never change things by fighting the existing reality. To change something, build a new model that makes the existing model obsolete.

R. Buckminster Fuller

The Skillful Means to Wisdom and Dialogue

Theology, Reason, and Science have each had their days of glory in the Middle Ages, the Age of Reason, and the Modern Age. Each era has brought many vital insights into our understanding of the world and ability to act on it. But these forms of knowledge and learning have also been responsible for negative legacies that affect how humans interact with Nature and each other. The institutions of religion, philosophy, and science have too often supported hierarchies that blindly served authority. The effects of such hierarchies ranged from domination of all life forms by human beings to ensuring that powerful interests prevailed over the common good.

The global epoch we have now entered will embrace many forms of wisdom and dialogue, or it will not be. While humans will continue to build on previous accomplishments, this new, global age must also rise to the challenge of creating better and more effective forms of civic and social engagement to solve problems on a world scale. It must create synergies among the living knowledge of people from all parts of the world. This includes the almost one billion poor or marginalized people wrongly branded as "have-nots" and "know-nothings" with little to contribute to human history.

The concepts and tools presented in this Guide contribute to a critical shift towards greater collective wisdom and democracy in the creation and mobilization of knowledge. The focus is on complex settings involving many stakeholders and knowledge systems where both careful reasoning and dialogue across boundaries are urgently needed.

Skillful Means

As you consider the ideas and tools presented below, keep in mind our central purpose: to help people develop the skills they need to inquire into situations that do not lend themselves to easy solutions designed by experts alone. Creating and mobilizing knowledge for the common good does not depend simply on sharing the right information, having the right concepts, or using the right techniques. It hinges on the competency or "skillful means" that people bring to situations that are inescapably messy and unpredictable.[1] "Skillful means" refers to any method or strategy that is helpful because it is attuned to the capacities, needs, and circumstances of the people involved. The Guide should be read in this spirit, as a helpful set of concepts and tools that promote the practical wisdom to engage with others and the world we live in.

More than ever, universities are called upon to develop the competencies that people require to create and mobilize knowledge that is socially relevant. To achieve this vital goal they must focus less on the art of mastering existing bodies of knowledge, performing literature reviews, and debating abstract theories or models of change detached from people and practice. Instead, universities should rethink the nature of thinking and learning. This is particularly pressing in the social sciences, a field that places too much emphasis on students applying theoretical reasoning to social issues, at considerable cost to teamwork and collaborative problem solving. University approaches in the hard sciences have a different problem: students typically learn to apply exact knowledge to problems stripped of their social aspects. Graduates in both fields end up applying narrow sets of concepts or technical frameworks to each and every new situation.

Institutions of higher learning are still in a position to provide leadership in the use of diverse forms of knowledge to **engage creatively** with problems and people in complex and uncertain environments. New approaches to learning must mobilize collaborative thinking among people working both in academia and in other sectors such as government, the non-profit and voluntary sectors, community organizations, the media, philanthropic foundations, think tanks, institutes, consulting firms, and international bodies working in different fields. Our Guide supports this reorientation of "higher learning" by building on skillful means to engage in forms of thought and action that are socially relevant and embrace dialogue.

People-Based and Evidence-Based Thinking

The sections that follow describe the skill-set people must develop when applying wisdom and dialogue to problem solving. These skillful means combine **people-based inquiry** and **evidence-based thinking** into a holistic approach, in support of a *careful action-learning* process

---

[1] The term "skillful means", also known as the craft of compassion, is a Buddhist concept, from Sanskrit upaya-kaushalya. It emphasizes context and process in the selection and use of ways to help others realize their potential and the potential within a situation.

that brings together two important ingredients: the ability to think carefully, with rigor, and genuine caring for others and the world we live in.

On one hand, the Guide supports people-based abilities to:

1. Manage and **mediate** different views and knowledge systems; and

2. Maintain a sense of purpose and social **grounding**.

   The people-based approach of SAS^2 inquiry draws on some of the lessons of participatory action research in the field of development. It also draws from social actor and political economy theory, by looking at issues of stakeholder power, interests, legitimacy, and histories of collaboration and conflict. Several SAS^2 techniques build on social anthropology and psychology in a socio-constructivist perspective, by exploring and tapping into local knowledge and value systems in different cultural settings.

   On the other hand, the Guide also stresses evidence-based thinking based on the art of:

3. **Navigating** through methods of data gathering and analysis, especially methods that can deal with complexity; and

4. **Scaling,** or calibrating the level and kind of evidence, and inquiry needed in each situation.

   To facilitate evidence-based thinking and dialogue in the context of complexity, the Guide builds on concepts and tools adapted from (*i*) formal economics and management science, and (*ii*) chaos and complexity theory. These adaptations show how to assess different resource-and risk-management strategies while also dealing with situations that are messy, that is, filled with uncertainty and the unknown.

   The last skill described in the Guide is perhaps the most advanced form of active learning within SAS^2. It involves the art of:

5. **Interpreting,** or making sense of complex information and situations.

   Interpreting the findings of a complex inquiry is not an easy task, as most researchers know too well. The task becomes less daunting, however, when it involves a mediation of different perspectives and is grounded in real situations that are meaningful to the people involved. Interpretation is also less arduous when the process of inquiry relies on techniques that are properly selected and combined to create sound and relevant evidence. The analysis becomes all the more meaningful when it is owned by all participants and managed at a scale that suits a common purpose.

THE SKILLFUL MEANS OF SAS²

MEDIATE: SAS² practitioners learn to support reasoning and dialogue among people with different perspectives, across disciplines and in many cultural settings. This requires an ability to suspend judgment, consider the views of others, and integrate the diverse interests and rich knowledge that people bring to problem-solving.

GROUND: To be relevant, inquiry needs to be systemic. That means ground thinking in the middle of ongoing events and processes meaningful to the people involved.

NAVIGATE: Complexity is the norm. Navigating in the uncertainty and unknown requires the means to select and combine multiple forms of inquiry, planning, and action.

SCALE: The level of evidence, analysis, participation, and planning needed by a group in a particular situation is not fixed. The art of scaling is in choosing the right mix of tools and adjusting their level of application to fit the job.

INTERPRET: Making sense of complex information involves analysis and telling a story. Dialogue and reasoning can do both. Together they create meaning that can bridge gaps between competing theories and perspectives and between quantitative and qualitative data gathering.

> When these conditions are met, the act of interpretation concludes a thinking process applied with skill through the efforts of all the parties involved.

People-Based Inquiry: Mediating and Grounding

Five skillful means must be combined to achieve a holistic approach to collaborative inquiry for the common good. The first skill involves being able to suspend judgment and **mediate** different views and knowledge systems. Instead of relying only on their professional understanding of reality, researchers, evaluators, analysts and planners must also learn to listen, mediate, and integrate different perspectives, including informed views not backed by institutional accreditation. They must learn to see and value other forms of expertise and the richness of all expressions of learning. People qualified to conduct rigorous inquiry and planning must develop a way of looking at the world and creating processes that allow diverse viewpoints and forms of knowledge to emerge in complex situations. Even as they offer their own views and knowledge, all experts must take up the challenge of making social inquiry, reasoning, and true dialogue possible, thus helping to break down the walls between theories, disciplines, cultures, belief systems, genders, castes, and classes. This can happen by bringing many voices and kinds of knowledge into the service of inclusive inquiry and decision-making. Dialogue is particularly important when power conflicts are acute and readiness for listening and reasoning is in short supply. Managing and mediating different views and knowledge systems then becomes essential to reaching viable solutions.

Enabling the social mediation of knowledge is not an easy skill to acquire. Institutions of higher learning can contribute to development of this skill as part of their own mission by questioning the tidy division of labor that separates the researcher from the teacher, the learner, the planner, the facilitator, and the activist. Instead of isolating people and their skills into slots, university programs should help students learn the art of wearing many hats. Future analysts and planners, in particular, must learn to apply their own professional skills while also acting as learners, citizens, and stakeholders in their own right. If universities are to help change the world, a complex and urgent task if ever there was one, they must encourage academics to change their own world, by taking on many and complex roles in the work they are called to do.

Managing and mediating the knowledge of different actors is really only feasible when it is done with a sense of direction and a good grasp of the history behind the immediate situation. This requires another skillful means, which is to **ground** inquiry in a social purpose or intention to act socially. Unfortunately, the skillful means to ground thinking are often ignored in academic settings and programs. In fact, questions about the relevance and broader impact of course-based learning and disciplinary research are seldom asked and poorly answered. Doing studies that are driven mostly by curiosity and personal interest is valid and should not simply be set aside for the sake of applied research. However, students and researchers should also acquire the skill to design questions and a process of inquiry that engage people involved in real events. This means integrating the inquiry into social actions that are part of broader processes. Only then will the knowledge created reflect "meaningful events", rather than producing "eventless" documents shelved in filing cabinets, bookcases, scholarly journals and libraries, real or electronic.

Participatory Action Research

The concepts and tools in this Guide promote inquiry that is socially mediated and grounded. They also incorporate lessons from current and past efforts to engage people in research for social change. These lessons include Participatory Action Research (PAR). PAR and its variants provide a strong body of theory and practice rooted in the social reform movements of the late 19th century, as applied in the fields of international development, social psychology, industry, agriculture, and education. The approach is based on the principle of inquiry into the actual or proposed actions of people, by and with those affected. As such, it differs from research conceived and executed by experts far from the people studied and the actions or processes under investigation.

The key challenge in both the theory and practice of PAR lies in the exercise of power by those who convene the activity. This is especially the case when PAR is started and directed by more powerful outside actors whose goals and methods are linked directly to their mandates and problem definitions. In principle, local people are then invited to contribute to decisions about projects by being part of a PAR process. In reality, they may have little scope to challenge the agenda or argue for other methods to approach the problem. As a result, a PAR exercise may simply uphold assumptions and solutions already built into the process.

The tendency to impose participatory structures and pre-defined goals may be compounded by other limits often observed in the practice of PAR. First, communities tend to be defined geographically, in keeping with a romantic concept of society that glosses over the internal differences and the external factors embedded in community life and social history. Second, PAR often takes for granted that the ideal level and form of participation is universal—things are done with as many people as possible, especially at the community level, regardless of their actual relationship to different project activities or goals. This can become a moral imperative that is time-consuming, creates many expectations, and can produce poor results. Third, techniques to facilitate participation in particular projects and events can wrongly be seen as a substitute for the larger and much more difficult exercise of democracy and justice in all spheres of life. These larger goals cannot be achieved simply by creating participation in a particular process, such as mapping existing assets or rating different options, for instance. Fourth, PAR tends to focus on quick-and-easy field research and a "cafeteria" approach to the techniques used. It offers few new concepts and practices to improve **evidence-based** research. This tends to marginalize it from mainstream learning and academic research institutions and from public policy-making processes. Finally, while PAR may be sensitive to community life and local knowledge, it lacks practical tools to delve into local culture and value systems and the distinct ways people create new knowledge and meaning.

The holistic approach adopted in this Guide seeks to overcome these problems by creating flexibly structured processes that support inquiry and dialogue in context and across social and knowledge boundaries. The approach uses concepts and tools from the social sciences to tap into the richness of culture and value systems and address broader issues of social structure and power. Participation is defined as the interactive engagement of stakeholder groups viewed as "communities of interest" (including those who convene the event, group representatives, and the community of all stakeholders). It involves doing the right thing with the right people at the right time, bringing together (*i*) fact finding and analysis by all knowledgeable parties, and (*ii*) negotiated views of problems and options for action. The objective of this approach to collaborative thinking and social engagement is to eliminate extractive and socially irrelevant inquiry managed "from outside".

Strategic and Progressive Engagement

The concept of "communities of interest" (as used in stakeholder theory) is central to the exercise of mediation and grounding and to many techniques offered in this Guide. Our usage of this concept is modified, however, in light of other ideas from political economy and social anthropology. Models based on the stakeholder concept contribute to collaborative inquiry and social engagement by helping to name the groups and institutions involved in a situation. They also show how existing or proposed actions may affect their interests. Stakeholder analysis looks at the resources, influence, authority or power that stakeholders can apply to a situation, and their real, or potential opponents and allies. It also considers the constant interaction of communities of interests, thus bringing together the local and global factors of social history and recognizing the critical role of differences in power and interests.

Stakeholder analysis is a social actor alternative to positivist methodologies that pay little attention to how people act on their own real life conditions. It also questions much of the standard wisdom of stratification theory and political economy based on handy class definitions that can be applied to all situations. Stakeholder analysis thus urges social thinking and inquiry that reflects particular contexts and is pragmatic. The focus is on specific social actors and what they can do to solve problems and achieve their goals using the power and resources they already have or seek to obtain.

There remain, however, many conceptual and methodological problems with stakeholder analysis. Tools for stakeholder analysis are descriptive and often too schematic. They assume that problems, interests and groups have clear boundaries and are stable over time. They tend to neglect issues of stakeholder domination, means to empowerment for marginal or voiceless groups, and public representations of the common good. As well, the analysis often ignores the question of who should conduct the inquiry and for what purpose—who is affected by the inquiry itself and who should be involved in that process? Social analysis is then done in a top-down fashion, with a neo-corporatist view that seeks to promote "dialogue" without challenging existing relations of domination and subordination operating at many levels within the increasingly integrated world we live in.

The Guide builds on and adjusts stakeholder analysis in several key ways. First, it suggests a **strategic** and **progressive** approach to **engagement** by focusing on (*i*) those parties that *can and should* be involved in the inquiry process, and (*ii*) those social relations where empowerment is needed and possible through the use of collaborative inquiry and social engagement for collective action. This change may appear to be minor, but it raises three tricky questions about **group boundaries**: (*i*) when to separate a group into various stakeholders, (*ii*) when to lump certain actors into one stakeholder group, and (*iii*) when to recognize the community of all stakeholders as a group with its own profile. These questions are not to be asked only by those who convene an event. They should be addressed by all those directly involved, or who will be affected by the answer. The way people respond to questions about how a group is composed and represented must reflect the context and purpose of the inquiry, and also the fact that some people may belong to more than one stakeholder group. Wearing many hats is often true of leaders and public officials who have their own stakeholder profile at the same time as they speak and act for broader groups.

Second, the Guide adds depth to stakeholder analysis by offering flexible tools to explore key factors shaping the course of social history. These factors include **power, interests, legitimacy**, and also:

(a) the positions, values, and commitments that stakeholders express in real situations,

(b) the networks of information that exist between them, and

(c) the record of trust, collaboration and conflict that apply to the situation.

The way these factors are played out in each situation affects the **stakeholder structure** and description of current and possible scenarios. By exploring these scenarios and the key problems they raise, **strategies** can be found to manage them. This may involve taking steps to transform certain social relations, including measures of cooperation and compromise to reduce conflict, efforts to empower weaker and vulnerable groups, or appeals to public values of justice and the common good.

Anthropology and Socio-Constructivism

The need to mediate and ground thinking for the common good raises another basic issue: the extent to which ideas borrowed from the social sciences reflect how actors view themselves and define social categories and relations in their own language and context. Can terms such as power, legitimacy, representation, collaboration, or conflict be carried from one cultural setting, or time to another setting, or time without a change in meaning? What should we do when the "stakeholder" concept does not fit with local values and practices that refuse to address individual, or group interests openly? Shouldn't stakeholders involved in the inquiry process make use of the knowledge and values embedded in their own language and the terms they use for social analysis? Shouldn't social scientists adapt their concepts to reflect how people construct their social worlds and the **cultural values** that guide their individual or group behavior?

Knowledge, Values, and Culture

Everyone who is committed to collaborative inquiry will recognize the importance of culture and local knowledge systems. But there are very few methods that provide the skills that people must apply if they are to "walk the talk". In this Guide, methods adapted from psychology provide unique answers to the crucial question of how to mobilize cultural values and systems of knowledge and learning. Techniques such as *Domain Analysis, Problem Domain, Social Domain, Value Domain and Option Domain,* with their roots in Personal Construct Psychology, offer both simple and advanced ways to build on local knowledge and value systems, using methods that avoid fixed terms and ideas and

Domain Analyses

make use of differences in language and culture. These techniques provide actor-driven exercises in ethno-sociology, ethno-politics, ethno-ecology or ethno-medicine, depending on the topic area that people choose to explore. Rather than simply finding out what views people share, social construct analysis offers the advantage that all parties may learn from each other and negotiate views across social and cultural boundaries. Participants, not just those who convene an event (or the expert), negotiate and construct their own knowledge and value systems and apply them to problems and solutions they define.

Domain analysis emphasizes the importance of tapping into the cultural richness and vitality of specific knowledge and learning systems. The techniques go far beyond current anthropological methods where local knowledge is reduced to describing and observing (the features and uses of plants, for instance). They also challenge anthropological views that ignore change in "traditional" systems or suggest that a local knowledge system remains authentic only when it remains intact. With social construct analysis, knowledge is inseparable from new learning based on problem solving and conversations across social and cultural boundaries. The approach embedded in these techniques recognizes that ideas and practices from mixed sources tend to be the rule rather than the exception.

System Dynamics

Our response to the challenge of collaborative inquiry and social engagement in different cultural settings also includes a set of techniques that focus on the complex and dynamic interaction of elements in social life and natural history. These include techniques to assess the interaction of actors (*Network, Role, or Social Dynamics*), skills (*Skill Dynamics*), values (*Value Dynamics*), problems (*Causal Dynamics*), activities (*Activity Dynamics*), and elements in nature (*System Dynamics*). These techniques to assess systems of interaction assume that every knowledge and learning system creates (*i*) differences between parts of a system that are thought to be distinct (social categories of actors, for instance) but also (*ii*) rules on how parts interact and relate to the whole and, (*iii*) opportunities to challenge and improve both the parts and the whole (transform class positions and class structure, for instance).

Many theories in the social sciences reflect on how to improve the dynamic integration of parts within a social reality (such as genders or classes, towards greater justice and equality). This may involve real efforts to create synergy and whole system harmony and adaptability. However, the contents and meanings of real systems and ways to harmonize them inevitably depend on how the elements are separated in the first place (into genders, classes, castes, life forms, and so on). Our view is that the drive to think "holistically" must always be expressed with local color and flavor and cannot be tackled through universal categories that apply to all possible settings.

In recognition of this fact, techniques described in this Guide *do not propose any particular version of what a complete or harmonious system should look like.* From a SAS^2 perspective, no complete theory or model applies to all situations. Instead, we propose a set of concepts and tools that is advanced and flexible enough to allow people to construct their own explanations, interpretations or theories of real life situations and dynamics. People can then use the models they develop to create new insights and act on reality at the same time. In our global age, whole system thinking (in health, education, development, or any other field) can "make a difference" only if it recognizes differences in the way that people actually think. SAS^2 tools are thus designed to support and ground the development and interactive engagement of different perspectives on real issues that shape the course of social history. This creates the possibility of authentic dialogue across boundaries and between people and knowledge systems.

Evidence-Based Inquiry: Navigating and Scaling

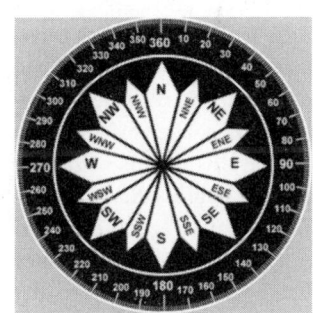

In this Guide, concepts and tools adapted from participatory action research, social actor theory, anthropology, and psychology support the involvement of key actors in an inquiry process that builds on different ways of knowing, learning, and acting. The thinking that results is socially mediated and grounded, allowing all subjects to speak directly and contribute to problem solving and social engagement in ways that reflect different value systems and cultural settings.

The Guide advocates a people-based approach to mobilizing and generating knowledge for social change. It also incorporates an evidence-based approach to inquiry, one that applies reason and judgment in complex and uncertain situations. To be more precise, the Guide suggests and illustrates two skillful means to advance evidence-based thinking in messy, real-life conditions: navigation and scaling. To act in our complex world, we need to learn the art of browsing and **navigating** in many fields and forms of learning, communication, and knowledge mobilization. Applying the same recipe or standard method of surveys or public meetings to all situations will not produce sound thinking based on solid information and reliable analysis. Today's researchers and planners must be able to find the information they need, select the correct tools, and then adapt and sequence those tools in ways that fit the situation. They must learn to sift through many sites and sources of knowledge, technology, methods of inquiry, and ways of facilitating dialogue and social engagement.

The Guide invites you to develop these important navigational skills. It supports "log navigation": users log in and out of different sets of inquiry techniques and engagement strategies, to combine forms of knowledge and learning. This flexible way of moving around extends to the task of browsing and navigating in and out of SAS[2] itself. The strategies for collaborative inquiry that we propose, must be combined with other learning and problem-solving methods, including expert consultation and local knowledge systems, that people may need to achieve their goals.

Building flexible navigation skills into the way knowledge is managed and created, is most critical when instability and uncertainty wreak havoc with plans. As in the medical profession, inquiries into messy problems require tools and methods that can adjust to change and the unforeseen. The mainstream approach to project management—analyze first, plan second, and implement third—is not well suited to complex human systems. You cannot predict the outcomes of trying to defuse a conflict or adapt to climate change so simply. In fact, it becomes irrational and may be very costly when plans are followed too rigidly, without adjustments to uncertainty and changing conditions. Most of the plans we create are in fact just working hypotheses colored with uncertainty; having to adapt to the unknown is actually how things are. Messy, real-life events call not only for logic and rigor but also for the kind of creativity and flexibility that allows people to move in and out of specific plans in response to new circumstances and information acquired along the way.

In complex situations, mediating and grounding the inquiry process calls for strategies of flexible navigation. They also require an ability to **scale** the process of collaborative thinking—knowing how to judge the level of evidence and public engagement required in each situation. In a perfect world, every inquiry would be complete and carry with it full agreement from all the parties involved. In reality, situations often need to be assessed quickly, with partial data and where views clash. When this happens, the only rational course of action is to scale the inquiry to meet the level of evidence and degree of consensus that can reasonably be achieved under the circumstances. This means using the knowledge that is already available and relevant while adjusting the collection of new data or information to a level that is "good enough" for key decisions. These estimates cannot be made mechanically. They require that all parties discuss and judge the situation and design the means of collaborative thinking accordingly. Doing this is particularly important in complex situations that involve moving between local, multisite and nationwide scales of information gathering, analysis and interactive engagement.

The Good-Enough Principle

Managing for Results and for Complexity

To adjust to situations of relative chaos and complexity, people engaged in the inquiry process must learn to scale up or scale down the kind and level of evidence, participation and planning that reflect their needs and the situation at hand. Being able to select from and scale (or calibrate) a flexible set of tools helps people design a process that works in the context.

Result-Based Management

Fields such as public administration, organizational development, and business management use a somewhat narrow range of methods to plan and manage projects. Famous among these methods, especially in the public sector, are those that involve managing for results—formally known as Result-Based Management (RBM). RBM begins with setting expectations that reflect common goals and specific objectives. Then, activities are designed and managed to achieve the expected results. The clear focus on results and the rational planning of ways to achieve results is a way to hold organizations and people accountable. The process involves a chain of causes and effects that unfold efficiently if based on the right inputs, such as sound analysis and the correct financial and human resources. Over the years, RBM and other planning and management methods such as Logical Frameworks have evolved to include critical reference groups in key stages of the project cycle, such as goal definition, information gathering, project planning and implementation. As such, they inject participatory principles into the planning process.

This way of doing management science, while rational, lacks reason in one important way: it brings rigidity into planning and management where **unpredictability** and **uncertainty** prevail. Reasoned planning where unpredictability and uncertainty exist, and with limited knowledge of key factors, leads to actions that are mechanical and linear. It deprives people of the flexibility they need to achieve desired results under changing circumstances. In complex situations, RBM produces closed-system plans that are too simple and that may hide reality behind defined goals and projects.

Process Management

This Guide provides an approach to planning called Process Management that can be used in complex, unpredictable situations common in the fields of development and social change. Process Management differs from RBM in many ways. For one thing, it allows gaps and details to be defined along the way, rather than planning everything at the start of a project when expectations may be too grand or vague to be rational. Process Management supports planning at the right level of detail, neither so general as to be of little use, nor so specific as to ignore the fact that some things are unknown, or hard to foresee. It also supports planning at the right time, which is any time it is needed, and not only

at the start of a project cycle. As in medical practice, planning becomes a form of continuous thinking grounded in ongoing activities. The result is a series of **working hypotheses** to be tested "in the middle" of complex situations that have no clear start or end. Outcomes (such as sustainable forest management) create new processes with goals and challenges of their own. Results cannot be fully defined in advance, and the need to adjust goals and actions is expected, even when well-crafted plans are implemented with due rigor.

Unlike RBM, Process Management does not assume that the same goals need to be shared by all the people involved. The method allows stakeholders to pursue different goals or activities within a common project. It also admits that in almost any situation, information is not complete and some actors have much better information than others. Action does and must proceed despite these gaps, uncertainties, and problems of asymmetric information. Under such circumstances, the planning process must respond to many interests, to information gaps, to ongoing needs for information, and to changing circumstances. With Process Management, plans are made at the right time and adapted to ongoing results, which means that each step of the process can create inputs for the design of later steps. People can then apply new learning to social action guided by practical wisdom and a sense of purpose.

Process Management helps planners bridge the gap between macro-management (focused on larger goals and processes) and micro-management (focused on precise events or activities). The approach can be combined with RBM-types of planning when parts of a project are predictable (such as organizing a public event or producing a publication).

Another key feature of Process Management is that it introduces the social dimension into project planning. The Guide shows how to achieve this: it combines Process Management with tools that support careful analysis of *the actors* involved in a project or situation, *the problems* they are facing, and *the options* for action they may use to solve these problems and achieve their goals. This blending of continuous planning and social inquiry allows people to take up the challenge of complexity in real life projects. It involves a reasoning process that can be used in completely different situations, without necessarily applying the same strategies or tools and without necessarily achieving the same results.

The overall approach proposed in this Guide is an open, complex systems approach to thinking, dialogue, and action. By combining Process Management with practical tools for collaborative inquiry and social engagement, SAS² addresses several problems common in the field:

(a) Methods that neglect social factors;

(b) Research and planning frameworks that are linear and rigid, to be followed faithfully even when they produce poor results;

(c) Inquiry that is limited to formal investigation and evaluation methods applied at fixed moments in a project cycle;

(d) Models and methods that are sketchy, or so conceptual that only experts can master them; and

(e) Techniques and toolboxes that are scattered.

Being Systematic and Being Systemic

Another common problem with conventional research is the length of time needed to complete a process of inquiry and the absence of interaction between all the key moments in a process of collaborative inquiry and project management. The key moments go from asking the right questions to gathering information, analyzing and interpreting the results, writing about the findings, sharing them with others, deciding on a course of action after the inquiry, implementing plans for action, and then evaluating the results on a periodic basis and at the end of a project. The long interval separating the different moments of the typical inquiry process reflects a bias towards systematic processes that are well planned, take a long time, and therefore seem more reliable. What is neglected are shorter, iterative processes that are directly grounded in real events and support human systems in action. Efforts to achieve systemic change must include these tighter cycles of knowledge turning into action and action into knowledge.

This Guide shows how collaborative inquiry can be both systematic and systemic, by supporting various cycles of thought and action that respond to both pressing needs and long-term goals, including those that are complex and hard to achieve. In our view, skillful means to adjust evidence-based inquiry to these different cycles of reasoning and adaptive behavior are essential to dialogue and social thinking.

Making Sense of Complexity

The Guide promotes abilities to mediate, ground, navigate, and scale the level of inquiry and dialogue needed for a process to become meaningful and powerful. It also calls for skillful means to **interpret** or make sense of complex information and situations, clearly and with flexibility. Interpreting the results of an inquiry involves bridging and combining the possible meanings of main findings with the theory and the "story" behind them. Without connection to a storyline that communicates the scope and significance of what we have to say, decisions and follow-up actions are hard to take.

Process-Based Learning

Sensemaking is a complex task. It cannot be made easy by simply choosing one theory or school of thought over another or relying on one method and source of information as a final statement of truth (for instance, either quantitative or qualitative findings). While defence of an interpretive theory or method receives great attention in the academic setting, the need to do so is often out of step with the diverse viewpoints and knowledge systems that must be factored into our understanding of complex issues and efforts to bring about social change. Developing firm, interpretive methods and positions should make room for a higher skill, namely, the art of combining dialogue and reasoning to create a story that is both analytic and meaningful, even emotional. This ability to connect to what is very important and must be communicated builds on the conditions created by the other skillful means. To convert the results of a collaborative inquiry into meaningful analysis, the whole inquiry process must mediate different views of reality, ground people's thinking in a context they are directly connected to, and then properly select and scale the tools that are needed to obtain relevant findings. All these skills, applied together, can lead to interpretive findings that will make sense of complex information in ways that are socially relevant.

The approach to interpretation in the context presented in this Guide draws lessons from many disciplines and viewpoints, including the educational insights of Problem, Process, Project, Product, and People Based Learning. Briefly, the P5BL approach centers on:

(a) Learning practical ways to solve complex **problems**;

(b) Using step-by-step **processes** to achieve expected results;

(c) Linking problems and processes with **projects** that are worth pursuing; and

(d) Creating tangible **products** that address real needs.

P5BL and this Guide also share a common commitment to **people**: *people* who construct and negotiate *project* goals, who set up the *processes* needed to meet these goals, who work together to resolve *problems* as they unfold, and who create *products* that express real achievements and the learning that occurs along the way. It should be noted that most experiences with P5BL focus on using existing bodies of knowledge to develop skills in a classroom setting. SAS[2] brings to P5BL an original collection of tools and a stronger focus on dialogue and on creating and mobilizing socially relevant knowledge in a real-life context.

This concludes our overview of the conceptual foundations and skillful means of SAS². Beyond the technical aspects of this Guide, there is a broader vision that readers and users should not lose sight of: shoring up the twofold "care-structure" embedded in the great adventure of human learning. By this we mean a learning approach that acknowledges the *careful precision* and intelligence that people must apply to understanding reality, and also the sense of *human caring* they must show in their engagement with other people and forms of life to achieve the common good.

Social Analysis and All-Purpose Techniques

Collaborative Inquiry

S AS² comprises a wide range of tools for collaborative inquiry and social engagement. The text below presents a general outline of SAS² techniques and software tools. Detailed descriptions of all 50 plus techniques are on the SAS² website (www.sas2.net).

There are two sets of SAS² techniques: All-Purpose Techniques, and Social Analysis techniques organized into various modules (Problems, Actors, and Options). Readers are encouraged to consult this overview to help them choose the techniques suited to their needs.

Note that we use the term inquiry to mean any explicit method used at any time to perform an investigation or analysis of the cause or nature of a condition, situation, or problem. We employ this expression instead of the conventional terms "research method" or "evaluation framework" which tend to be associated with expert forms of investigation limited to specific moments in a project or program cycle (usually at the beginning, at the end, or periodically during the implementation phase). In a SAS² perspective, inquiry, using techniques of various kinds, can be organized at any time it is needed and with all the people who should be involved.

All-Purpose Techniques

The All-Purpose Techniques are generic in nature and can be applied to any topic, including people's knowledge and views of nature and society, using the forum and participation strategies appropriate to their needs. They are divided into five sub-sets of techniques:

Participation and Forum

Participation and Forum helps you choose the forum options (*Forum Options*), the stage, form and level of participation (*Participation*), and the form of assistance (*Third Party*) that are appropriate to the activities you are currently planning.

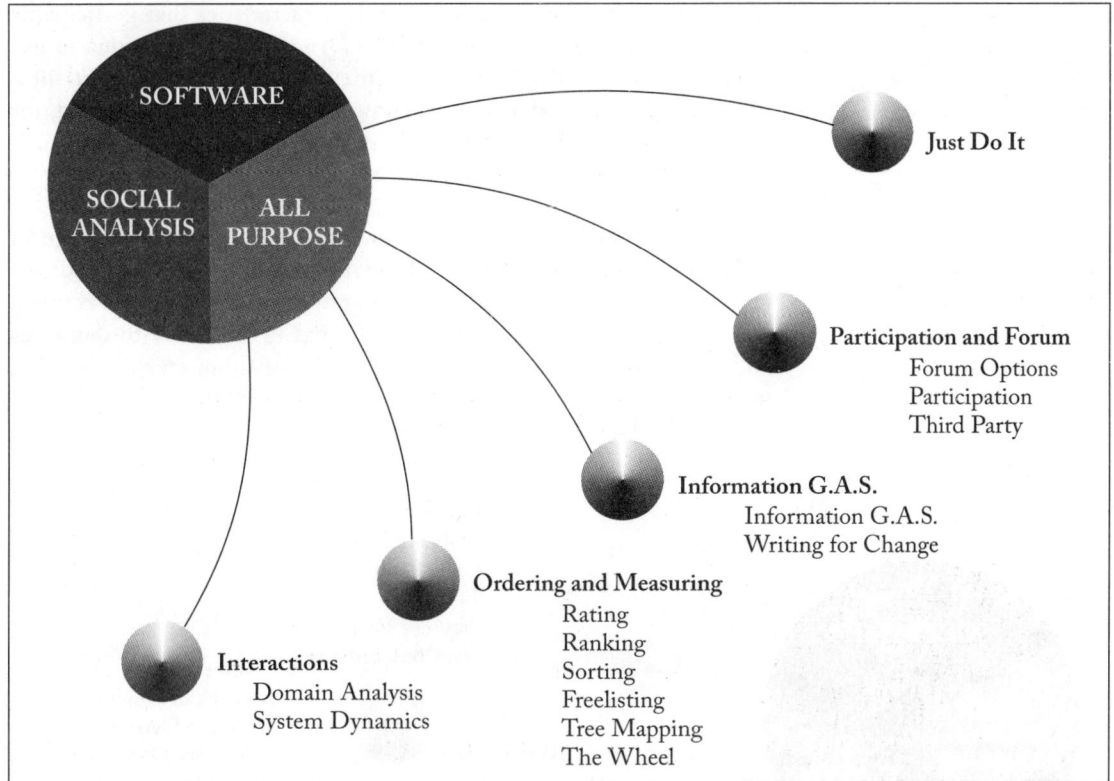

Information G.A.S.	Information G.A.S. (Gathering, Analysis, Sharing) includes two techniques. The first, also called *Information G.A.S.*, helps you choose the techniques you need to gather, analyze, or share information for the activities you are planning. The other is *Writing for Change*, a CD and Website that demonstrate effective writing skills, with a focus on writing for science and writing for advocacy.
Ordering and Measuring	Ordering and Measuring techniques—such as *Rating, Ranking, Sorting, Freelisting, Tree Mapping, The Wheel*—provide instructions on how to create and organize the elements of a list, identify priorities, and compare the views of different parties.
Interactions	Interactions consist of two generic versions of advanced techniques used elsewhere in SAS[2] for social analysis (looking at problems, actors, and options for action). The generic versions can be applied to the assessment of the relations between virtually anything (including plants, animals, soils, etc.). *Domain Analysis* helps characterize and compare the elements

of a topic or domain using words and characteristics that participants themselves choose and define. *System Dynamics* is a technique to explore the ways in which elements interact with other elements in a topic area (the interaction of cultivated plants in a farmer's field, for instance). Both techniques may be used to test people's views against experience, solve problems, and learn in the process.

Just Do It!

Just Do It is an important reminder that people regularly engage in collaborative inquiry and social engagement in ways that may be formal or informal and that will vary according to cultural setting and context. It encourages you to consider applying the existing day-to-day rules and procedures to gather and analyze information, create priorities, make plans, resolve problems, take action, and interact with others in the process. Just do what people normally do.

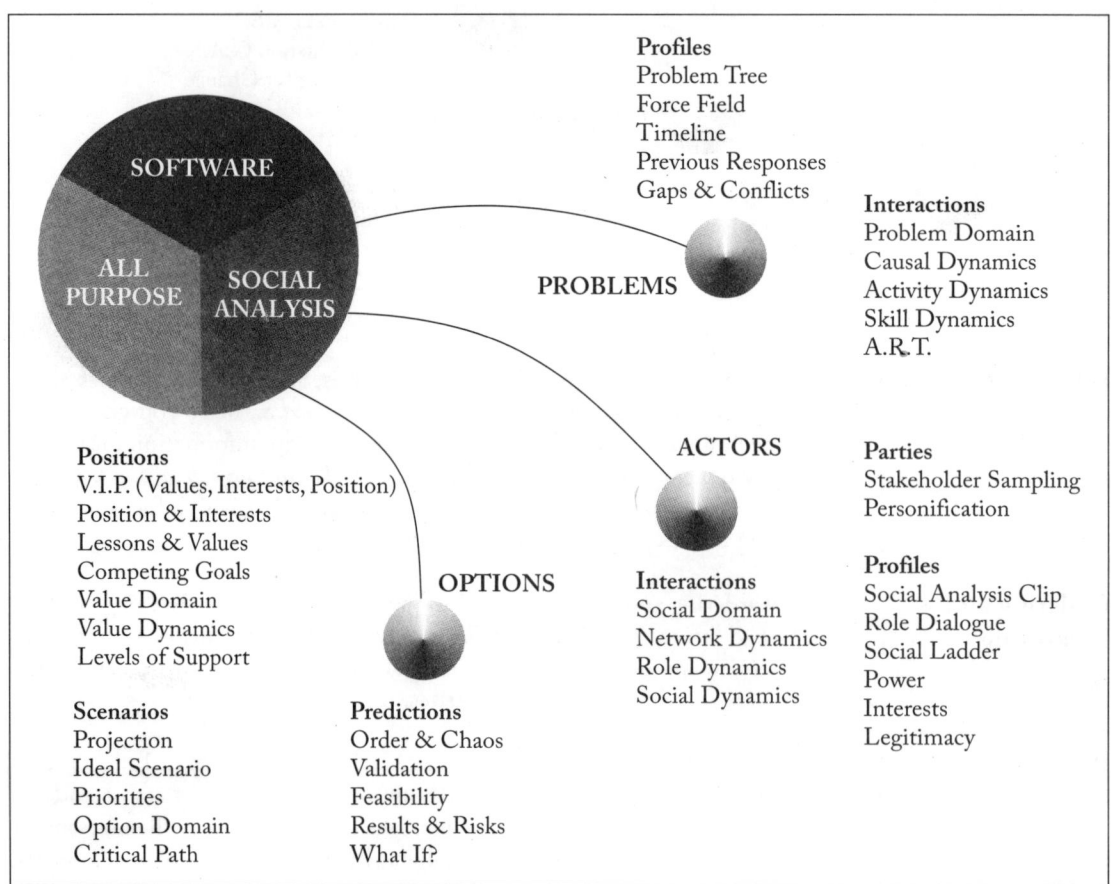

SOFTWARE

ALL PURPOSE

SOCIAL ANALYSIS

PROBLEMS

Profiles
Problem Tree
Force Field
Timeline
Previous Responses
Gaps & Conflicts

Interactions
Problem Domain
Causal Dynamics
Activity Dynamics
Skill Dynamics
A.R.T.

ACTORS

Parties
Stakeholder Sampling
Personification

Interactions
Social Domain
Network Dynamics
Role Dynamics
Social Dynamics

Profiles
Social Analysis Clip
Role Dialogue
Social Ladder
Power
Interests
Legitimacy

OPTIONS

Positions
V.I.P. (Values, Interests, Position)
Position & Interests
Lessons & Values
Competing Goals
Value Domain
Value Dynamics
Levels of Support

Scenarios
Projection
Ideal Scenario
Priorities
Option Domain
Critical Path

Predictions
Order & Chaos
Validation
Feasibility
Results & Risks
What If?

Social Analysis Techniques

The Social Analysis techniques are organized into *modules* that reflect three basic questions applicable to any situation: what are the problems that people face, who are the actors or stakeholders affected by a situation or with the capacity to intervene, and what are the options for action?

Problems

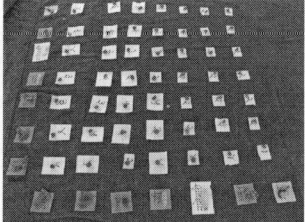

This module presents 10 different techniques to describe or *profile* a set of problems and understand their *interactions*.

Profiles includes five widely used participatory techniques such as *Problem Tree* (assessing the first and second level causes and effects of a core problem), *Force Field* (examining the factors that cause a problem and those that counteract it), and *Timeline* (identifying how a problem has evolved over time). In this set of techniques you will also find *Previous Responses*, a technique to assess the ways that key parties have managed core problems in the past, and whether these responses involved local customs, legal-administrative measures, or Alternative Dispute Resolution. The technique also explores whether past responses involved the use of necessary force, authority and social pressure, concession and accommodation, withdrawal and defusion, give-and-take compromise, third party arbitration, or mediation and collaboration. Another technique to describe a problem is *Gaps and Conflicts*. It asks whether a core problem is mostly about gaps or conflicts in particular areas such as power, interests (gains and losses), values, or information and communication.

Interactions comprises five original techniques that are central to SAS[2] theory and practice: *Problem Domain, Causal Dynamics, Activity Dynamics, Skill Dynamics, A.R.T. (Action, Research, Training)*. As their titles suggest, these techniques help users characterize, compare and look at the interactions of problems, their causes, the activities or the skill sets in a project, an organization or a particular situation.

Actors

This module consists of 10 techniques that are divided into three subsets: Parties, Profiles, and Interactions.

1. **Parties** are tools to identify, sample or describe the stakeholders involved in a core problem or action (*Stakeholder Identification, Stakeholder Sampling, Personification*).

2. **Profiles** are more advanced assessments that revolve around *Social Analysis CLIP*, a technique and software tool to examine how the factors of **C**ollaboration, **C**onflict, **L**egitimacy, **I**nterests, and **P**ower shape the stakeholder structure in a certain situation and possible strategies to manage social problems or actions. If you need to assess each CLIP factor in detail, you can consult the corresponding techniques entitled *Power* (wealth, force, authority,

information), *Interests* (net gains or losses), *Legitimacy* (rights, responsibilities, resolve), *Social Ladder* (the advantages and disadvantages of holding higher or lower positions), or *Role Dialogue* (the different roles that a party plays in a concrete situation).

3. **Interactions** comprise four tools to compare and assess the ongoing relations between actors. *Social Domain* can be used to characterize and compare actors using terms and characteristics chosen by the participants. *Network Dynamics* explores the network of influence, trust or information that exists between stakeholders involved in a core problem or situation. *Role Dynamics* focuses on what stakeholders expect of each other in a particular situation, and how much these expectations are actually satisfied. *Social Dynamics* brings together stakeholder analysis with problem and option assessment in a single technique that asks how each principal stakeholder, problem and activity (proposed or real) influences and is influenced by other stakeholders, problems and activities.

Options

This module offers the choice of 17 techniques organized into three sets: Scenarios, Predictions, and Positions.

1. **Scenarios** are tools to manage a core problem or action with a sense of vision and with efficiency. They help visualize the future that actors can expect if current trends continue and no actions are taken to change them (*Projection*); imagine an ideal future that builds on current strengths and accomplishments (*Ideal Scenario*); compare options and identify priorities (*Priorities*, *Option Domain*); and identify the shortest path to completing step-by-step tasks together with parallel tasks that may be done at any time in the process (*Critical Path*).

2. **Predictions** allow users to assess different options by looking at the upstream conditions or the downstream effects associated with each option. *Feasibility* is an upstream assessment. It focuses on the favorable factors (strengths, opportunities) and the unfavorable conditions (weaknesses, limitations) associated with each course of action. By contrast, *Results and Risks* evaluates the positive and negative effects that are likely to result from each proposed action.

    Three other risk-management techniques evaluate the knowledge needed to assess a situation, make plans or monitor their implementation: *What If?*, *Validation*, and *Order and Chaos*. The first technique (*What If?*) helps users track factors that are difficult to predict and that may greatly affect the outcome of their activities. The other two techniques point to key ideas about knowledge mobilization from a SAS² perspective. *Validation* suggests that the results of an assessment can be evaluated using two criteria:

the extent to which the assessment is based on evidence (sound and sufficient information and analysis), and the extent to which it achieves consensus through collaborative thinking. *Order and Chaos* advances another important principle: the planning approach you adopt—flexible process management and/or detailed result-based engineering—must reflect the degree to which your plans are well-informed as well as the level of difficulty you anticipate when trying to achieve your goals.

3. **Positions** consist of seven techniques to understand and respond to the positions that stakeholders hold in a certain situation. They allow SAS² practitioners to examine and discuss the positions, the values, and the goals of different stakeholders involved in a core problem or action. *V.I.P.* (*Values, Interests, Positions*) is usually a good place to start as it combines these different issues in a single technique: it compares the positions that stakeholders take on a problem or action with their actual interests as well as the moral values they hold. If the *V.I.P.* analysis shows that positions do not reflect existing interests, the technique *Positions and Interests* can then help to reveal the interests underlying the positions that stakeholders take on a core problem or action. If the analysis shows instead a gap between the positions and the values or principles that stakeholders hold, SAS² users can then apply *Lessons and Values* to see how stakeholders can build on the lessons they have learned regarding how to apply their own values with positive results. Note that the software version of *Social Analysis CLIP* (www.sas2.net) incorporates *V.I.P.* to produce a comprehensive analysis of stakeholder positions, values, interests, power, legitimacy, and ties of collaboration and conflict. The findings of this full *CLIP* assessment can be used to plan actions that better reflect the interests and the values of the parties concerned.

Positions include four other tools to assess people's value systems and commitments to plans for action. *Value Domain* examines how people view the relationship between their own **values** and a specific set of objectives, actions, events, problems, objects or people that express or contradict these values. *Value Dynamics* focuses on the degree of interaction between the values that people hold— the degree to which their values are organized in a coherent system or a hierarchy where each value contributes to and depends on other values. *Competing Goals* helps rank stakeholders' goals (objectives or values) in order of importance, and understand disagreements or misunderstandings that people may have in relation to these goals. Finally, *Levels of Support* is a technique to identify the level of support or commitment that may be obtained for particular activities and options for action.

Process Management

Process Management (PMt) and Process Manager (PMr)

Process Management (**PMt**) is an approach to planning and managing single events or a series of events organized into projects or programs. The principles of PMt and how they relate to frameworks such as Result-Based Management (RBM) are summarized in the Table below. PMt is the *point of entry and practical grounding* of the social analysis and all-purpose techniques described in the previous section.

The PMt approach can be turned into a collaborative planning and management technique described below called Process Manager (**PMr**). How this is done depends on the kind of planning being undertaken. Three likely scenarios can be distinguished with the help of the Social Analysis technique *Order and Chaos*.

Scenario 1: Plan First, Implement After

The first scenario involves situations that are sufficiently predictable for you to be able to plan most project activities (including Monitoring & Evaluation assessments) in advance with considerable detail, producing plans that are result-based and reliable in most respects. Many project and management tools such as Result-Based Management (RBM) operate assuming this high level of information and certainty regarding the chances of achieving particular goals. Under these conditions, use PMr and SAS^2 techniques to do four things in sequence:

RBM

(a) Assess the initial situation using collaborative SAS^2 techniques (combined with other assessment methods);

(b) Use PMr to make detailed activity plans based on your findings (when confident that you can predict the linkages between your project activities and the expected results);

(c) Include plans to use SAS^2 (and other methods) to monitor the on-going results of your project implementation against your baseline information (your initial set of observations or findings); and

(d) Evaluate the final results of your project against your initial objectives using SAS^2 techniques (and other methods).

Many organizations require projects to follow the RBM approach. SAS^2 and PMr can support this RBM approach and achieve greater efficiency and accountability in the process, by providing tools for collaborative thinking and planning. However, this plan-first and implement-after approach (using SAS[2] and PMr or not) has its limitations. It works well only in situations of relative order characterized by high levels of certainty and predictable linkages between causes and effects (or between inputs, outputs, outcomes, and impact). This linear approach to planning and management imposes sharp distinctions between research, planning, action, and evaluation.

If you choose this approach, consult the PMr instructions below, and then the instructions on how to incorporate SAS[2] techniques in Process Manager (*Guidelines for SAS[2] Events and Process Design*). Note that you can also use this approach to plan a full research project, by selecting in advance the appropriate SAS[2] techniques to be applied throughout your research process.

Scenario 2: Continuous Planning

The second scenario consists of situations that are not fully predictable but still lend themselves to planning in a continuous mode—by making plans along the way or adjusting plans in light of unforeseen events and new information. These are complex situations of relative chaos characterized by the **unexpected and the unknown** where the results of prior activities, the performance of key factors, and stakeholder interventions cannot be assumed or fully predicted.

SAS[2] and PMr

For this kind of situation, use several SAS[2] techniques and PMr to support a series of events in a project where some actions and analyses may be planned in advance and other plans must be made along the way (in response to ongoing project results, stakeholder interventions, and key factor performance). This approach allows you to make full use of SAS[2] in complex situations where you have incomplete knowledge of the key factors and their future behavior. To help you assess whether or not this continuous planning (or Process Management) approach fits your needs, see *Order and Chaos*. If you adopt this approach, consult the instructions below.

Note that when using this approach you may choose to progressively compile and reflect on the results of your actions and inquiry activities to produce an applied research document such as a report, a thesis or a scholarly publication.

Scenario 3: Single Events

The third scenario involves situations that are so uncertain that you can only plan relatively immediate events, as opposed to making broader project plans in advance. PMr or other planning tools are not really needed in this scenario. Rather, you can simply use one or several SAS[2] inquiry techniques when you need to, for a single or one-off event. If you adopt this approach, go directly to *Guidelines for SAS[2] Events and Process Design*.

RESULT-BASED MANAGEMENT (RBM)	PROCESS MANAGEMENT (PMt)
RBM uses a linear *conception→implementation* model or the **plan-and-execute** approach of the engineer. The model involves making assumptions and calculating risks as they relate to the conditions and methods that will help to achieve project or program goals. This closed-system approach allows projects to have a clear beginning and a clear ending. It works when there is relative order, low levels of uncertainty, and high levels of **predictable links** between causes and effects (or between inputs, outputs, outcomes, and impact).	PMt incorporates the *action→reaction* model or **testing-and-monitoring** approach of the medical profession. Interventions are done "in the middle" of complex situations that have no clear beginning or ending. This adaptive approach is suited to open systems characterized by the **unexpected** and the **unknown**. The approach works in situations of relative chaos where the results of prior activities, the performance of key factors, and stakeholder interventions cannot be assumed or fully predicted.
In RBM most of the decisions and planning occur when the project cycle begins and are done with considerable detail.	In PMt, decisions are taken and plans for next steps are made at the right interval, in light of ongoing results, key factor performance, and stakeholder interventions. Plans are made at the **optimum level**, with gaps and details that are left unspecified until the conditions for further planning are met.
RBM uses pre-established and **expert-led** methods, suppported by **comprehensive** planning and **strict accounting** of the resources used. Formal assessments are done at **fixed moments** in the project cycle. They include upstream diagnoses, midstream reports on the work in progress, and downstream accounts and evaluations of the final results.	PMt incorporates **collaborative inquiry** into ongoing activities, using methods that are either planned in advance or improvised to meet unexpected needs. Assessments are done for accounting purposes but also to **guide social action** in circumstances that evolve over time.
RBM assessments focus on the need for **reliable data**, measurable indicators, and ways to verify results applied at the global project level.	PMt promotes the use of multiple and flexible inquiry tools to assess different parts of a project at the **optimal level of detail** (simple, intermediate, or advanced). The optimal or good-enough application of inquiry tools takes into account what is feasible in each case (given limitations in time and resources) and what level of evidence and agreement is actually needed for the assessment to achieve its purpose.
RBM starts by defining the **objectives** and expected end-results, and then decides what actions are needed to achieve them.	PMt identifies ongoing and projected **activities** informed by experience, goals, and the desired results explicitly or implicitly embedded in them.
RBM is based on a logical ladder of general and specific objectives shared by all parties and **stable over time**.	PMt tracks complex multistakeholder situations where general and specific objectives interact and evolve, subject to negotiations, compromises, and **change over time**.
RBM tends to highlight the interests of the **beneficiaries** and to apply measures of accountability and ownership of results to those who lead the project.	PMt accommodates a **plurality of stakeholder interests** and contributions to project results.

How to Use Process Manager (PMr)

Activity Mapping

Step

1. Identify a **project or a series of activities** that needs planning.

2. Use brainstorming to **list all current and/or proposed activities** within your project. Make sure to include the inquiry activities that you need as part of your project (including SAS[2] assessments).

3. Describe each activity on a card using a few key words (one activity per card) and organize them into **sets of activities and subsets**, if necessary (see Sorting under All-Purpose Techniques). Create a card and a label for each set and for each subset. Be sure to use concrete words and verbs that describe an activity or set of activities instead of topics or objectives. For example, use "workshops" instead of "capacity-building", "fund raising" instead of "resources", or "lobbying" instead of "policy impact".

4. Begin your activity map by drawing a **central bubble** (Level 1). This bubble represents your project as a whole. Label the bubble.

5. **Add** smaller **bubbles** at Level 2, Level 3, and Level 4 if necessary. These bubbles represent sets and subsets of activities. Identify the bubbles using the labels created in Step 3. To prevent your map from becoming too complex, do not create more than six lower-level bubbles for each higher-level bubble.

6. Place the **activity cards** that cannot be subdivided at the last level of your activity map, close to the set or the subset that represents them.

7. **Trim down** your activity map by reducing it to those activities that are important and feasible.

Here's an example of an activity map involving three levels (using MindManager):

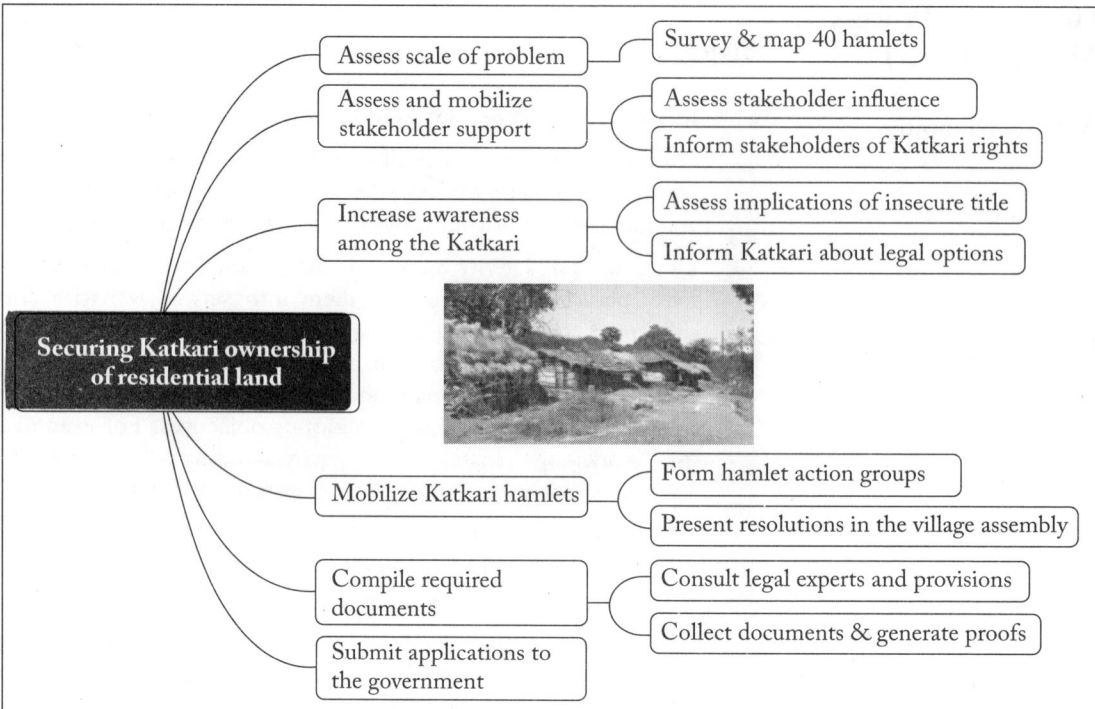

Assess scale of problem — Survey & map 40 hamlets

Assess and mobilize stakeholder support — Assess stakeholder influence / Inform stakeholders of Katkari rights

Increase awareness among the Katkari — Assess implications of insecure title / Inform Katkari about legal options

Securing Katkari ownership of residential land

Mobilize Katkari hamlets — Form hamlet action groups / Present resolutions in the village assembly

Compile required documents — Consult legal experts and provisions / Collect documents & generate proofs

Submit applications to the government

Summary of this example: The tribal Katkari of India used to be hunters, gatherers and fishers living in the hills and forests of the Western Ghats of Maharashtra. Most now live in abject poverty, and work as bonded labor at brick-making kilns in the region. They move from place-to-place, from season to season, to find work, leaving their homes vacant for months at a time. Many Katkari do not have legal title to the land on which their hamlets are located, even though they have lived there for many generations. This restricts Katkari access to government programs for housing, water, schools and other services. Recently, Katkari in some hamlets have been forced to leave their homes by landowners.

Two non-governmental organizations, Academy of Development Science (ADS) and SOBTI, have been working in Katkari communities in Raigad and Thane Districts for many years. They decided to join forces in a study of how to help the Katkari own the lands where they live in several townships. An assessment of the chances of achieving this goal (see *Order and Chaos* example in this Guide) suggested that detailed project plans could be made. ADS and SOBTI felt that their chances of success were high because it was a precise and narrow problem with clear legal standing. They also felt sure about their prior knowledge of the conditions or factors affecting the plan, such as local land tenure systems, legal rights, the location of Katkari hamlets, and the stakeholders involved.

ADS and SOBTI project staff (5 men and 1 woman) met during a SAS[2] workshop. The purpose of the meeting was to plan the project. Proposed activities were listed on cards and organized into sets around the project title. The activities were then reduced to those that were deemed important and feasible. These cards were then ordered in a line and sequence by participants. The resulting plan was to: (*i*) assess the problem through a survey and maps of 40 Katkari hamlets in three townships, based on a broader assessment of the scope of the problem; (*ii*) assess and mobilize stakeholder support for Katkari land claims; (*iii*) increase awareness among the Katkari of their legal options and the effects of insecure title; (*iv*) mobilize Katkari hamlets to present resolutions in village assemblies; (*v*) compile documents and legal proofs; and (*vi*) submit applications to government agencies.

Operational Details

8. Identify the details (people, expected results, knowledge, methods, time, resources) of your **project as a whole**. You can do this by filling out an **Operational Process Card** for the project level bubble using the following 6 headings. *Choose the level of planning detail that corresponds to your needs.*

People

The *people* involved in the activity, their *roles* and the level of *effort* expected from them (the number of days they will dedicate to the activity).

Expected Results

The expected results of an activity and the *status of the results* already obtained (are the results partly achieved?). Results can take many forms, ranging from real products (outputs) to changes in behavior and relationships (outcome). Results may also include how stakeholders are affected or how systems are changed (impact). Note that different expected results corresponding to different stakeholder interests may be assigned to the same activity.

Knowledge

Input or *output* information, documents (electronic or printed), as well as reports, archives, statistics and websites.

Methods

Ways in which you and others will implement the activity, including how you will meet; the facilitation methods and decision-making procedures you will use; the ordering, measuring, and *Information G.A.S.* (*Gathering, Analyzing, Sharing*) techniques you will need for the activity (see All-Purpose Techniques). (The Social Analysis Techniques available in SAS^2 may be integrated into plans as activities in their own right, not as methods within an activity.)

Time

Start and *finish* dates

Resources

Budget and *equipment*

9. For each activity, choose from three planning options: Plan Now, Plan Later, or No Plan Needed.

Plan Now

Identify the activity bubbles where the immediate planning of precise details (Operational Process Card) is *needed and possible*. This is the Plan Now option. To help you decide if you should choose this option, ask yourself if you have enough information about:

(a) The results of **prior activities** (for example, do you need to see the results of your fund-raising campaign before you plan a public meeting?)

(b) The performance of a **key factor** (for example, do you need to wait until the municipal elections are over before you plan a public meeting?)

(c) The nature of a particular **stakeholder intervention** (for example, should you wait to see how the newly elected municipal leader responds to your project before you plan a public meeting?)

Plan Later

There may be some activities that you cannot plan fully because you cannot anticipate the results of prior activities, the performance of a key factor or stakeholder interventions that may have a direct bearing on the activities. In this case, choose the Plan Later option. Indicate at which time you should revisit the activity to see if you have enough information to plan the activity.

No Plan Needed

There may be some activities that require no formal planning, because implementation details are clear to all concerned. In this case, choose the No Plan Needed option for that activity. The activity remains in the overall project plan but no Operational Card is created.

You may record the option you choose—Plan Now, Plan Later or No Plan Needed—on a **Ready-to-Plan card** if necessary. Attach the card to the activity.

Level of Planning Detail

10. If you are ready to plan an activity at any level (Plan Now decision), fill out an Operational Process card for the activity. Choose the **level of planning detail** that corresponds to your needs. Make sure that the details recorded for lower-level activities (expected results, and so on.) are compatible with the details recorded at higher levels of your activity map. If some details (people, time, and methods, for instance) are exactly the same at different levels, you can save time by recording them only at higher levels of your activity map.

You may decide to focus on the activities that require immediate or short-term planning, leaving some more distant activities unplanned for a while and other activities without formal plans at all. This allows for a continuous and flexible approach to planning that can actively integrate relevant information into the planning process as it becomes available.

Visual Codes

To make it easier to interpret your map, organize the activities that will be done in sequence (step by step) vertically, according to the order in which you plan to implement them. You can place those that are continuous activities or not scheduled in a separate area of your map. You may also create and use your own **visual code** to highlight important aspects of your activity management map. For example, you can use numbers to indicate levels of priority, ticks and small clock markers to describe the status of each activity, or callouts to identify the inquiry technique you are planning to use.

Here is an activity map that uses the example introduced in Step 7:

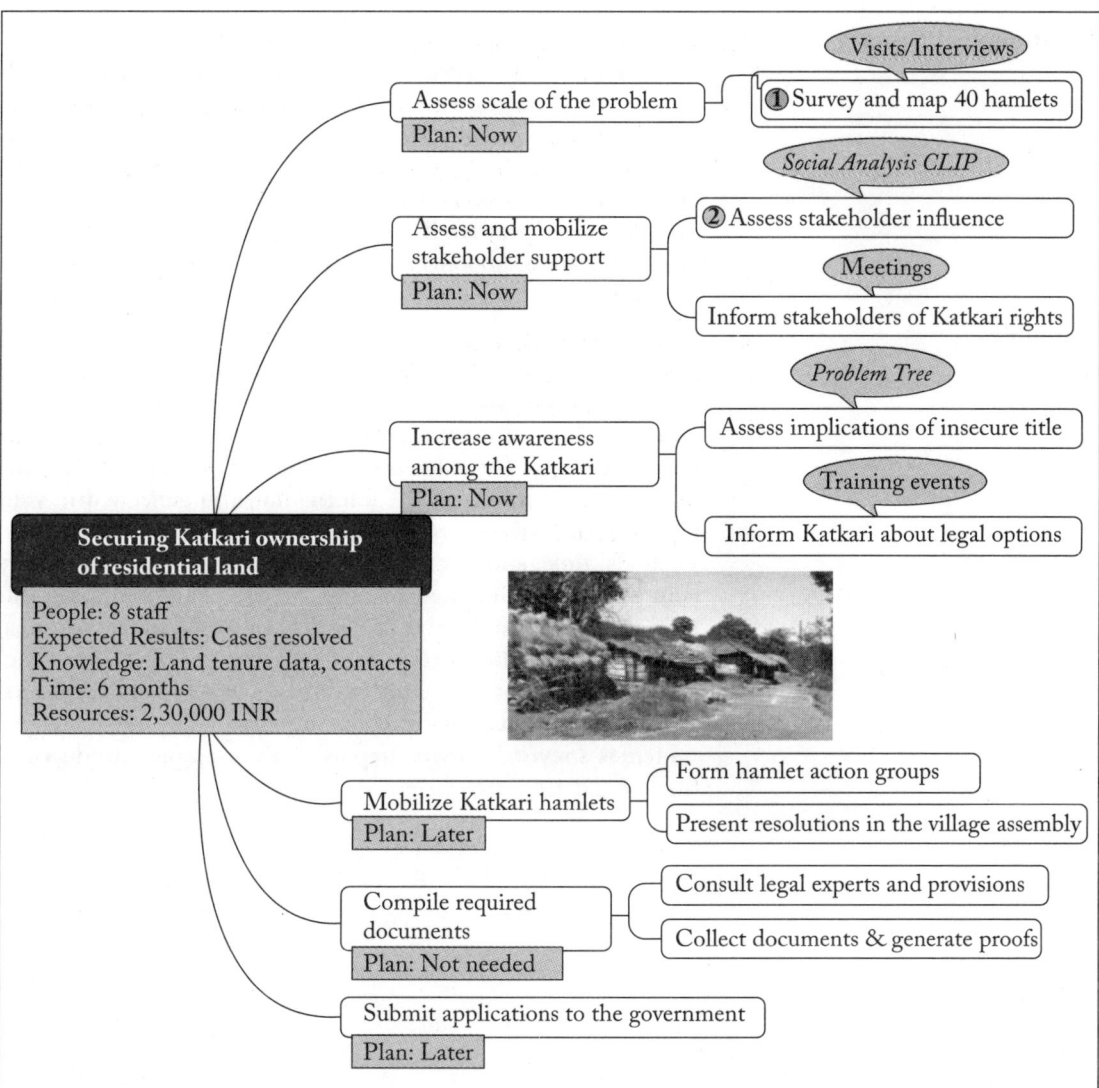

Visits/Interviews

① Survey and map 40 hamlets

Assess scale of the problem
Plan: Now

Social Analysis CLIP

② Assess stakeholder influence

Meetings

Inform stakeholders of Katkari rights

Assess and mobilize stakeholder support
Plan: Now

Problem Tree

Assess implications of insecure title

Training events

Inform Katkari about legal options

Increase awareness among the Katkari
Plan: Now

Securing Katkari ownership of residential land

People: 8 staff
Expected Results: Cases resolved
Knowledge: Land tenure data, contacts
Time: 6 months
Resources: 2,30,000 INR

Form hamlet action groups

Present resolutions in the village assembly

Mobilize Katkari hamlets
Plan: Later

Consult legal experts and provisions

Collect documents & generate proofs

Compile required documents
Plan: Not needed

Submit applications to the government
Plan: Later

Summary of this example: Enough information was available during the planning session to plan three of the major activities in detail. SAS[2] methods were chosen for two sub-activities (*Social Analysis CLIP* and *Problem Tree*). Other methods (visits, interviews, meetings, and training events) that built on the detailed knowledge ADS and SOBTI have when it comes to land tenure in Katkari villages in the Raigad district were also selected. Planning for two tasks (mobilize the Katkari and apply to government officials) was left for a later date, once the results of plans to build awareness and assess the scale of the problem were known. One activity did not need to be planned because the details of how it would be done were clear to all concerned (compile documents and legal proofs). Assessing the scale of the problem and the power of key stakeholders were identified as first steps that would provide information needed to further refine plans for other activities. These first assessments would also provide a baseline for monitoring changes in the stance of different stakeholders as a result of project activities.

Continuous Planning

11. Individuals or groups may create, fill out, record, and revise activity bubbles, Ready-to-Plan cards, and Operational Process cards at any time to meet their **continuous planning** needs. When you cannot plan an activity because of a factor you cannot predict, you may still decide to do some planning and revise your **tentative plan** at a later date, when you have the information you need. You may also develop a **Plan B**, to be followed in case the original plan does not work or no longer applies because of events you did not anticipate.

Compile

12. You can **compile** Operational Process information from several activities to produce a table of who does what, why, when, and how. To do this, you can use software such as MindManager or create a table with seven columns. In Column 1, list all your project activities (or only some of them, if you prefer). Use the other columns to record the information you generated in your Operational Process cards (people, expected results, knowledge, methods, time, and resources) for each activity. You can **modify your table** every time new or more precise plans are made. This kind of table is similar to a Logical Frame used in conventional planning approaches (except that it can be modified over time) and provides a way of linking your plans to other organizational requirements such as reporting on activities.

Here is a revised activity map using the example introduced in Steps 7 and 10:

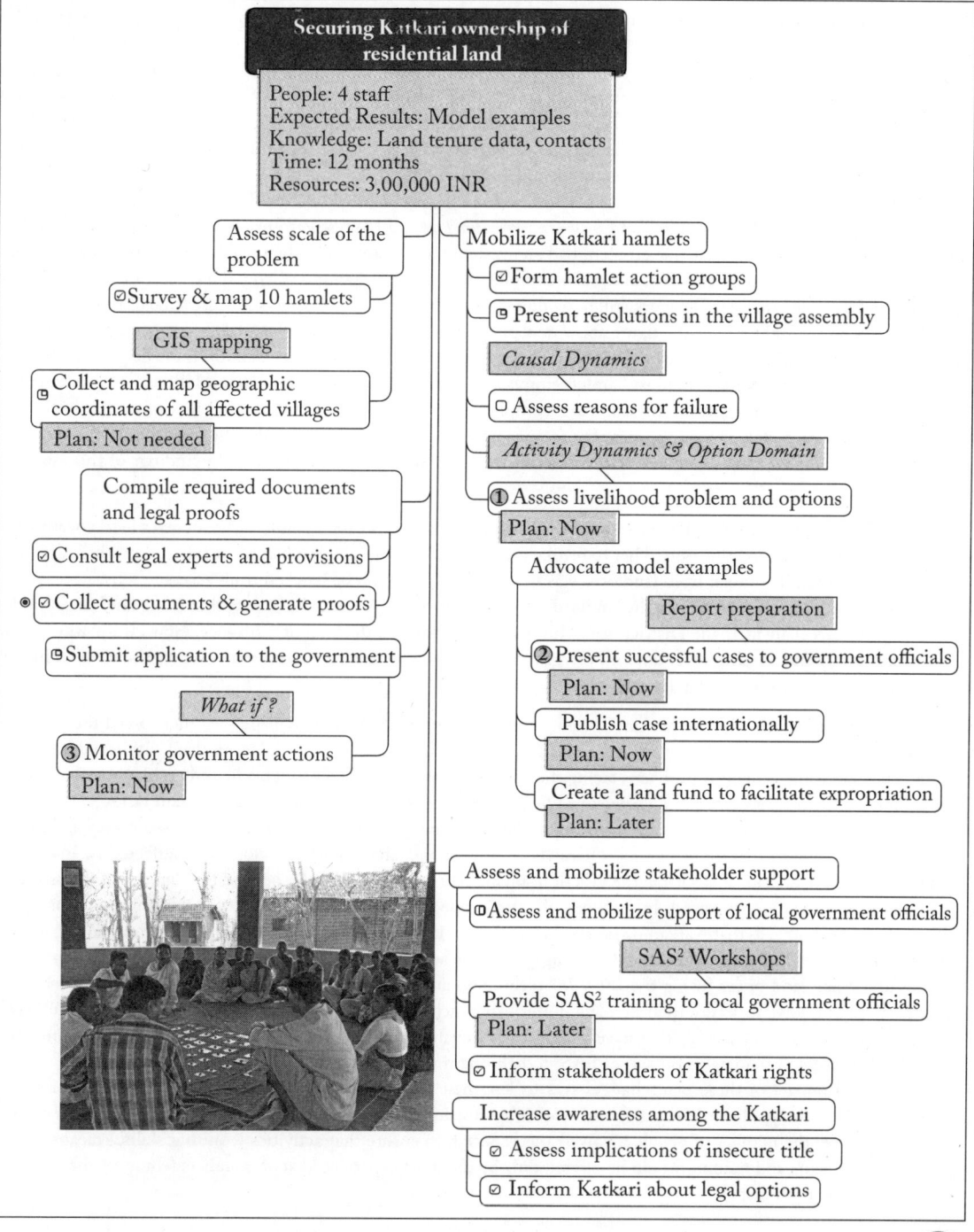

Securing Katkari ownership of residential land

People: 4 staff
Expected Results: Model examples
Knowledge: Land tenure data, contacts
Time: 12 months
Resources: 3,00,000 INR

Assess scale of the problem

☑ Survey & map 10 hamlets

GIS mapping

Collect and map geographic coordinates of all affected villages
Plan: Not needed

Compile required documents and legal proofs

☑ Consult legal experts and provisions

☑ Collect documents & generate proofs

Submit application to the government

What if ?

③ Monitor government actions
Plan: Now

Mobilize Katkari hamlets

☑ Form hamlet action groups

Present resolutions in the village assembly

Causal Dynamics

☐ Assess reasons for failure

Activity Dynamics & Option Domain

① Assess livelihood problem and options
Plan: Now

Advocate model examples

Report preparation

② Present successful cases to government officials
Plan: Now

Publish case internationally
Plan: Now

Create a land fund to facilitate expropriation
Plan: Later

Assess and mobilize stakeholder support

Assess and mobilize support of local government officials

SAS² Workshops

Provide SAS² training to local government officials
Plan: Later

☑ Inform stakeholders of Katkari rights

Increase awareness among the Katkari

☑ Assess implications of insecure title

☑ Inform Katkari about legal options

Summary of this example: This figure shows the revised Katkari project plan six months later. It had to be revised because of unforeseen events and new information. Activities on the left side of the figure are complete or about to be completed, with some changes to the original plans. Record rainfall in the Katkari townships and much flooding cut many hamlets off from major roads and greatly constrained the movements of ADS and SOBTI staff. Also, the time needed to apply activities in chosen villages was much greater than planned. These two problems delayed the project and forced project staff to reduce the number of hamlets surveyed and mapped from 40 to 20, and then to 10. The project also had to adjust by relying less on detailed interviews and more on short visits by project staff and the use of a Global Positioning System (GPS) to map the scale of the problem. While the Katkari were initially skeptical about the importance of the residential land issue (see *Problem Tree* and *Ideal Scenario* examples in this Guide), by this time they were fully aware of how this problem had an impact on many aspects of their lives. All documents and legal proofs required to make their case had also been compiled for 10 target hamlets. Geographic coordinates for some 200 villages had been amassed. The work still to be done was to prepare a final map to show the scale of the problem.

Activities on the right side of the figure show new plans that had to be made when stakeholder meetings did not unfold as expected. While the Katkari were prepared, and fully in favor of presenting resolutions in village assemblies, when the day arrived the Katkari in most hamlets simply stayed away. Only four out of 10 resolutions were presented, and one of these was later revoked. This came as a complete surprise to the project team, and was a major setback.

Plans were immediately revised to assess the reasons why the Katkari did not present the resolutions. The project team used the SAS[2] technique *Causal Dynamics* (see oval on the top right of the figure). Key findings of this assessment were:

1. The Katkari were very afraid that landlords might strike back. In one case, a landlord threatened a local government official with violence; this caused her to revoke the resolution even though it had passed. In many other cases, the spoken or implied threat from landlords was that the Katkari would be blocked from access to jobs.

2. While the project had expected the landlords to resist, it had not foreseen the impact that rising land prices in the region (especially in Thane District near Mumbai) would have on the level of resistance. New information about land prices and a much lower amount the government was now able to provide when expropriating land had to be added to the stakeholder assessments.

Assessing the reasons why the Katkari did not present resolutions at planned village meetings forced the project team to challenge its early assumptions that the specific problem of insecure tenure could be resolved without addressing many other social and economic problems facing the Katkari. Broader assessments of livelihood problems and options for addressing them (using *Activity Dynamics* and *Option Domain*) were planned as new and urgent tasks.

Research results that showed the scale of the problem also changed the project plan. The revised survey and GIS mapping work showed that more than 200 hamlets in Raigad and Thane Districts alone were affected by insecure tenure. This new data made it clear that the task of resolving these situations was far beyond the capacity of the project and the two organizations involved. In response, the project decided to produce models of successful resolutions, to show government officials that Katkari ownership of residential land was possible. This became a second priority, to be planned right away. The project also decided to support these actions with immediate plans to monitor government actions and rising land prices (using the *What If?* technique) and to publish details about the scope of the problem and the Katkari resolve to secure their hamlets. Later plans include a proposal to (*i*) create a land fund that will pay expropriated landowners for lands that have risen greatly in value, and to (*ii*) continue to provide local government officials with access to training in the use of SAS[2] to help them work more effectively.

The overall impact of these plan changes was to lengthen the project time frame, and more funding for new activities such as the publishing venture, and workshops for local government officials. While the project became broader in scope, the number of people involved was reduced, to ensure that activities requiring skillful means such as SAS[2] assessments and training would be offered only by the most experienced staff members (compare the central project bubble in both maps).

**Process Manager
Tips**

1. Work with cards for activity bubbles, Ready-to-Plan cards, and Operational Process cards that you can move around easily to produce a readable map.

2. To prevent your map from becoming too complex, do not draw lines between same-level bubbles. Use the Operational Process cards to record connections between same-level activities.

3. When working on complex projects, you can divide participants into groups, ask each group to use Process Manager to map out their own set of activities, and then adjust group plans through discussions and negotiations between all groups.

4. For simpler versions: Focus on one activity bubble or one planning period, such as the next month. Omit the Ready-to-Plan or Operational Process cards, or some elements within them. For example, do not fill the Expected Results, Information, and Methods columns on the Operational Process card.

5. For more advanced versions: Attach a descriptive text to each activity label. Divide your expected results into outputs, outcomes, and impacts. Produce detailed budgets. Describe the methods you intend to use, or the knowledge input and output assigned to each activity. Explain the observations and decisions recorded on your Ready-to-Plan cards. Convert your Operational Process cards into a MindManager map or into a Logical Framework or Microsoft Project document. Use the appropriate database and archival system to support the information inputs and outputs of your project or program activities.

Guidelines for SAS² Events and Process Design

SAS² practitioners can use the following guidelines to design the way they apply SAS² techniques to a single event or a broader process of collaborative inquiry and social action. How you choose SAS² techniques and adjust them to an inquiry is not a science involving strict rules. Rather, it is an art that requires the exercise of judgment, creativity, and a lot of practice. To make full use of SAS², practitioners must have a clear idea of the setting, the purpose, and the expected results of each inquiry. They must identify the main questions to be asked, the prior knowledge and decisions that can help answer these questions, and the amount of time and the resources that are available or needed to get the work done. Practitioners must learn how to make the right decisions on when to apply particular techniques, what other methods they should use together with SAS², how to organize the techniques and steps in sequence, and how in-depth the inquiry should be. They should also decide what supporting technology is needed, how to combine story telling with tables and diagrams, and whether the technique(s) used should be made explicit or not. Finally, practitioners must decide when to divide participants into subgroups, what role(s) should the facilitator(s) play, and how to document the inquiry process and its results.

Two figures organize these decisions into steps to follow when designing a SAS² event or specific inquiry within a broader process (Figure 1), and choices to make when selecting the techniques (Figure 2). Keep in mind that the steps outlined below are not always linear and may require **going back and forth** (between defining the setting and the purpose of the inquiry, clarifying the main questions, and then selecting the techniques, for instance).

**Identify SAS²
Activities Ready
to be Designed**

To begin a design process, you must identify the specific event or activity that may require using SAS² and that you're ready to plan in some detail. If the inquiry extends over time, you can use Process Manager to plan the overall process and identify the short-term assessment that you should design immediately (using the instructions below). Process Manager will help you situate each SAS² assessment in the broader inquiry process.

Figure 1: SAS[2] Events and Process Design

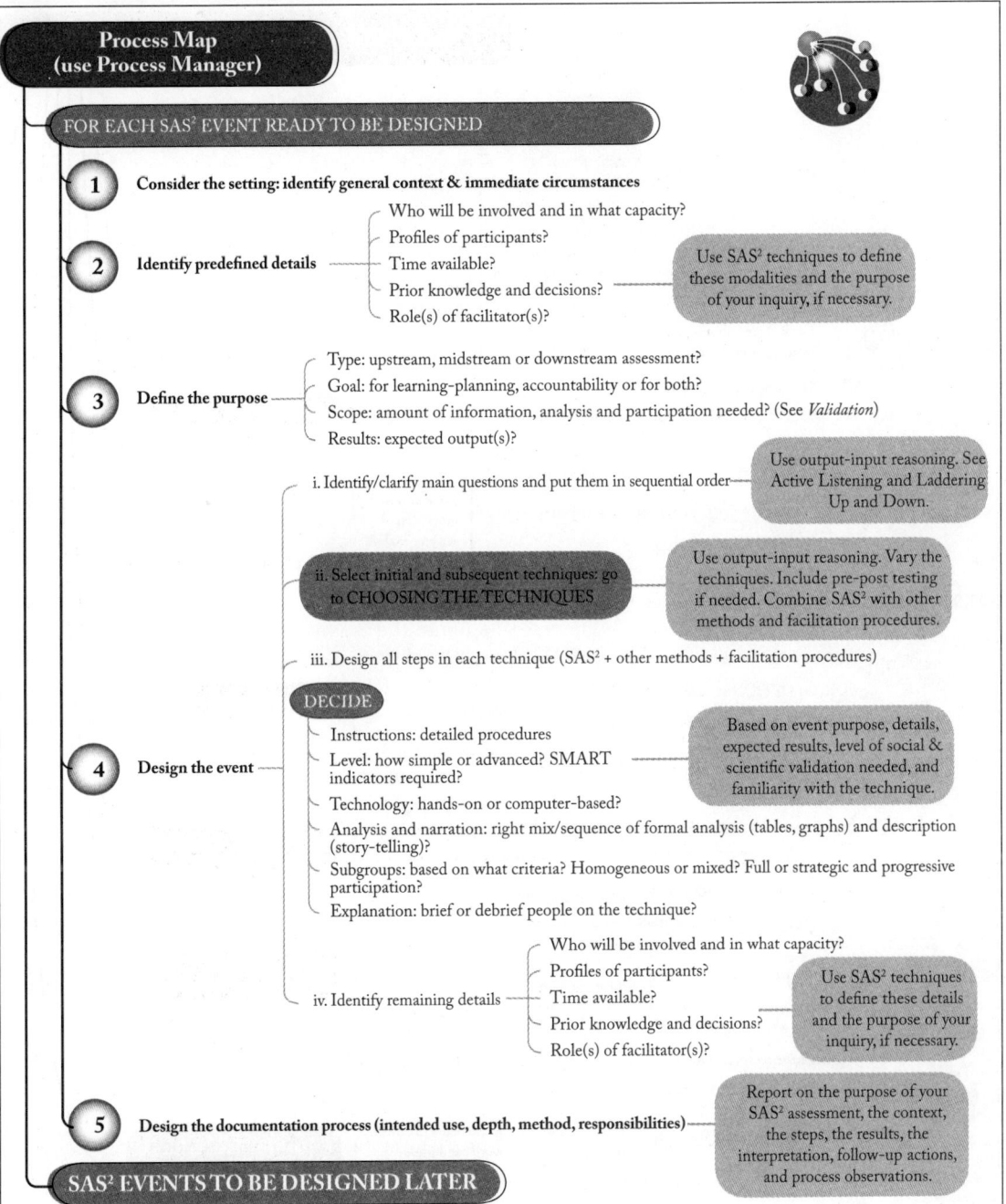

Process Map (use Process Manager)

FOR EACH SAS[2] EVENT READY TO BE DESIGNED

1 Consider the setting: identify general context & immediate circumstances

2 Identify predefined details
- Who will be involved and in what capacity?
- Profiles of participants?
- Time available?
- Prior knowledge and decisions?
- Role(s) of facilitator(s)?

Use SAS[2] techniques to define these modalities and the purpose of your inquiry, if necessary.

3 Define the purpose
- Type: upstream, midstream or downstream assessment?
- Goal: for learning-planning, accountability or for both?
- Scope: amount of information, analysis and participation needed? (See *Validation*)
- Results: expected output(s)?

4 Design the event
- i. Identify/clarify main questions and put them in sequential order
  - *Use output-input reasoning. See Active Listening and Laddering Up and Down.*
- ii. Select initial and subsequent techniques: go to **CHOOSING THE TECHNIQUES**
  - *Use output-input reasoning. Vary the techniques. Include pre-post testing if needed. Combine SAS[2] with other methods and facilitation procedures.*
- iii. Design all steps in each technique (SAS[2] + other methods + facilitation procedures)
- **DECIDE**
  - Instructions: detailed procedures
  - Level: how simple or advanced? SMART indicators required?
  - Technology: hands-on or computer-based?
  - Analysis and narration: right mix/sequence of formal analysis (tables, graphs) and description (story-telling)?
  - Subgroups: based on what criteria? Homogeneous or mixed? Full or strategic and progressive participation?
  - Explanation: brief or debrief people on the technique?

  Based on event purpose, details, expected results, level of social & scientific validation needed, and familiarity with the technique.

- iv. Identify remaining details
  - Who will be involved and in what capacity?
  - Profiles of participants?
  - Time available?
  - Prior knowledge and decisions?
  - Role(s) of facilitator(s)?

  Use SAS[2] techniques to define these details and the purpose of your inquiry, if necessary.

5 Design the documentation process (intended use, depth, method, responsibilities)

Report on the purpose of your SAS[2] assessment, the context, the steps, the results, the interpretation, follow-up actions, and process observations.

SAS[2] EVENTS TO BE DESIGNED LATER

Figure 2: Choosing the Techniques (Step 4, ii)

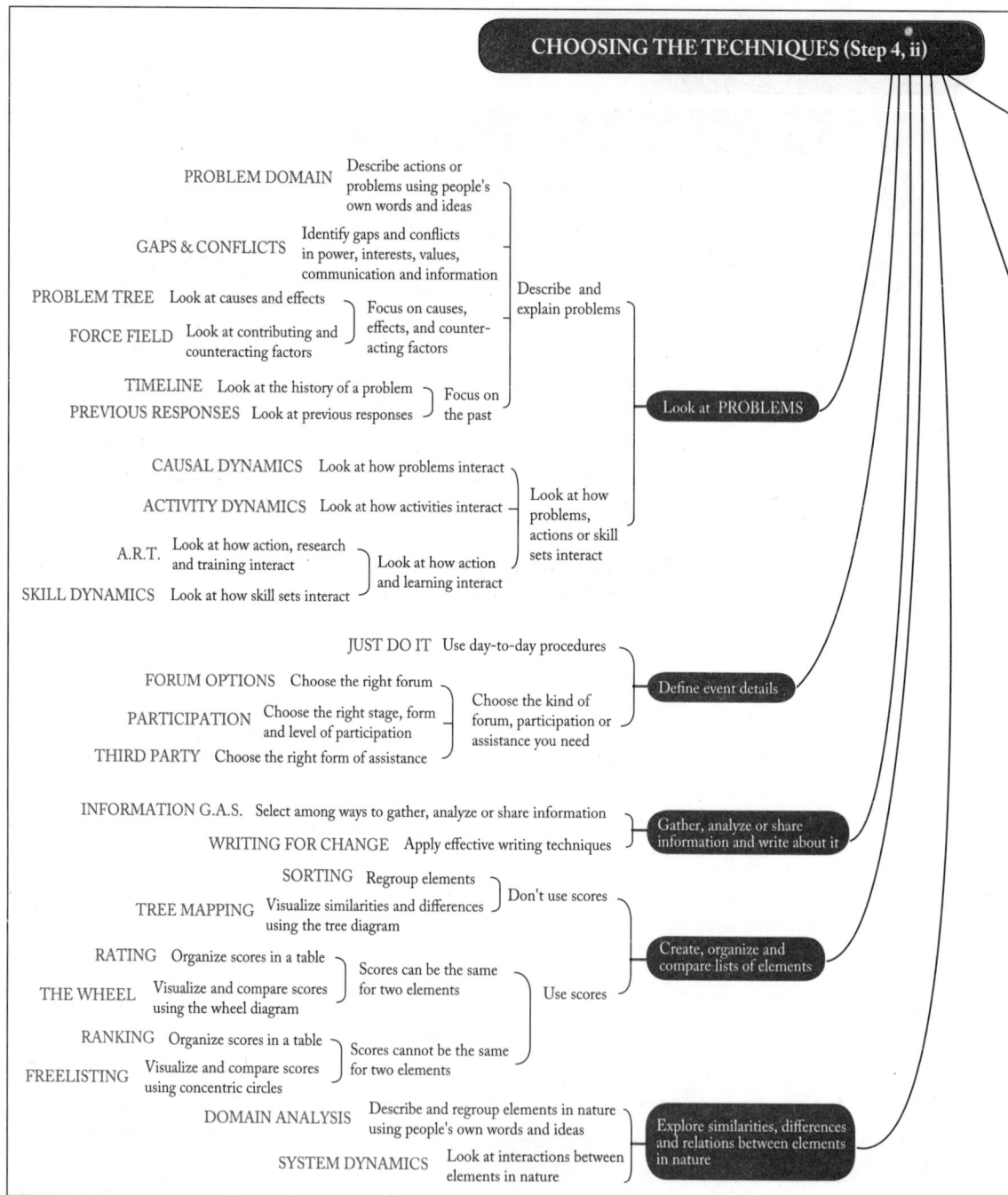

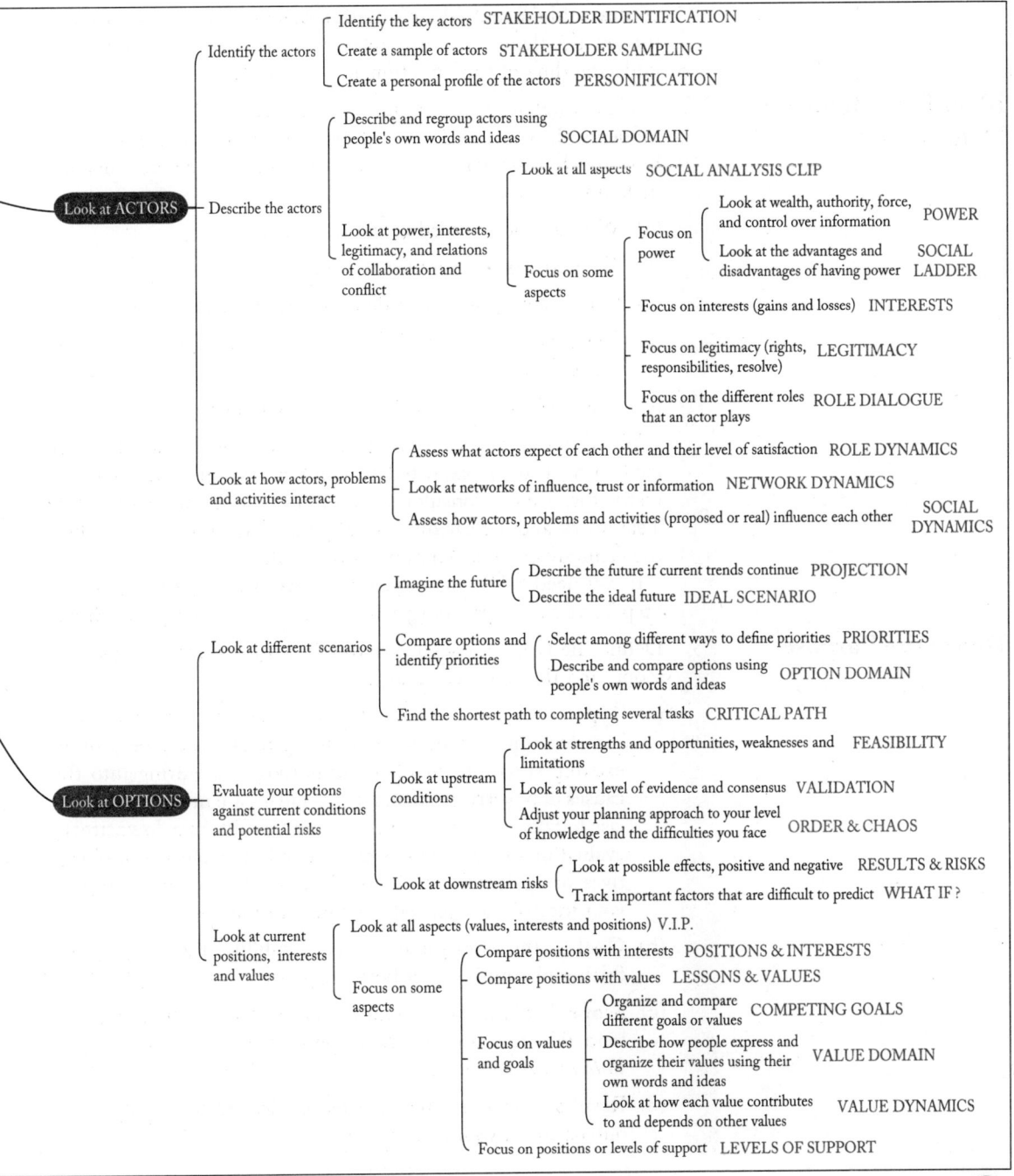

Look at ACTORS

- **Identify the actors**
  - Identify the key actors — STAKEHOLDER IDENTIFICATION
  - Create a sample of actors — STAKEHOLDER SAMPLING
  - Create a personal profile of the actors — PERSONIFICATION

- **Describe the actors**
  - Describe and regroup actors using people's own words and ideas — SOCIAL DOMAIN
  - Look at power, interests, legitimacy, and relations of collaboration and conflict
    - Look at all aspects — SOCIAL ANALYSIS CLIP
    - Focus on some aspects
      - Focus on power
        - Look at wealth, authority, force, and control over information — POWER
        - Look at the advantages and disadvantages of having power — SOCIAL LADDER
      - Focus on interests (gains and losses) — INTERESTS
      - Focus on legitimacy (rights, responsibilities, resolve) — LEGITIMACY
      - Focus on the different roles that an actor plays — ROLE DIALOGUE

- **Look at how actors, problems and activities interact**
  - Assess what actors expect of each other and their level of satisfaction — ROLE DYNAMICS
  - Look at networks of influence, trust or information — NETWORK DYNAMICS
  - Assess how actors, problems and activities (proposed or real) influence each other — SOCIAL DYNAMICS

Look at OPTIONS

- **Look at different scenarios**
  - Imagine the future
    - Describe the future if current trends continue — PROJECTION
    - Describe the ideal future — IDEAL SCENARIO
  - Compare options and identify priorities
    - Select among different ways to define priorities — PRIORITIES
    - Describe and compare options using people's own words and ideas — OPTION DOMAIN
  - Find the shortest path to completing several tasks — CRITICAL PATH

- **Evaluate your options against current conditions and potential risks**
  - Look at upstream conditions
    - Look at strengths and opportunities, weaknesses and limitations — FEASIBILITY
    - Look at your level of evidence and consensus — VALIDATION
    - Adjust your planning approach to your level of knowledge and the difficulties you face — ORDER & CHAOS
  - Look at downstream risks
    - Look at possible effects, positive and negative — RESULTS & RISKS
    - Track important factors that are difficult to predict — WHAT IF ?

- **Look at current positions, interests and values**
  - Look at all aspects (values, interests and positions) — V.I.P.
  - Focus on some aspects
    - Compare positions with interests — POSITIONS & INTERESTS
    - Compare positions with values — LESSONS & VALUES
    - Focus on values and goals
      - Organize and compare different goals or values — COMPETING GOALS
      - Describe how people express and organize their values using their own words and ideas — VALUE DOMAIN
      - Look at how each value contributes to and depends on other values — VALUE DYNAMICS
    - Focus on positions or levels of support — LEVELS OF SUPPORT

Consider the Setting

1. To design a SAS^2 inquiry, you should first explore the general **context** and the immediate **situation** that needs attention. Talk to the key people and read the relevant documents to validate your understanding of this situation and its context.

Identify Predefined Details

2. Some key details of your inquiry may already be decided and may influence the way you design the assessment process (for instance, how much time you have). Identify these predefined details, including:

   (a) **Who** will be involved in the assessment;

   (b) The participants' **profiles** and **roles**;

   (c) How much **time** will be dedicated to the assessment;

   (d) The available **inputs** (knowledge, decisions) from previous events; and

   (e) The role(s) that the **facilitator**(s) should play.

   When defining roles, decide whether or not the facilitator or facilitating team is expected to combine various roles, such as instructor, expert-consultant, researcher, note-taker, or actor. Teamwork and a clear division of labor may be necessary when the facilitator(s) must combine several roles.

   If you need SAS^2 techniques to answer these questions, go to Step 3 and start your inquiry with the assessment of key modalities.

Define the Purpose

3. Define the type of assessment you wish to perform, its goal, its scope, and the expected results.

   (a) **Type**: does the assessment stand alone or form part of a broader inquiry process? Is it an upstream assessment of an existing situation for planning purposes (inquiring into the causes of poverty, for instance), a midstream monitoring exercise to take stock of progress towards results, or a downstream evaluation of the outcome of your actions against your objectives or against your observations on the situation prior to your intervention (called baseline information)?

   (b) **Goal**: is the assessment for accountability, for learning and further planning, or for both purposes?

   (c) **Scope**: What is the amount of information, analysis and participation that are needed to perform the assessment? (See *Validation*)

   (d) **Results**: What are the expected or desired results (outputs, outcomes) of your assessment?

Make sure that the type of assessment you wish to perform, its goal, its scope, and the expected results are compatible with the predefined details identified in Step 2.

Design the Event

4. You are now in a position to design your inquiry in some detail. There are several steps to this process.

Identify and Clarify Your Main Question(s)…

(i) The first step consists in identifying the **main questions** that your inquiry is expected to answer. To do this, explore and unpack the different questions that may seem relevant, and clarify each of them. Then identify the question(s) that are the most important and that reflect the purpose and the key details of your assessment, as defined in Step 1 and Step 2. Make sure to clarify each question and the main ideas to be used in your inquiry, using terms that are meaningful to the participants.

For tips on how to clarify the main question(s), see *Active Listening*. If the questions are too general, use the **Laddering Down** technique to make them more concrete. Ask "What do you mean by this?" or "Can you think of a situation where these questions must be answered?" If the questions are too concrete, use the **Laddering Up** technique to make them more general. Ask "Why are these questions so important?", "What do they have in common?" or "Is there something we should know to help us answer these questions?"

…and Organize Them in Sequence

As you are clarifying the main questions to be explored, try to put the questions in the right **sequential order** using output-input reasoning (where the answer to one question serves as the input to the question that follows). For instance, the question you may ask about what your options are, should be answered first before you can raise the next question—what are your preferred options?

Select SAS² Techniques…

(ii) You have now reached an important step in the design process, which consists in selecting and sequencing the SAS² techniques and other methods that you need for your inquiry. To help you choose the right SAS² techniques, consult:

(a) Figures 1 and 2 (SAS² Events and Process Design, Choosing the Techniques), describing the reasoning that guides you when selecting the appropriate techniques; and

(b) The overview of *Social Analysis and All-Purpose Techniques* in Part 1 of this Guide (pages 32–37).

To be fully effective, SAS² must be combined with the learning systems and the facilitation procedures that are appropriate to the situation. There is no SAS² technique to do chemical soil analysis or to provide legal advice on land tenure issues, for instance. Nor does SAS² provide extensive tips and techniques on how to facilitate group discussions in all possible contexts. These topics require particular forms of knowledge and inquiry that must be combined with SAS² tools if collaborative inquiry and social engagement is to achieve the expected results. Choose the **combination of methods** that suits your needs, including the existing day-to-day rules and procedures to gather and analyze information, create priorities, make plans, resolve problems, take action, and interact with others in the process (see *Just Do It* and *Information G.A.S.*).

Vary and Order the Techniques

When using several techniques involving tables or diagrams, **vary the techniques** and the kinds of tables or diagrams you will be using so as to avoid fatigue.

You should also **identify the order** in which you plan to apply each technique. The way you organize the techniques in sequence should match the way you ordered the questions in Step 4.1 using output-input reasoning. If you are using Process Manager to plan an inquiry process extending over time, you can decide how to order the techniques at different stages in your project and when to plan them in detail, when you are ready to do so.

When sequencing the techniques, you may plan to pretest the technique with key parties involved in the process, if needed. Also, if you plan to use SAS² techniques to evaluate a project when completed, you may choose to do some **pre-post testing** by applying the same assessment technique twice: at the beginning of the process, before the activities are started, and then at the end to see if things have changed as planned.

Point of Entry and Iteration

To select the right module and techniques, a good question to ask is whether you should focus on assessing the *Problems*, profiling the *Actors*, or exploring the *Options* for action? Decide this in light of the main question(s) you're asking as well as the setting, the purpose and the predefined details of your inquiry. Focus on what is *more pressing* and leave the other issues (and modules) in the background until you're ready to explore them in detail. **Going back and forth** between *Problems*, *Actors*, and *Options* for action when managing a complex and dynamic situation may be important. Be aware that the inquiry you do may have to be revisited again later in light of changing circumstances or new information from other assessments.

Use Predefined or Elicited Concepts?

Some SAS[2] techniques such as *Gaps and Conflicts*, *Social Analysis CLIP* or *Legitimacy* can help you explore problems, actions, and relations by using predefined concepts adapted from the social sciences (power, legitimacy, gaps in values or information, for instance). Other techniques, including those entitled "Domain" or "Dynamics", involve elements, characteristics, and relations that are fully elicited by the participants. When looking for the right technique to apply in a particular situation, decide whether you should start with and validate predefined concepts or generate relevant concepts with the participants themselves.

Look at Characteristics or Interaction?

SAS[2] includes 13 techniques with either the word "Domain" or the word "Dynamics" in their titles. The "Domain" techniques are social adaptations of Personal Construct Psychology. They can be used to describe or **characterize** a series of elements (problems, activities, actors, skills or options, for instance) and levels of similarity between them, with the optional support of Cluster Analysis and Principal Component Analysis using Rep IV software. By contrast, the "Dynamics" techniques focus on the **interaction** between elements, including actors (*Network, Role or Social Dynamics*), problems (*Causal Dynamics*) or activities (*Activity Dynamics*). SAS[2] practitioners should keep this distinction between "domain characterization" and "dynamic interaction" in mind when selecting a technique.

Design All Steps

(iii) Define all the **steps** and the **procedures** used in each technique. Adjust each technique by choosing the right level of application and technology and adjusting the relative weight of formal analysis and description, narration or story telling. Decide how explicit the instructions should be and how participants should interact and contribute to the inquiry. The following guidelines can help you make these decisions.

Define the Level of Application

Use the instructions provided in each SAS[2] technique and your assessment of the following factors to decide how simple or advanced each application of a SAS[2] technique needs to be:

(a) How much **time** and **resources** do you have to apply the technique?

(b) How **familiar** are you with the technique?

It is usually safer to start with simpler applications of the technique you select and become familiar with it before you make full use of it.

(c) How **complex** are the issues? Can you address the issues using simple indicators of key factors, or do you need to divide these factors into their component parts (for instance, power can be divided into control over wealth, political authority, the use of force, and access to information and communication)?

One way to apply a technique at an advanced level consists in dividing a key variable into its component parts—looking at the various expressions of the **power** variable in *Social Analysis CLIP*, for instance. By contrast, you can reduce the level of application of a technique by focusing on some key indicators that summarize what the assessment is about. These indicators should be SMART—specific, measurable, applicable, realistic, and timely.

(d) How **reliable** do you want the results to be? Do you need to ensure that the analysis is valid by providing sound and detailed information and by making sure stakeholders agree with the findings? (See *Validation*)

(e) How much **dialogue** do you want there to be between knowledge systems (such as local knowledge and the natural sciences)?

(f) What are the **expected results** and how important are the decisions that will follow from the exercise? Are the **decisions reversible** if they prove to be wrong?

The level at which you apply a technique should be based on your answers to these questions. It is a good idea to avoid extremes: one, where you apply SAS^2 techniques at such advanced levels that real stakeholder participation becomes difficult and action is always pushed back into the distant future, once all factors are fully analyzed; and two, where you use the techniques in a mechanical and superficial way, without providing the details, nuances and analyses that you need to make the inquiry meaningful and reliable. To assess whether or not you're applying a SAS^2 technique at the right level, see *Validation* and *Order and Chaos*.

Choose the Right Technology

For each SAS^2 technique you use, you must decide what kind of facilitation equipment you will need, such as cards, flipcharts, drawing material, a projector, and so on. You should also decide whether you should use the technique in software or interactive online form, if available (*Social Analysis CLIP* and *Domain Analysis* techniques are currently supported by software).

Combine Formal Analysis and Narration

Think of the best way to combine and move between narration (describing events, telling stories) and formal analysis supported by diagrams and tables.

The role of formal analysis is to organize your information and findings in ways that are clear, logical, and succinct. Narration (whether oral or written) gives you the context, the sequence of events, *a sense of purpose*, and some details that add richness and texture to your understanding of the situation. When using SAS² techniques you can start with narratives and then convert the findings into formal analyses, or vice-versa. The important point to remember is to combine the two modes of understanding and communication, and adjust the relative weight of each mode to suit your needs. You should also carefully read the instructions provided in each technique on how to integrate the collection of quantitative data (ratings for instance) with the analysis and the interpretation of your findings in light of group comments and discussions.

Form and Move between Groups?

Decide whether you will divide all participants into subgroups and how each subgroup will contribute to the exercise (for example, by getting groups to complete the ratings for different rows in a table). Decide whether each subgroup should be homogeneous (using the specialized knowledge they have on the subject, for instance) or heterogeneous (to make sure the exercise expresses views that are representative of the entire group). Use the option of subgroups only if all participants don't need to be involved in all parts of the assessment.

Pay special attention to differences that may affect how people assess the same issues. You may create subgroups based on age, gender, marital status, ethnic origin, religion, education, the amount of time they have lived in a certain place, their place of residence (such as rural and urban, old and new immigrants), their occupation (such as non-agricultural workers in a farming area), or their role in an organization or project.

Plan realistic ways to help people participate in an inquiry process. This includes deciding whether all the key actors should be present or not. In some cases you may prefer to work only with actors that are keen to cooperate. You can then help them analyze the relevant issues and develop plans suited to their needs. In other cases you may prefer to ask a third party to facilitate the exercise by interviewing individuals or small groups separately, and then presenting the results at a general meeting where all the parties are together (with their prior consent).

Explain the Technique?

Decide when to share the step-by-step instructions of a technique, and when to avoid explaining these instructions to the participants so as not to detract their attention from the exercise and the substance of the discussion. In the latter case, the technique should be used discreetly to guide an interview or group facilitation process, and to organize the findings in the facilitator's mind or notebook (during or after the event). If you're using a technique that requires participants to complete a table, you can ask participants to compare and score cards that represent different elements (such as problems, activities, options or actors), and later enter the scores in the table.

Identify Remaining Details

(iv) Identify the remaining details of your inquiry process, those that were not predefined and identified in Step 2, including:

(a) **Who** will be involved in the assessment;

(b) The participants' **profiles** and **roles**;

(c) How much **time** will be dedicated to the assessment;

(d) The available **inputs** (knowledge, decisions) from previous events;

(e) The role(s) that the **facilitator**(s) should play.

Make sure that the decisions you take in regard to these details are compatible with the purpose of the assessment and all other decisions you have taken when designing the activity.

Plan the Documentation Process

5. Define the steps you will take to document the results of your SAS^2 assessment during and after the exercise (for example, by taking notes, voice recording, videography, and so on) and assign the related responsibilities (note taking, report writing, and so on). Decide how extensively you will report on the group discussions, and determine the exact purpose or use you will make of the documentation after the exercise (towards a formal report or an online publication, for example).

Documentation of the exercise should at least include the following elements:

(a) The purpose of the assessment;

(b) The context requiring the assessment;

(c) Process specifications;

(d) A descriptive analysis of the results;

(e) An interpretation of the results;

(f) Follow-up actions identified by the participants;

(g) Observations regarding what went well or difficulties encountered during the process.

See *Writing Guidelines* in this Guide for suggestions on what can be covered under each element.

Monitoring and Evaluation

This Guide shows how to design evidence-based and people-based inquiries that address the questions that people ask, at the right time and with the proper tools. The questions may be part of a problem or needs assessment, a strategic planning exercise, a risk assessment or a feasibility study. Monitoring and evaluation (M&E) questions such as "What are the results or impacts of our program or project thus far?", or "How well is the program or project using its resources?" can also be answered using SAS² concepts and tools. As with any SAS² inquiry, the skills needed to ask and answer M&E questions for a certain context include knowing how to ground the inquiry in a real learning process, select the correct techniques, scale the inquiry to the right level, and mediate different views of the M&E process and its findings.

M&E plays an important role in many projects and programs. The exercise usually involves a review of progress along the way (mid-stream monitoring) and then an assessment of the results of the project or program once it has ended (downstream evaluation). The goals and activities people want to monitor and evaluate are as varied as the projects and programs they are involved in. So are the baseline conditions against which the activities are assessed. Each project and program must decide what to monitor or evaluate. Sometimes, all activities must be evaluated against their expected results and goals. In other cases, a set or sub-set of activities needs to be looked at, each with its own objective and expected results. How M&E is done also depends on the context and purpose of the exercise. No single set of M&E steps or methods is useful in all situations. That's why we believe M&E is more of an art than a science.

Art or Science

Despite the need for flexibility in the design of M&E, almost every major development agency and institution has its own approach and language that staff and partners must use. Some common problems with these methods are that:

(a) The process is driven by outside experts, and the people directly involved are mostly excluded from design of that process;

(b) The methods make poor use of the actors' own knowledge and local forms of evaluation and learning;

(c) They focus on accounting for resources and neglect learning and adapting to changing circumstances;

(d) They use questions and ways of answering questions that are fixed in advance and do not evolve over time or adjust to the people's real needs;

(e) They assume high levels of certainty and predictable links between causes and effects (or between inputs and outputs, outcomes and impact);

(f) They draw sharp lines between research, planning, action, monitoring and evaluation, and often isolate people doing these different tasks from each other;

(g) They span a long time, require a high level of effort, and may not interact with other aspects of project or program processes, such as planning.

Asking the Right Questions

While some methods try to address these problems, we believe that efforts to create comprehensive M&E methods that work in all contexts are misguided. This Guide does not treat M&E as a special form of inquiry that requires unique concepts or special bundles of techniques. Instead, it defines M&E as any inquiry that addresses, at any time, the relationship between planned action and observed results. From this viewpoint, there are no M&E frameworks or methods per se, only M&E questions. Any tool or technique, whether it's a soil test or a conflict assessment using local stories, can be used to monitor or evaluate relationships between planned action and observed results, provided it is the right technique to answer the right question at the right time.

M&E Design

The Process Management method described in the previous section of the Guide is a flexible planning approach that helps design M&E procedures for specific project plans. It introduces rigor in project planning and at the same time integrates M&E into broader processes that are grounded in real learning situations. You can incorporate M&E into your *Process Manager* plans by following four basic steps:

1. Identify and record the specific project **activities** in your *Process Manager* map or other planning framework that require formal

evaluation during the project or at the end. Be aware that some activities do not need to be evaluated formally because there is no pressing need or the results are clear.

2. Ask **why** monitoring or evaluation is needed in each case: is it for accounting to the funding agency, for ongoing planning by project members, or to tell your project story to a broader audience? Make sure that you know how the M&E results will be used in each case.

3. Decide **who** you're doing M&E for and who you should do it with.

4. Based on your response to the previous points, determine **how** to do the M&E for each activity or set of activities (and related objectives or expected results), with what information and techniques, at what time, and at what level of detail?

Focusing on Actions

This approach to M&E design starts with project activities (goal-oriented actions) rather than the general and specific objectives (action-oriented goals) typical of Result-Based Management frameworks. While both planning strategies connect activities and their objectives or expected results, action-oriented goals (such as promoting democratic management of forest resources in a certain region) tend to be abstract and overly ambitious compared to goal-oriented actions (for example, setting up a multistakeholder committee to manage a region's forest resources more fairly). This makes the former difficult to monitor and evaluate. Goal-oriented actions are more grounded, and closer to the day-to-day language that people use to make plans and assess their progress.

Selecting

The *Guidelines for SAS² Events and Process Design* and techniques such as *Information G.A.S* help you **select** and combine the right techniques and the evidence you need based on a clear idea of the context, purpose, and expected uses of your M&E process. The right tool for a certain M&E process may come from SAS², or it may come from another source. When possible, M&E plans should use local methods that are already in place and have worked well (see *Just Do It!*). When it's time to select the technique, determine how best to combine qualitative analysis (such as storytelling) and quantitative information (data displayed in tables and figures). If you need precise data, you can decide to create SMART indicators (specific, measurable, applicable, realistic, and timely) that can reduce complex results to simpler forms, thus helping you measure progress.

Scaling

The *Guidelines* and a technique such as *Validation* also help you **scale** your M&E process, by defining the level of information and consensus that is "good enough" in a certain context. Deciding to scale your assessment up or down will depend on the purpose of your M&E, as well as the time and the resources available. It will also depend on the real scale or complexity of a program or a project. For example, unlike single-site assessments, multi-site evaluations often require a scaling up of M&E tools, to produce findings that capture not only the similarities and differences between local activities but also their complex interactions at broader levels.

Timing

The art of M&E involves selecting the right techniques, and then scaling the information to be gathered and analyzed according to your needs. M&E is also a matter of proper **timing**. Where project and program goals are mostly technical or where you can predict key factors, detailed planning of M&E activities in advance may be possible (see *The Wheel* example on page 305). The M&E process may then include plans to do the assessment twice: at the start of a process, before action begins, and then at the end to see if things have changed as planned. More often, however, projects and programs involve many goals and stakeholders interacting in unpredictable settings. Some goals may not be shared by all parties and may not be stable over time. This may force people to respond to unforeseen circumstances "in the middle" of complex situations (as in the Katkari example for *Process Manager* mentioned above). Process Manager helps manage these complex situations. Some techniques, such as *Order and Chaos*, will help assess how predictable things are and how sure stakeholders are that they can attain their goals. The less certain they are, the more monitoring and continuous planning they may need. The technique *What If?* also helps track factors that people find hard to predict and that may greatly affect their planned actions and the results they desire.

Process Manager helps you respond flexibly to both pressing needs and longer-term goals. This allows people to design M&E processes that evolve along the way, as project needs change, and in response to situations that may not have been foreseen. Whether the M&E process is for accounting purposes or to support learning and social action, a rigid package or method cannot replace judgment and creativity in combining methods and techniques and using them in the right circumstances. To succeed, M&E must be systematic as well as grounded and "systemic", which means doing the assessment at the right time, when it is truly needed.

SAS² Facilitation and Active Listening

SAS² Facilitation

The following tips suggest ways to facilitate SAS² assessments and apply active listening skills during the process. They apply to SAS² as a whole and are not meant to cover all aspects of group facilitation and active listening. For tips that apply to certain techniques, see the instructions for those techniques.

Pretesting

Start with simple applications of a technique and become familiar with it before you make full use of it.

If possible, design and pretest the technique with key parties involved in the assessment.

Explaining the Technique

Clearly state the main question and the key terms and ideas of a technique. If necessary, restate the question and key terms using words that are more meaningful to the participants.

If using the technique in a language into which it is not yet translated (versions exist only in English, Spanish and French), do some preliminary translation.

Don't try to explain the full technique before using it. Outline and seek agreement on the assessment's expected results, and then proceed step by step, with breaks during the process as needed.

Managing Time

Plan enough time for participants to go through all the steps of a technique.

You may decide at any time to stop so that participants can find more information about the issues being raised. Once the information is collected people can always return to the assessment and revise their findings, as needed.

To save time, you may divide the group into smaller groups, and then ask each one to complete one part of the assessment (for example, by having groups complete the ratings for different rows in a table). Decide whether each group should be homogeneous (using the special knowledge they have on a subject, for instance) or heterogeneous (to make sure the assessment represents the views of the entire group). Use the option of smaller groups only if all participants don't need to be involved in all parts of the process.

Numbers and Measurements

Keep in mind that numbers and measurements are not ends in themselves but rather means to provide information, clarify people's views or knowledge about a topic, define their priorities, direct their attention during a group discussion, and facilitate dialogue and learning. Do not let the numbers overshadow the discussion. While the questions contained in surveys are designed to generate numbers and evidence, the point of SAS[2] is to use numbers and measurements to generate questions and support discussions.

When planning several assessments that use tables or diagrams, vary the techniques and the kinds of tables or diagrams you will be using so as to avoid fatigue.

Creative Expression

Building awareness, energizing the group and connecting to emotions through humor, games, improvisation and other forms of creative expression (art, magic, stories) can help facilitate teamwork, problem solving, and learning grounded in real life situations. They are all the more effective when they are selected or designed to support and complement the immediate learning process or inquiry.

Group Differences

If participants disagree about some issues that may affect the results of an inquiry, decide how important this is to the analysis and make a list of points to discuss further or research later.

Be aware that the same people may be members of different groups that may have different views on the issues being raised. For instance, some people may have their own views on certain problems or actions at the same time as they belong to broader groups (for whom they act or speak) that have other views.

When you compare the analyses of different groups and look for possible disagreements and misunderstandings, ensure that group differences are clearly defined and relevant to the exercise. This means that the members of the same group should share similar characteristics. When people initially form separate groups, you may regroup them if you and they think their similarities are more important than their differences (this is called aggregation). On the other hand, if the differences within a group are more important than the similarities, divide the group into meaningful subgroups (this is called disaggregation). Pay special attention to differences that may affect how people assess the same issues. You may create subgroups based on age, gender, marital status, ethnic origin, religion, education, the amount of time they have lived in a certain place, their place of residence (such as rural and urban, old and new immigrants), or type of occupation (such as non-agricultural workers in a farming area).

Think of realistic ways to help people participate in an inquiry. Doing some analyses when all the key actors are present may not always be possible or desirable, especially when there is intense conflict and little interest in resolving it. In some cases you may prefer to work only with actors that are keen to cooperate. You can then help them analyze the relevant issues and develop plans suited to their needs. In other cases you may prefer to ask a third party to facilitate the exercise by interviewing individuals or small groups separately, and then presenting the results at a general meeting where all the parties are together (with their prior consent).

If you do the assessment with some stakeholders but not all of them, be aware that any resulting plans may reflect mostly the views of the participants and others who have similar views or interests.

Keep in mind that you will not dispel a misunderstanding or disagreement simply by identifying it. Knowing the probable cause(s) is just as important.

Social Effect

Keep in mind that doing a group assessment is a social interaction among participants, and also between the facilitator and the individuals or groups doing the assessment. This social effect may influence the views that participants will express, especially when the views involve sensitive issues. Participants will then express views that reflect what they believe they should be saying, not what they actually think. When this happens, you can discuss the problem openly with the participants. Or you can facilitate the assessment by interviewing individuals or small groups separately and then presenting anonymous results at a general meeting where all the parties are together (with their prior consent).

Making Suggestions

Usually, the facilitator should not express his/her own personal views about the issues being raised, unless he/she is an actor and a member of the group doing the exercise. In this case, you need to be careful about taking on the dual role of actor and facilitator.

Some techniques allow the facilitator to suggest ways to resolve certain problems and learning opportunities (as in all Domain analyses). When making these suggestions, be brief. Let the participants decide what is relevant, and make sure there is enough time for the participant(s) to reflect and respond.

SAS² Active Listening

Authors	J.M. Chevalier, M. Bourassa, and D.J. Buckles
General Listening Tips	The following tips are offered to help you do active listening when using SAS², whether you are working one-to-one or with a group.

The Verbal

Open Questions

Pose open questions, such as *Tell me about your experience...* or *What do you think would happen if....* Open questions do not lend themselves to "yes" or "no" answers. Make sure the person or group understands your question. If not, restate it using other words.

Paraphrases

Restate what someone has said, using the speaker's key words and starting your sentence with phrases such as *What I'm hearing is that...,* *I see that..., If I understand you well...,* or *In other words what you're saying is that...*

Summary

Summarize the main ideas expressed during a discussion, as needed. Use key words and begin your sentence with *To sum up this point...*

Note Taking

Gather ideas on flipcharts. Decide whether to take notes on one, two or three flipcharts. The first could be used to capture all the points that are made, the second to summarize and organize the main points, and the third to list issues that may have to wait until later to be discussed. If possible, have one person write on the flipcharts while the other listens and summarizes what should be written.

Synthesis and Validation

End the discussion with a synthesis and validate the synthesis (*Can we conclude that...? Is it fair to say that...?*).

The Non-Verbal

The Implicit Body Language, Emotions

Reflect on and draw out the implicit meanings, feelings and non-verbal messages that people are expressing (without being aware of it). These may add meaning to what is being said (*If I hear you well, it seems that... Perhaps we should talk about...?*).

Self-Awareness and Empathy

Self-Awareness

Take time to reflect on your state of mind before you begin active listening. Be aware of and let go of immediate concerns that may affect your ability to listen.

While listening to what others have to say, be aware of any bias, feelings or immediate reactions you may have. Take stock of these when you breathe in, and let go when you breathe out. Be aware of your verbal and non-verbal language, and adjust if necessary.

Be aware of your own gaps in knowledge. Acknowledge information held by others and invite them to share it.

Empathy

Show empathy and appreciation while listening (*I understand… I see/hear what you're saying… I appreciate the fact that…*). Avoid being judgmental (*Lucky you! I envy you! Poor you! How awful!*). Do not describe similar experiences you have had in the past.

Be aware of moments that are intense. Do not try to rush through them.

Dialogue

Encourage active listening and empathy toward third parties that are being talked about (*How would you state, in one sentence, what they are trying to tell you?*)

To support listening in a group, allow time for people to reflect on the topic (best, if in writing) before the dialogue begins. Encourage people to listen with presence of mind and to let go of planning what they will say.

Suspended Judgment

Avoid making positive or negative judgments. Don't start your sentence with *Yes but…*, *I believe that…*, *In my opinion….* At the start of a new discussion, start with a brainstorming task where all ideas can be expressed freely, without being judged or interrupted by others.

Rhythm and Silences

Avoid rapid speech and frequent interruptions. Slow down. Make sure to listen instead of preparing what you're going to say next. Don't try to fill silence. It's a time for people to pause and think. Accept and welcome silence, either when the group calls for it, or when it arrives on its own.

Welcome good humor, laughter, and enjoyment of the process.

Orientation

Clarifying the Goals

Discuss and clarify what the group expects from a process. (*What do you expect from this meeting? If I understand you well, you'd like to…*). Take into account how much time is needed, and available, to achieve these goals. Apply active listening tips to make sure you clearly understand what people expect.

Selecting a Technique	Select a SAS^2 tool or any other technique that fits people's expectations. Make your own judgment of what is needed and timely.

Framing

Unpacking	Keep track of and note different lines of thinking (*I'm hearing three topics being raised. They seem to be…*). When several issues are raised in a discussion, unpack them so that you can address each of them separately and establish priorities.
Sequencing	Identify the issue that should be addressed first (and those to follow). Choose the right moment to end one topic and proceed to the next (*Perhaps we could move on to the next topic concerning…*).
Parking	Identify topics that may need to be "parked" or discussed later.
Prior Information	Plan in advance so that the documents, facts or evidence needed to conduct a well-informed discussion are on hand for the group.

Reframing

Positive Reframing	If needed, restate negative statements as positive statements (*If I understand you well, you'd like your team meetings to be short and to the point…*).
Congruency	When statements seem to contradict each other, try to clarify them, without expressing judgment (*It makes me curious to hear that…. What surprises me in what you're saying is that…*). When needed, note areas of both disagreement and likely agreement (*Some people seem to be saying that… Others think that…*).

Scaling

Laddering Up or Down	When statements seem too general or vague, use laddering down questions to make them more specific or concrete. (*For instance? Can you give an example? What makes you say that? What do you mean by this? Can you tell us about a situation that describes what you're saying?*) When statements seem too specific or concrete, use laddering up questions to make the meaning clearer. (*Why is it so? What have you learned from this? Why does this matter? What do these things have in common?*)

The Good Enough Principle	Make sure that the information and analysis that are part of a discussion are "good enough" to meet people's needs and expectations, without being exhaustive or exhausting (see *Validation*).
Process Observations	Welcome questions or comments about the process being used in a discussion. State what needs to change in a positive way, and adjust when possible.
	If you are not sure how to proceed, share your doubts and ask for help. While you are fully responsible for how you respond to situations, the active listening experience is co-created.

Writing Guidelines

You can use the following guidelines to create a report on a **one-time application** of a SAS² technique or to **compile a series of SAS² assessments** that are part of a larger inquiry (such as a project report or a thesis, which may have additional formatting requirements). For examples of reports using these guidelines, see Part 2 of this Guide.

When you report on a SAS² assessment, you are helping others learn about your findings and how they were made. Writing also helps sharpen your thinking about the results and ways to improve how you use SAS² techniques. By writing technique reports first, you may find that writing a larger project report is easier.

The guidelines provide a logical structure for reporting on the results of each SAS² assessment. They consist of headings that describe what needs to be reported in each topic, with an emphasis on: how you applied the SAS² technique, key findings, and actions that emerged from the inquiry. We recommend that you use these headings to avoid repeating information within the report.

Title

Express in the title what the assessment was about, why you did it, and where it happened.

For example, your title might be: Creating Strategic Alliances in the Tobacco Farming Areas of Southern Bangladesh.

Key Words

List key words that describe important ideas or people that you are writing about in the report. Include the name of the technique as it appears on the SAS² website under Tools.

For example, key words might be: Social Analysis CLIP, Bangladesh, Agriculture, Tribal People, and Stakeholder Analysis.

Reference and Acknowledgements

Provide the **full reference** for your report so that it can be correctly cited and found by others. The reference should include the author(s), the title of the report, the year it was written and where it is published or posted online. You can also **acknowledge** people or other research reports that helped you complete the assessment or the report itself.

We suggest you refer to the *IDRC Style Guide*. It sets out standard rules for citations and referencing research reports in the English language. It also provides useful guidelines for punctuation. In the world of publishing it is important to use one style consistently.

For example, a full and correct reference for an unpublished report is: "Suazo, L. 2006. Assessing the profile of organizations doing joint research on watershed management in Honduras. Social Analysis Systems[2] Technique Report #1, 5 pp."

Who is an Author?

An author is someone who plays an important role in many of the key steps of an inquiry. Those steps are (*i*) conception of the research; (*ii*) design of the inquiry; (*iii*) data collection and analysis; (*iv*) interpretation and explanation of results; and (*v*) writing the final document. Normally, to be an author, a person must have been part of at least 3 steps, including writing the final document.[1]

Who Should be Acknowledged?

You should acknowledge people who provided strong support to several steps of an inquiry but are not authors. For example, an acknowledgement might be: "The author wishes to acknowledge the efforts of Rafiqul Huq Titu who helped to design the inquiry and collect data."

Context

Describe the circumstances that surround the problem to be solved or the action to be taken. If the assessment is a **one-time application** of a SAS[2] technique, provide enough information that a reader will be able to understand what the assessment was about and why it was needed. If the assessment is part of a **series of SAS[2] assessments** within a broader inquiry project, provide only the information that directly relates to the situation that led to the assessment. Indicate where the initiative for the assessment comes from and the role of the event convenors.

Within this heading, you can refer to documents that provide more information on the problem or situation, the people involved, and the place where the problem or situation is happening. This helps to avoid repeating the same information when two or three SAS[2] reports build on one another.

An example of a context statement for an assessment done as part of a series of SAS[2] activities might be: "Lama is a township of tribal people and Bengali settlers in Bandarban District of southern Bangladesh. The British American Tobacco Company (BATC) and other tobacco buyers have been promoting the production of tobacco in the villages of

---

[1] Adapted from Don Peden, Guidelines to Authorship. 2001. In Barker, A. and F. Manji. Writing for Change. International Development Research Centre/Fahamu, Ottawa/London.

the township since 1984. UBINIG, a Bangladeshi non-governmental organization that supports ecological farming in a nearby township, has recently contacted a few farmers in Lama that want to stop tobacco farming. UBINIG wonders whether it should launch a broad campaign to promote ecological farming in this region. For more information on the project, see: UBINIG; Carleton University, 2006. From Tobacco to Food Production: Assessing Constraints and Transition Strategies in Bangladesh. First Interim Technical Report to IDRC, 18 pp."

Purpose

State the immediate reasons for doing the SAS[2] assessment, as understood and shared by those who were part of it.

For example: To identify the strategic alliances that UBINIG might use to support farmers who want to stop tobacco farming.

Process Summary

(a) Name who hosted the assessment, describe briefly where the event was held, list the different stakeholder groups who were invited to participate, and state the number and gender of participants.

(b) Summarize the steps you followed when doing the assessment, making special note of how you modified or adapted the technique to the setting. Your observations on problems that arose and positive aspects of the process should be given in Observations on the Process (see final step, below).

(c) Indicate who is reporting on the process and what steps were taken to inform participants about planned reports and uses of their information.

An example of a process summary is: "UBINIG invited three male farmers from Lama to their Cox's Bazaar Center for a meeting. One of the farmers had been working with UBINIG for a year and had already stopped tobacco farming, in favor of horticulture. He identified and invited to the meeting two tobacco farmers who were open to doing the same. The merits of shifting out of tobacco into horticulture and other forms of agriculture were discussed, along with the challenges that both they and UBINIG have in the region. The farmers created a list of stakeholders and used *Social Analysis CLIP* to discuss characteristics for each stakeholder until there was a common understanding. The group then discussed the history of conflict and collaboration among stakeholders, followed by actions UBINIG could take to mobilize support for a shift to ecological farming. The process was facilitated by the report author, with permission to report on the findings given by the participants."

Analysis

(a) Describe the information (such as elements in a list and their characteristics) and comments made during the assessment.

(b) Summarize the findings or patterns that emerged from this information. In writing the analysis, focus first on the main findings, then describe less important or finer patterns, relationships or comments made during the assessment.

(c) Indicate who contributed to the analysis.

The following **example** focuses only on the main findings of an analysis: "The profile of 15 different stakeholders is based on ratings of three factors that can affect the proposed action—interests, power, and legitimacy (as shown in Table 1). The overall stakeholder structure shows that more powerful stakeholders have opposing interests, and that some also have lower-class allies. A large block of forceful stakeholders led by the BATC would be strongly opposed to the proposed shift from tobacco to ecological farming. An opposing block of three stakeholders holds similar power to this group, and they support the shift to ecological farming. Between these two blocks lies a block of three vulnerable or marginalized stakeholders (labelled Tobacco Farmers, Laborers, and Food Farmers) whose interests would be negatively affected by or neutral to the proposed action".

Interpretation

Explain why you think you got the findings that you did or the implications that follow from the assessment. The reasons may reflect explanations that participants know and consider valid, or they may express new insights that emerge at the end of the assessment. The interpretation involves taking a step back from the analysis and using a broader viewpoint to understand the implications or the reasons behind the findings. Indicate who contributed to the interpretation.

An example of an interpretive statement might be: "The scenario is a challenging one for UBINIG because tobacco farmers do not believe their interests will be served by the proposed action, and food farmers are neutral at best".

Action

State the course of action participants decide on at the end of the assessment. If the assessment is a one-time application of a SAS^2 technique, the information you provide should be complete, to enable a reader to see why the action matters. If the assessment is part of a series of SAS^2 assessments within a broader inquiry, state the course of action that will be taken immediately, based on the analysis and interpretation. In some cases, the course of action may be to consult further or to plan a new assessment on an issue that is still not resolved.

An example of an action statement might be: "Despite the challenges, the following actions were identified. UBINIG could indirectly influence tobacco farmers through its recent, positive link with food farmers who have close ties with tobacco farmers. While promising, this action would have little influence on tobacco farmers unless the campaign was supported by new information on the net economic benefits of farming options. UBINIG and the farmers decided to research the economic gains and losses from tobacco farming and compare these to various forms of ecological farming. The participants also discussed building closer relations with the Chittagong Hill Tracts Regional Council and the BADC irrigation scheme as a way to create support for the shift both from the Zone Commander and the marginal stakeholders. They decided, however, that this action should come later, once the perceived interests of tobacco farmers and food farmers change in ways that show more support for the proposed action".

Observations on the Process

(a) Describe positive lessons and the problems that arose during the assessment and how these problems have been managed at each step of the process.

(b) If relevant, give the results of any validation exercise applied to the results of the assessment (see the SAS² *Validation* technique).

An **example** of an observation on the process is: "The main question 'To what extent does A cause or contribute to B' was initially confused with 'To what extent does B cause or contribute to A'. This problem was managed by using the tree metaphor and drawing. The analysis generated a lot of enthusiasm for experiments and provided some direction regarding what crop features to consider. The result of the exercise was considered a key turning point for participants interested in pursuing alternatives to tobacco. They noted that it provided them with a clear explanation of their situation that would be useful as well to discussions with other farmers not yet convinced of the kinds of investments they need to make to shift out of tobacco".

PART 2
SAS^2 Techniques and Learning

Thinking Across Boundaries

The real voyage of discovery consists not in seeing new landscapes but in having new eyes.

Marcel Proust

The concepts and skillful means of collaborative inquiry call for new ways to support thinking and learning across boundaries. The approach we propose is one that fosters understanding and dialogue across institutions, classes, professions, disciplines, generations, and genders, in pursuit of common ground. It also bridges tensions between quantitative versus qualitative information, efficiency versus participation, accountability versus adaptability, and simple versus advanced methods. Our belief is that by moving beyond these divisions we can arrive at the essential points common to all genuine forms of human inquiry.

This section of the Guide provides practical ways to support social thinking and learning, in institutions, communities, and workplaces. The 18 techniques outlined here represent about one-third of the techniques available on the SAS^2 website (www.sas2.net). They focus on ways to assess three kinds of issues: problems, actors, and options. The techniques help to identify and analyze real-life problems, examine relationships among people, or explore alternative options, the conditions needed to achieve them, and the values, interests, and positions that different people hold in certain situations. Also included here are techniques to assess projects and plans and validate the results of an inquiry.

The skillful means that support collaborative inquiry are built into the design and step-by-step instructions for each technique. Efforts to mediate and ground an assessment start with Process Manager, and the process and event design guidelines described in Part 1. Part 2 continues with techniques that focus on identifying the situation or action to be assessed, defining the actors, and adapting the categories and terms used in the assessment. Detailed instructions in each technique help guide the assessment. Suggestions for simpler and more advanced versions at the end of each technique point to ways to scale the technique based on the resources and goals of the people involved. This kind of flexible design lends itself to using SAS^2 techniques with other day-to-day rules and methods people use to gather and analyze information, set priorities, make plans, resolve problems, take action, and interact with others along the way. Finally, all techniques include a series of guidelines and scenarios that can help add analytical and narrative depth to the results and decisions people take.

The way we have presented the techniques follows the standard design for a SAS^2 Introductory Workshop. This design supports a hands-on, incremental and holistic approach to learning that seeks to balance and integrate action, research and training. All workshop participants, and people who choose to use this section as a self-study guide, are encouraged to work in real teams and do real work while they learn new skills. Each time you apply a technique, it can be grounded in the problem(s), project(s) or situation(s) you currently engage in or plan to work on in the near future. When people use SAS[2] with real, multi-stakeholder groups, the learning process becomes meaningful and useful right away.

An example that shows how a technique was used and key learnings that came from that process immediately follows the description of each technique. Most examples are drawn from groups in South Asia and Latin America. Some examples involve Canadian organizations doing international work. Each example was written using the Writing Guidelines offered at the end of Part 1. Those Guidelines urge writers to be clear and brief.

All examples used here are based on real issues faced by organizations and groups. Topics range from land issues and local economic development to project planning. While grounded in these broader issues, the reports on the assessments are for single events, not a series of assessments that form a larger collaborative inquiry. Those more detailed and nuanced accounts are available elsewhere, in project reports, video clips, graduate theses, books, and peer reviewed articles.

Workshop and Self-Study Guidelines

This chapter describes the steps in a SAS² Introductory Workshop. The Workshop covers many key concepts and techniques in the context of real-life applications and with the guidance of a certified Instructor. Independent study of these techniques requires an **incremental learning** strategy inspired by the rule of practice-makes-perfect. Potential users should start with simpler versions of those techniques they are not familiar with, preferably in low-risk situations.

To understand **SAS² as a whole** without mastering all the techniques, learners can do four things: read carefully the conceptual foundations presented in Part 1, become familiar with the modular organization of SAS² techniques (*Problems, Actors, Options, All-Purpose Techniques*), incorporate Process Management in their own work, and start using the *Guidelines for SAS² Events and Process Design*.

Your Action-Research-Training Profile (A.R.T.)

A.R.T. (Action-Research-Training) is a good place to start learning basic SAS² concepts. You can use this Venn diagram technique in the Problems module to assess the balance and integration of three project components: (*i*) Actions, aimed at achieving project goals, (*ii*) Research, consisting of data collection and analysis, and (*iii*) Training, involving capacity-building events and strategies.

A central goal of SAS² concepts, techniques, and training workshops is to help users integrate all three components in their own work.

Introduction to SAS²

You should have a quick look at Part 1 of this Guide, especially the two bubble maps showing the *Social Analysis* and *All-Purpose Techniques* and then *How to Use Process Manager (PMr)* and *Guidelines for SAS² Events and Process Design*. These will help you become familiar with SAS² tools and strategies to integrate action, research, and training. For those who would like to start with an overview of SAS² concepts, see the section entitled *Foundations and Skillful Means*.

What Are Your Plans?

Now that you've been briefly introduced to SAS², you can use Process Manager to map out your immediate project plans or activities. This is a major step that will help you ground your learning of SAS^2 concepts and tools in concrete situations. See *How to Use Process Manager* (*PMr*) in Part 1 of this Guide.

Levels of Planning: Order and Chaos

The next step involves choosing the right planning approach, using *Order and Chaos* (in Options). You can apply this technique to the project plans or activities identified when you used Process Manager. *Order and Chaos* asks two keys questions:

1. How do you assess your chances of achieving your project goals?
2. How confident or certain are you in the knowledge that you have about the conditions or factors affecting your plan?

Whereas Result-Based Management (RBM) applies to situations of relative order, where your chances of achieving project goals are good and the level of confidence in your knowledge is high, the Process Manager approach developed for SAS^2 works better where there is relative chaos involving uncertainty and the risk of failure. See *Process Management* in Part 1.

Where to Start: Problems, Actors or Options?

Now that you've mapped out your project activities using Process Manager, you need to decide which SAS^2 techniques to apply. This raises a general question: when applying SAS^2 to a project, what should be your point of entry? Should you start by looking at the Actors (stakeholder analysis), their Problems, or their Options for action (see the corresponding Modules in Social Analysis Techniques)?

When people discuss the point-of-entry question in a training workshop, all participants can divide themselves into groups that take different positions on this issue. Each group can then explain its position and try to recruit members from other groups. Participants can also identify well-known methods that support each position (for instance Appreciative Inquiry starts with the options or visions of the future). The exercise can end with a short discussion of the SAS^2's position on this issue: where you start depends on where you are!

What's the Problem?

If project activities call for problem analysis, begin with the Problems module. To become familiar with these tools, you should start with a quick review of those techniques that are well-known in participatory action-research, including the following:

Problem Tree

Problem Tree helps you analyze the first and second-level causes and effects of a core problem.

Force Field	*Force Field* helps you understand people's views about the factors that cause a problem and those that stop it from becoming worse.
Timeline	*Timeline* helps you identify the events that have created a certain problem or situation. It explores people's views and knowledge about how a problem or situation has evolved over time, and changes that have occurred in the process.
Gaps and Conflicts	*Gaps and Conflicts* helps you find out if your key problem is mostly about gaps or conflicts in power, interests (gains and losses), moral values, or information and communication.
Key PMr Questions	If time permits, you can apply one or two of the preceding techniques to a concrete problem you are faced with in your project. Practise techniques that you are not already familiar with. Answer the **two key PMr questions that SAS^2 instructors ask at the end of every exercise:**

1. What new plans should you make and include in your Process Manager Activity Map based on the results so far?
2. Can you plan to use the technique you have just learned in upcoming project activities?

Causal Dynamics	The next step uses *Causal Dynamics* to assess the causes of a key problem, and the way that each cause affects other causes. This important technique is a SAS^2 adaptation and novel development of input-output analysis, a well-known technique used in economics, and economic policy and planning for the past half-century. You should apply this technique (in the Problems Module) to a concrete problem you are faced with in your project. You should also answer the **two key PMr questions** that come at the end of each exercise (see above).
How Good Is Your Analysis?	When using SAS^2, you need to ask yourself at the end of each assessment: how valid are the results of this assessment? To answer this question use *Validation* (in the Options Module). Learn this technique by applying it to the *Causal Dynamics* analysis you just did.
Validation	*Validation* asks two questions:

(a) To what extent is your assessment based on evidence (sound and sufficient information and analysis)?
(b) To what extent does your assessment achieve consensus through collaborative thinking?

The extent to which your assessment should be based on evidence and consensus depends on various factors, such as how much time and information you have, whether it is urgent that you act, the impact the assessment will have on your project activities, how much stakeholder approval and involvement is needed, and so on.

Good Enough Principle

Validation implies that you should use each assessment tool at the best possible level of detail (simple, intermediate, or advanced). An assessment is *good enough* when it takes into account what is feasible in each case (given limits on time and resources), and what level of evidence and agreement you need for the assessment to achieve its purpose. (See "Defining the Level of Application" in *Guidelines for SAS² Events and Process Design.*)

Who Are the Actors?

Stakeholder Identification

SAS² offers many tools to define and address relationships among people involved in real-life problems, situations and project activities (see the Actors Module). *Stakeholder Identification* is a technique to help you choose the method that you need to identify the key parties or stakeholders involved in a core problem or action. You can also use this technique to visualize the differences between stakeholders who may influence a situation or course of action and stakeholders who may be affected by it.

Social Analysis CLIP

Another important technique for stakeholder analysis, with its own on-line software tool (www.sas2.net), is *Social Analysis CLIP.* This technique helps create profiles of the parties involved in a core problem or action. These profiles are based on four CLIP factors:

(a) Existing relations of **Collaboration and Conflict;**

(b) **Legitimacy;**

(c) **Interests;** and

(d) **Power.**

You can use this technique to describe the characteristics and relationships of key stakeholders in your project. Once you are finished, you should answer the **two key PMr questions** (see above), and explore what you can do to resolve social problems, such as managing conflict, building trust or empowering marginalized groups.

Social Domain

Social Domain helps you characterize and compare actors using terms and characteristics chosen by the participants themselves. It also helps you look for ways to negotiate views of actors across social and cultural boundaries, test people's views against experience, solve problems, and identify learning opportunities. It is a SAS[2] adaptation and development of the concepts and techniques of Personal Construct Psychology, and a powerful means to make visible knowledge areas that are neglected or hidden from the view of expert-based assessments.

You are encouraged to enter the results you obtain from *Social Domain* in the Rep IV software available through the SAS[2] website. This user-friendly software allows you to do statistical analyses of the results of all SAS[2] techniques that have the word 'Domain' in their titles.

What Are the Options?

SAS[2] also provides many tools that explore options for action (see the Options Module in *Social Analysis and All-Purpose Techniques*).

Values, Interests, Positions

A good place to start is *V.I.P.* (*Values, Interests, Positions*). You can use this technique to compare the positions that stakeholders take on a problem or action with their actual interests and the moral values they hold. Use these findings to plan actions that better reflect the interests and the values of the parties involved.

As with previous exercises, use the results you obtain here to create inputs for the next exercises and project plans.

Ideal Scenario

Ideal Scenario (in the Options Module) offers ways to develop visions of an ideal future using current strengths and accomplishments. You may already know about some of these techniques. They include the *Tree of Means and Ends*, a drawing that turns your analysis of a core problem and its causes and effects (using *Problem Tree*) into a statement about your main objective, the ways to achieve it, and the reasons you wish to pursue it. *I Have a Dream!* starts with a provocative idea and explores its implications. The *Vision Circle* helps you create a statement about the ideal future, using guided visualization for the group and input from individual participants. The *Ideal Scenario Tapestry* collects vision drawings using real or imagined life forms or scenes. Another option is *Two Truths and a Lie*, a game where you describe three impressive goals you have achieved, one of which is a lie that others must detect.

Look at the *Ideal Scenario* techniques, and do one you are not familiar with, if time permits.

Option Domain and Rep IV

By now you should have a good understanding of the problems you have in your project, as well as the key actors and their values, interests, and positions. You should also have an *Ideal Scenario* in mind. The next technique (in the Options Module) involves looking at concrete options to achieve your vision or mission. *Option Domain* examines how you view options in a situation using words and characteristics that you choose and define. It also shows how you negotiate these views of options across social and cultural boundaries. The technique may be used to test your views against experience, solve problems, and learn in the process.

The Rep IV software can add an additional level of analysis, as needed.

Competing Goals

Once you have identified your main options, you can use *Competing Goals* (in the Options Module) to invite different stakeholders to rank the goals they wish to reach, in order of importance. This allows the group to understand and plan how it might resolve disagreements or misunderstandings among stakeholders involved in the project.

Stakeholder Expectations: Role Dynamics

Role Dynamics (in the Actors Module) is another technique that you can use to clarify what different stakeholders may expect. This technique helps assess what stakeholders expect of each other as a result of a contract, a promise or a moral responsibility, and how satisfied they are with the way other stakeholders perform in a given role.

How to Assess Levels of Support?

You can assess all project decisions and stakeholder plans with the help of *Levels of Support*. This technique (in the Options Module) will allow you to choose the decision method and level of support that are appropriate to your final plans for action.

SAS² Skills: The Wheel

To apply SAS² with success, you must develop skills that are central to the SAS² approach to collaborative inquiry and social engagement. These skills include an ability to mediate different views of reality, navigate within your use of SAS² tools, be grounded when doing an inquiry, scale the way you use techniques, and interpret complex information and findings (see *Foundations and Skillful Means* in Part 1). You can use *The Wheel* technique (in All-Purpose Techniques) to set your learning goals for these skills, and to assess your progress in acquiring them. The technique can also help create an important learning impact known as the Socratic effect: *I have learned that I know less (or more) than I had thought.*

Training, Certification, License, and Communities of Practice

If you are interested in learning more about SAS² or becoming a member of a Community of Practice, a Certified SAS² Practitioner or Instructor, or a Licensed Partner, visit these sections of the SAS² website: Training, Certification and Licensing; and SAS² International, Institutional Partners, and Communities of Practice.

Advanced Practice and Learning

To strengthen and deepen your skills and knowledge in using SAS^2, you must focus on the "A.R.T." of combining Action, Research, and Training within ongoing activities. You can do this by talking with other practitioners or Advanced Workshop Instructors about problems you have had when using SAS^2. You can also explore new techniques, and co-design the use of SAS^2 concepts and tools in new situations (see *Guidelines for SAS^2 Events and Process Design*). The design process involves learning to select and sequence inquiry tools in real projects, and adapt SAS^2 techniques to many contexts and groups of people. It also involves "scaling" of techniques for different purposes, and becoming more familiar with advanced SAS^2 tools that describe and assess the dynamics of a situation. (See website information on advanced workshops in the section entitled Training, Certification and Licensing.)

A.R.T. (Action-Research-Training)

Author   J.M. Chevalier

Acknowledgement   *A*.*R.T.* is a SAS² adaptation and development of the principles of problem-based learning and learning by doing (see *Readings and Links*).

Purpose   *A.R.T.* helps you assess the balance and integration of three project components: (*i*) **actions,** aimed at achieving project or program goals, (*ii*) **research,** consisting of data collection and analysis, and (*iii*) **training,** involving capacity-building events and strategies.

Guiding Principles

1. Actions are goal-oriented interventions where people reach decisions, implement them, and interact with others in the process. Research is any inquiry where people systematically gather and analyze information on a topic. Training is any learning activity that provides instruction and practice in a skill.

2. The precise balance of action, research, and training should reflect project or program objectives.

3. Projects or programs that achieve a strong integration of all three components may achieve better results because:

   (a) Action is more effective when it is based on sound research and good training;

   (b) Research is more reliable and useful when it is informed by action and is shared with others through training events; and

   (c) Training creates better learning when it is directly applied to problem-solving research and action. This is capacity building grounded in "action learning" or "learning by doing".

Process

Using a Venn Diagram

1. Identify an activity or a group of activities (actual or proposed) where you need to use *A.R.T.* Clarify the purpose of your analysis.

2. Draw a **Venn Diagram**. Use the three intersecting circles to represent the three *A.R.T.* components (Action, Research, Training) and all their possible combinations (see example in Step 4).

3. Discuss and compare the **importance** given to action, research, and training in the activities you identified in Step 1. Use one of the following categories from your Venn Diagram to describe these activities:

   • Action mostly
   • Research mostly
   • Training mostly
   • Action and research mostly
   • Action and training mostly
   • Research and training mostly
   • Action and research and training

   You can use one of these categories to describe your **project or program in general**. Another option is to use the appropriate category to describe **each activity** within your project or program.

4. If the activities identified in Step 1 focus on action, research or training mostly, discuss what **contribution** this makes to the objectives of other activities. For instance, do you focus on the kind of research that others can use mostly for training (but not for immediate action)? If so, divide the circle for research in half and put your answer in the half that intersects with the circle for training (see the upper right corner of the diagram below).

   Here is an example of a Venn Diagram involving a Survey Institute that mostly does research through public opinion polls. In this case, the research is used mostly for political decision or action by other groups.

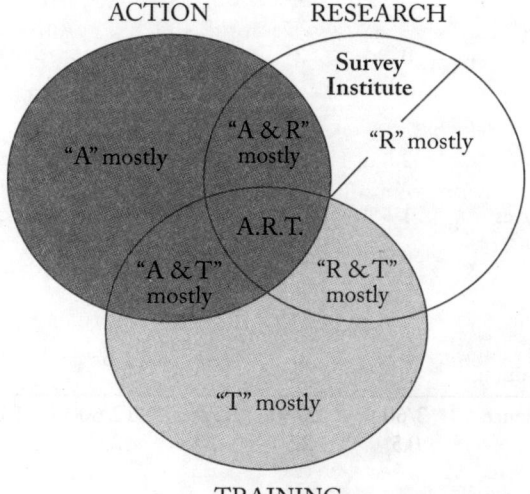

ACTION   RESEARCH

Survey Institute

"A & R" mostly

"R" mostly

"A" mostly

A.R.T.

"A & T" mostly

"R & T" mostly

"T" mostly

TRAINING

5. If the activities identified in Step 1 combine more than one focus, assess the extent to which each component affects the other(s). For instance, if you combine R & T mostly, can you use the results of your research in your teaching, and is your teaching useful to your research? If you combine research with both action and training, how is each component useful to the other two? Use your own code to describe the **level of interaction** among the components of your *A.R.T.* profile (such as a long dash for a weak integration, as in R – T, and a plus sign for a strong integration, as in R + T).

Calculating the Level of Interaction

6. You can use *Activity Dynamics* to measure the **level of interaction** among the components of your *A.R.T.* profile. Here is an example of an *Activity Dynamics* table and diagram that show the contribution that each project activity makes to other activities (the activities are categorized by components, in order of importance):

Activities	Research			Action			Training	
	Data collection & analysis	Pub-lishing	Reports	Green manure project	Local initiatives	Lobbying	Partici patory research training	Total contribution
Research								
Data collection & analysis	x	8	6	1	3	8	3	29/60, 4.8
Publishing	0	x	2	1	1	6	0	10/60, 1.7
Reports	0	2	x	0	0	2	0	4/60, 0.7
Action								
Green manure project	2	3	5	x	2	3	1	16/60, 2.7
Local initiatives	1	2	4	2	x	4	2	15/60, 2.5
Lobbying	0	0	0	2	4	x	7	13/60, 2.2
Training								
Participatory research training	0	0	0	6	3	0	x	9/60, 1.5
Total dependence	3/60 0.5	15/60 2.5	17/60 2.8	12/60 2.0	13/60 2.2	23/60 3.8	13/60 2.2	96/420 23%

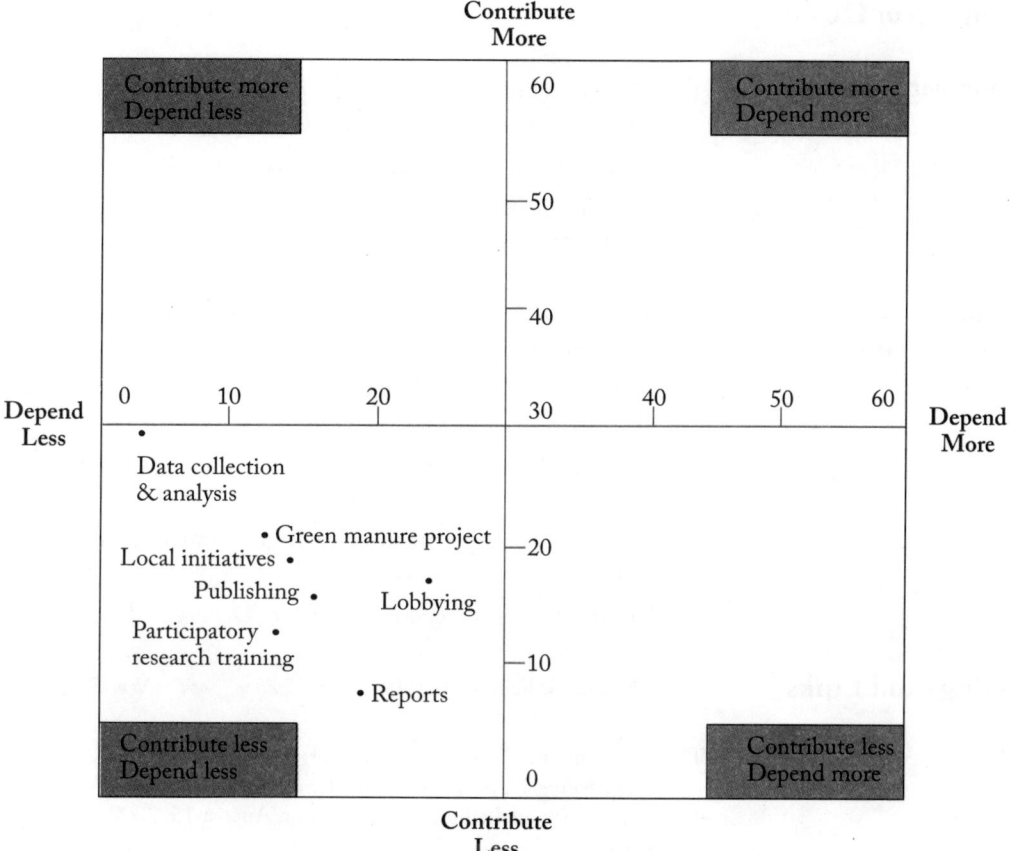

Summary of this example: This project involves research and action mostly, with some training. But the overall interaction between the corresponding activities is generally weak; each activity makes a limited contribution to other activities. Data collection and analysis contributes the most, and lobbying depends the most on other activities.

Interpreting the Results

7. Discuss how satisfied or dissatisfied you are with your *A.R.T.* profile that results, and where you would prefer your activities to be located in the Venn diagram (Step 4) and the interaction diagram (see example in Step 6). Explore what you can do to achieve this **ideal profile**.

8. Discuss the guiding principles presented at the beginning of this technique.

Scaling Up or Down

For Simpler Versions

1. Use the technique to assess your project or program in general but not each activity within the project or program (see Step 3).

2. Do not divide your circles into halves (Step 4).

3. Do not calculate the dynamic interaction among the components of your project or program (Step 6).

For More Advanced Versions

1. Take more time to gather the information you need to complete the exercise.

2. During the exercise, discuss and record the views that participants express.

3. Write a short description for each component of your *A.R.T.* profile.

4. Evaluate the importance of each component using *Ranking* or *Rating*.

5. Use the advanced version of *Activity Dynamics*.

Readings and Links

Boud, D.; and G. Felleti (eds). 1991. *The Challenge of Problem-Based Learning*. London: Kogan Page.

ITUE (Institute for Transforming Undergraduate Education). 2006. *Problem-Based Learning*. Newark, DE, USA: University of Delaware. Available online at http://www.udel.edu/pbl/, accessed on August 15, 2007.

MCLI (Maricopa Centre for Learning and Instruction). 2001. *Problem-Based Learning*. Tempe, AZ, USA: Maricopa Commmunity Colleges. Available online at http://www.mcli.dist.maricopa.edu/pbl/info.html, accessed on August 15, 2007.

PBLI (Problem-Based Learning Initiative). 1999. *Problem-Based Learning Bibliography*. Springfield, IL, USA: PBLI. Available online at http://www.pbli.org/bibliography/index.htm, accessed on August 15, 2007.

Rangachari, P.K. 2002. *Problem-Based Learning in the Sciences and Liberal Arts*. Hamilton, ON, Canada: McMaster University. Available online at http://www.fhs.mcmaster.ca/pbls/#Sean, accessed on August 15, 2007.

Woods, D. R. 1994. *Problem-Based Learning: How to Gain the Most from PBL*. Hamilton, ON, Canada: McMaster University. Available online at http://www.chemeng.mcmaster.ca/pbl/PBL.HTM, accessed on August 15, 2007.

A.R.T.: Assessing the Profile of Organizations doing Joint Research on Watershed Management in Honduras

Key Words

A.R.T., Honduras, watershed management research, organizational profile

Author and Acknowledgement

L. Suazo-Gallardo. The author wishes to acknowledge the efforts of Raul Zelaya (IDRC) who helped facilitate the assessment and Daniel Buckles (Carleton University) who helped to write the report.

Context

Three organizations are jointly implementing a research project in the San Juan watershed on the Atlantic coast of Honduras, a mountainous area vulnerable to landslides. The project goal is to study how local institutions and people manage the resources of the watershed, and design a training process to improve practices. CURLA is a branch of the National Agricultural University of Honduras. REHDES is a network of ecologists that protects a number of natural reserves in the region. MAMUCA is a regional association of small municipalities. The organizations know each other well, but this is the first time they have worked together on a common project. The contribution of each to joint project goals had not been assessed.

Purpose

To find out and adjust the balance of action, research, and training the organizations can use to meet joint project goals.

Process Summary

The International Development Research Centre (IDRC) hosted the assessment during a SAS[2] Introductory Workshop in La Masica, Atlántida, Honduras. Teams of 5–6 people from CURLA, REHDES and MAMUCA discussed and compared the importance their organizations give to action (goal-oriented activities), research (data gathering and analysis), and training (capacity building). The way action, research and training (A.R.T.) interact in each institution was assessed by ranking how much one type of activity impacts on others, on a scale of 0 to 10. Each organization's profile and the joint profile were then discussed in relation to the project's goals. A report on the workshop and the assessment was prepared by IDRC consultant Laura Suazo-Gallardo. The participants agreed to share their information in the report.

Analysis

The profile of A.R.T. that best describes the work of each organization is shown in Figure 1. CURLA has a strong focus on research and training; for instance, it does agronomic field trials on campus and offers

Figure 1: The Profile of Action, Research, and Training of Three Organizations in Honduras

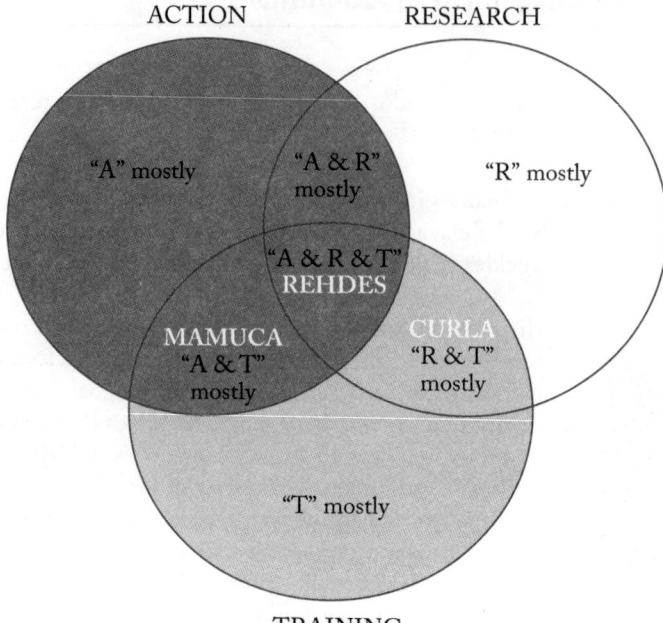

ACTION   RESEARCH

"A" mostly   "A & R" mostly   "R" mostly

"A & R & T" REHDES

MAMUCA "A & T" mostly   CURLA "R & T" mostly

"T" mostly

TRAINING

university courses. The work of REHDES is more wide-ranging, and includes environmental education with school children, monitoring of illegal use of natural resources in national forests, group planning for natural resource management, and tree planting campaigns, among others. Thus, action, research, and training are all parts of its organizational profile. MAMUCA is responsible for a large development project with international funding; this project focuses mostly on action and training. All three organizations share a common interest and experience in training, an organizational profile relevant to project goals.

Tables 1, 2, and 3 show how much one type of activity currently contributes to others within the organization, on a scale of 0 to 10. The ratings for CURLA are relatively high compared to the other two organizations and overall the integration of the three activities is high (66.6 percent integration). This reflects their view that all three aspects of A.R.T. interact with each other in the work they currently do. By contrast, the ratings for REHDES and MAMUCA are relatively low, as is the overall level of integration (30 percent and 35 percent, respectively).

Table 1: The Interaction of Action, Research, and Training in the Activities of CURLA

Activity	Action	Research	Training	Average
Action	x	5	6	5.5
Research	6	x	8	7.0
Training	7	8	x	7.5
Average	6.5	6.5	7.0	66.6%

Table 2: The Interaction of Action, Research, and Training in the Activities of REHDES

Activity	Action	Research	Training	Average
Action	x	2	4	3.0
Research	2	x	3	2.5
Training	4	3	x	3.5
Average	3.0	2.5	3.5	30.0%

Table 3: The Interaction of Action, Research, and Training in the Activities of MAMUCA

Activity	Action	Research	Training	Average
Action	x	2	3	2.5
Research	4	x	4	4.0
Training	5	3	x	4.0
Average	4.5	2.5	3.5	35.0%

Graph 1 shows the balance of the three activity components for all three organizations. The vertical axis plots the extent to which one activity contributes to other activities (using the row averages from the tables). The horizontal axis shows the extent to which the activity depends on the contributions of other activities (using the column averages from the tables). The resulting profile for CURLA, falling in the top-right quadrant, is relatively well integrated. Their action, research, and training activities all contribute to and depend on each other. By contrast, the profiles for REHDES and MAMUCA are less integrated. Different types of organizational work are done without a large impact on each other. Some organizational work may focus on training while other work will focus on action or research. The different activities are independent of each other (bottom-left quadrant).

Graph 1: The Interaction of Action, Research, and Training in the Activities of Three Organizations in Honduras

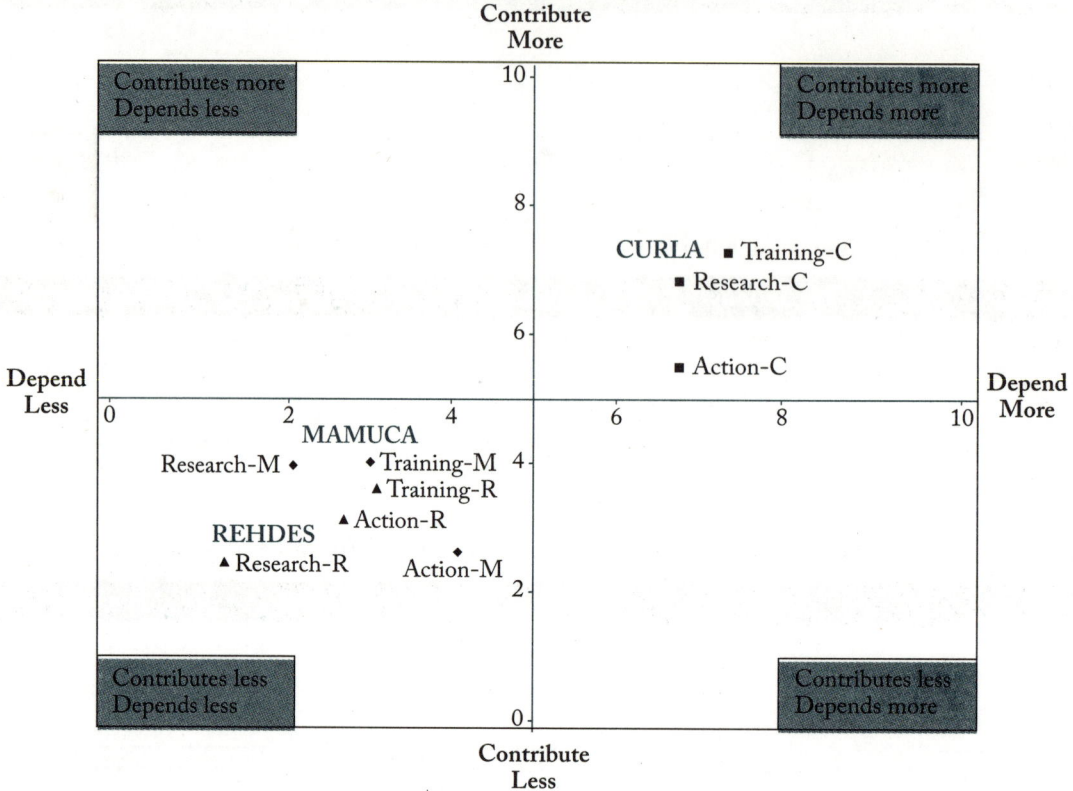

Interpretation
: The distinct profiles and ways that A.R.T. interacts reflects each organization's mandate and history. CURLA, while mostly a research and training organization, has for many years involved professors and students in goal-oriented project activities. The other two organizations mostly work on specialized projects (action, research or training projects), each of which has a distinct budget, plan and reporting requirement.

Action
: The organizations decided to adjust their joint project activities by integrating research activities led by CURLA into project activities that mostly involved action and training and were led by the other organizations. This was seen as a way to make the best use of their individual and joint profile to meet project goals.

Observations on the Process

No problems emerged during the assessment. Long-standing friendships and personal contact among people in the three organizations made it easy for them to challenge and then verify the ratings they had provided. They considered the result useful to their planning as well as a positive contribution to evolution of an institutional profile. Some participants said that while they had considered their work to be appropriately balanced before the exercise, they now appreciated the relevance of doing different activities in ways that strengthen or reinforce each other.

Order and Chaos

Author   J.M. Chevalier

Purpose   This technique helps you to identify the planning approach you need by answering two questions. The questions are: how do you assess your chances of achieving your project or program goals, and how confident are you in the knowledge that you have about the conditions or factors affecting your plan?

Guiding Principles

1. The way you make plans depends on how you assess your chances of achieving your project or program goals. This is your estimate of your **chances of success**—how you view the conditions or factors affecting your plans and whether they are favorable or not.

2. Your plan of action also depends on your **level of certainty**—how confident or certain you are of the information you have about the conditions or factors affecting your plan.

3. Plans made in difficult conditions and with limited knowledge of the key factors (affecting your chances of success and level of certainty) require *process management* tools adapted to situations of relative **chaos**.

4. Result-Based Management tools based on fixed objectives and details on how to achieve them are suited to plans made in favorable conditions and with sufficient knowledge of the key factors. This planning approach works in situations of relative **order**.

Process

1. Identify a plan of action where you need to use *Order and Chaos*. Define the objectives of your plan as clearly as possible, and clarify the purpose of your analysis.

2. Create a diagram by drawing a vertical line that crosses a horizontal line (see example in Step 6). This creates a cross inside a square. Write 0 and 10 at opposite ends of the vertical line. The value 10 indicates that you have very high chances of achieving the objectives identified in Step 1. The value 0 shows the opposite (your **chances of success** are very low). If you want to be more precise, identify **indicators** that define the meaning of each number on the scale.

3. Write 0 and 10 at opposite ends of the horizontal line. The value 10 indicates a high **level of certainty** or confidence in the information you have about the conditions and factors affecting your plan. The value 0 shows the opposite (your level of certainty that the information is sufficient is very low). If you want to be more precise, identify indicators that define the meaning of each number on the scale.

   Focus discussion on the quality or precision of all the information that went into making the estimate of your chances of success, not how confident you are in the estimate of success *per se*. A statistical concept similar to level of certainty is the notion of a margin of error, used when reporting on election polling data: the poll taken September 8–11 of 614 registered voters showed Mrs Gonzalez would win 57 percent of the vote if the election where held now, with a margin of error of plus or minus four percentage points.

4. Discuss the chances of success and the level of certainty associated with your plan of action identified in Step 1. **Plot** the chances of success on the vertical line, and the level of certainty on the horizontal line. Connect the values from the two lines, using the letter 'X' to mark the place where they meet. See example in Step 6.

   Instead of assessing your plan in general, you can identify several objectives or activities that are part of your project or program, and then use the diagram to plot the chances of success and the level of certainty *for each objective or activity*.

5. Use the same diagram to plot the chances of success and the level of certainty that you need and should aim for, in order to proceed with your plan. Use another "X" to mark the place where the two **values that you are aiming for** meet. Draw an arrow from the first "X" to the second.

6. To help you analyze the results of your analysis, use key words to characterize the combination of outcomes represented in each corner of the diagram. Since each outcome represents a different planning approach, with its advantages and disadvantages, try to use neutral terms. For example, if you are certain that your plan of action is feasible but with difficulty, call your plan a **challenge** (as in the bottom right corner of the diagram). If you think your plan has a good chance of succeeding but you have limited knowledge of the key factors involved, call your plan a **wager** (as in the top left corner of the diagram). If you feel your plan has little chance of succeeding and you do not know all the factors involved, you might call it a **dream** (as in the bottom left corner of the diagram).

Note that plans involving *wagers*, *challenges* or *dreams* are all "working hypotheses" developed in situations of relative **chaos** (where factors of success and certainty are weak). By contrast, plans developed in situations of relative **order**, as in the field of **engineering** (where factors of success and certainty are strong, as in the top right corner of the diagram) are plans likely to succeed for reasons that are well known.

Be aware that each planning approach offers advantages and disadvantages and should be the preferred strategy in certain conditions. Imposing the same planning approach in all situations is inappropriate. Before starting a project or program, it may be wise not to move too quickly from an exercise in dream-like visioning to detailed plans using the Logical Framework, for instance. If your plan of action is "challenging" because of many obstacles and some key factors you cannot predict (as in medical practice, for instance), you may prefer to use a continuous planning strategy (see *Process Manager*) instead of a detailed result-based approach to project management.

Here is an example of an *Order and Chaos* diagram:

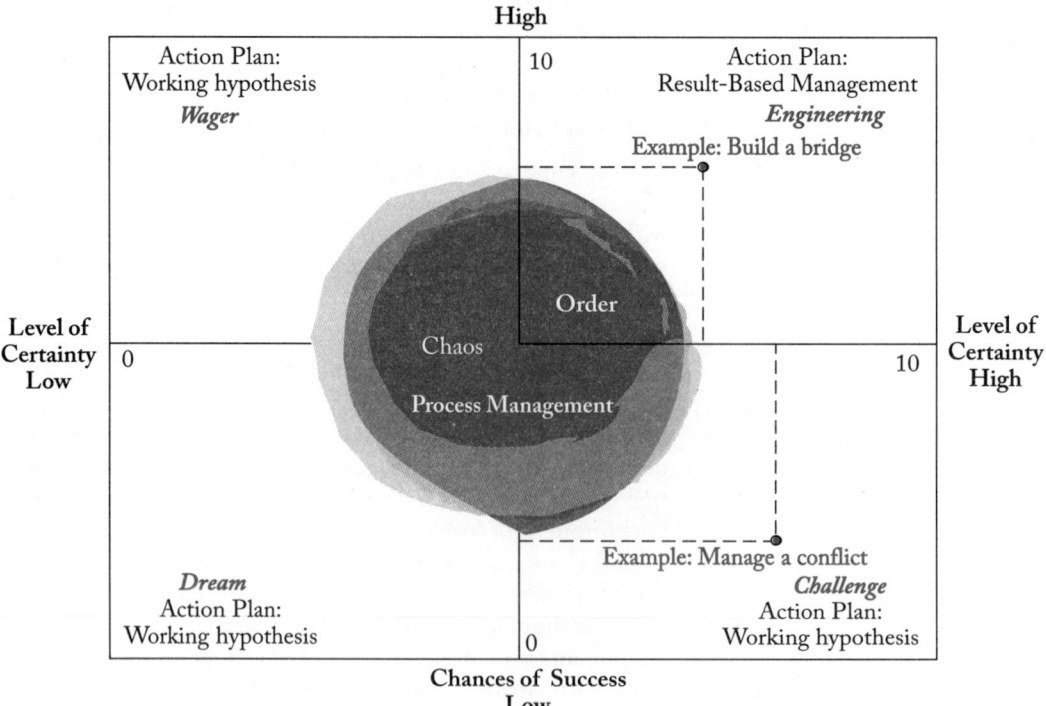

7. Use the results of your analysis to identify the **planning approach** and management tools that suit your needs. Also, identify the ways you can improve your knowledge and the conditions of success you need to achieve your project or program goals.

8. Each party (such as gender groups) may do its own *Order and Chaos* exercise and then discuss its results with other parties.

Scaling Up or Down

For Simpler Versions

1. Do not use indicators to define the meaning of each number on your scales (for chances of success and levels of certainty).

2. Do not assess the chances of success and the level of certainty associated with different objectives or activities.

For More
Advanced Versions

1. During the exercise, discuss and record the views that participants express.

2. Use indicators for the chances of success and the level of certainty.

3. Assess the chances of success and the level of certainty associated with different objectives or activities (see Step 4).

Order and Chaos: Insecure Village and Housing Land among the Katkari, Maharashtra, India

Key Words   *Order and Chaos*, India, tribal population, Katkari, project planning

Authors   D.J. Buckles, R. Khedkar, D. Patil, and B. Ghevde.

Context

The Katkari are a tribal population in Raigad and Thane districts of Maharashtra, India. More than 200 of their hamlets do not have legal title to the land where their homes have been for decades. The land is owned mostly by non-tribals living in nearby villages. Some of the hamlets are located on government lands (generally the Forest Department). By and large, the landowners do not allow Katkari families to improve or build new houses, to grow backyard gardens, to keep cattle in the hamlet, or even to develop basic amenities like drinking water wells, schools, approach roads, or dispensaries. As a result, conditions in most of the villages are primitive, cramped, and filthy. Families live as well with the constant fear of eviction, an ever-increasing occurrence in Thane district where land prices are rising rapidly due to proximity to Mumbai. In some cases entire hamlets have been surrounded by barbed wire fences to prevent any further expansion by the Katkari families and to intimidate them into moving to another location. Most healthy men, women, and children in the hamlets work as bonded labor at brick-making kilns in the region. They move from one place to another, from season to season, to find work, leaving their homes unattended for months at a time.

Governments at both the State and Federal levels have put in place a great deal of legislation to secure village and house sites for families from so-called "backward" classes (including tribal communities). They have also periodically issued Government Resolutions, Circulars, Orders and Letters pertaining to village and housing land, based on legal instruments such as: The Bombay Tenancy and Agricultural Lands Act, 1948; The Maharashtra Land Revenue Code, 1966; and the Bombay Village Panchayats Act, 1958. Implementation of these measures has been poor, however, as evidenced by government correspondence criticising the Collectors and Tahsildars for failing to implement the Village and Housing Site schemes.

The non-governmental organizations Academy of Development Science (ADS) and SOBTI have been working in Katkari communities for many years, and have accumulated a great deal of information regarding the legal rights of the Katkari. They joined forces to secure

Katkari ownership of housing land in a few hamlets, with a view to showing that it could be done and providing a model for the government to follow. Funds were acquired from an international organization to engage a team of people, including several Katkari, to undertake the project.

Purpose

To characterize the project and select the planning approach and management tools needed to achieve project goals.

Process Summary

Staff of ADS and SOBTI met to develop a plan for securing housing land in a few Katkari hamlets. After reviewing project goals and outlining plans in general terms, they estimated the chances of achieving these goals and the level of certainty or confidence in the knowledge they had about the conditions and factors affecting the plans, using a scale of 0 to 10. The character of the project was identified and a planning approach and management tool was selected. Six months later, a second assessment was done and project details adjusted. The report was co-authored by all participants in the exercise.

Analysis

The participants said during their first meeting that the problem they are addressing through the project (legal title to housing land in a few communities) is very precise and narrow, and that project resources are adequate. While intervention of government officials in support of the project goal could not be assured, they noted the substantial legal support for the position of the Katkari and favorable political climate for minority rights. They consequently considered their chances of achieving the project goal to be quite high, meriting a score of 7.5. They also gave a high score (8) for the level of certainty they felt regarding the assessment of probability. This reflected their considerable knowledge of the legal issues and of the hamlets and actors involved. Based on this assessment (Graph 1) the participants characterized the project as a straightforward "engineering" project that could be planned now in detail. They subsequently developed a linear and sequential plan with specific and measurable objectives involving a detailed series of activities and sub-activities leading toward their goal.

Six months after initiating the project, no hamlet had acquired legal title to village land and only one had submitted the requisite petition to the village council. The main reason for this situation was that while individual Katkaris wanted to secure their tenure, collective will was undermined by fear of retaliation from the landowners. This apparent failure led to a reconsideration and reassessment of the character and plans of the project.

The new score given for probability of success was much lower than before, dropping from 7.5 to 4. The experience of the previous six months had shown that insecure tenure over housing land, while a very specific problem, is embedded in a much broader and complex situation involving interrelated factors such as insecure livelihoods, rapidly changing land prices in Thane district, the political and social marginalization of the Katkari, and other considerations affecting the willingness of the Katkari to actively and collectively petition village and housing land.

The confidence they have in this new assessment is high (8), reflecting their view that the experience of the previous six months had revealed all of the likely hurdles and barriers to project goals. Information gaps remain, however, regarding the best timing for submitting petitions to government officials and the capacity of ADS and SOBTI to assess and respond to the problem of insecure livelihood. The participants concluded that the situation is a "challenge" because it seems that the situation of the Katkari needs to change on many fronts simultaneously, before later steps can be planned.

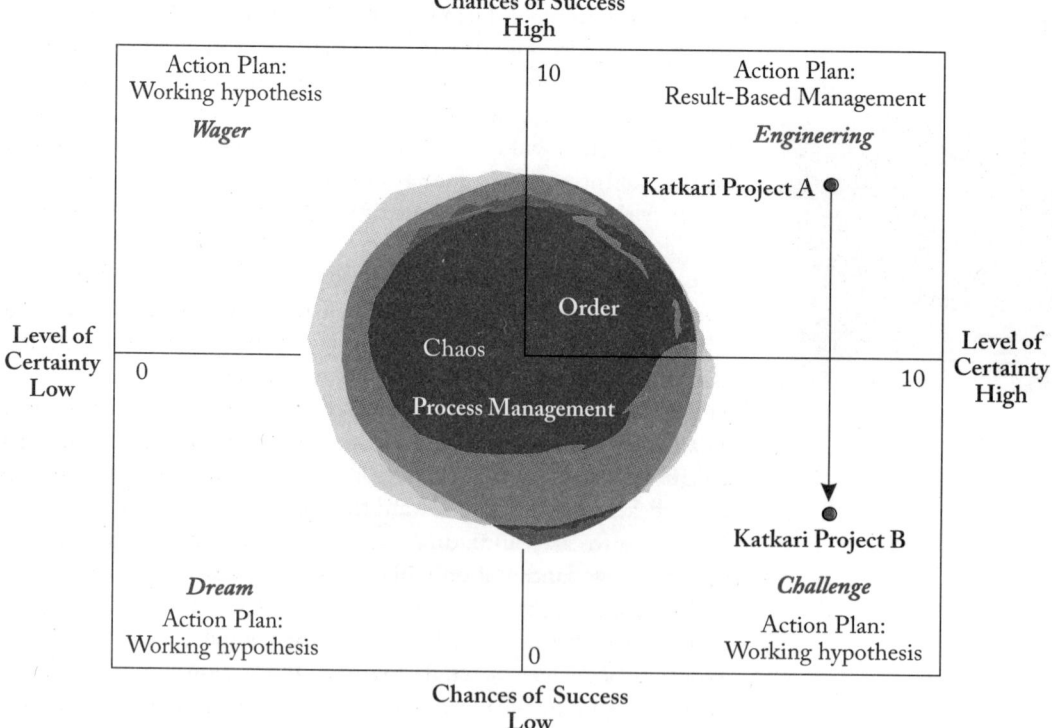

Interpretation	The development of detailed project plans at the outset reflects the orderly situation anticipated by the organizations and funding agency involved. The impact of factors like insecure livelihoods and rapid pace of changes in land prices on project goals could not have been predicted before actually engaging with the entire community on the issue, testing plans in some settings, and collecting information on emerging trends and alternative legal strategies. The revised assessment reflects the need for iterative and continuous planning of activities in response to a challenging situation.
Action	The organizations decided to focus their attention on Katkari hamlets in Raigad district where land prices are more stable and the organizations have funded projects offering livelihood options for the Katkari. Detailed plans for this district were developed for a one-year period. Ongoing work in Thane district was planned for the short term only, with a focus on monitoring both local and statewide political developments with the potential to impact the timing of future petitions for village and housing land.
Observations on the Process	Differences in the knowledge base of the two organizations involved were not considered during the first assessment. One organization had a history of working in both Raigad and Thane district while the other organization had only worked in Thane district. This was corrected prior to the second assessment by organizing cross-visits between the two regions, to ensure that when assessing the chances of success and the level of certainty, the representatives of both organizations were intimately familiar with the conditions affecting the project as a whole.
	Both organizations were satisfied with the result of the assessment and considered it to be a useful lesson for planning of this and other projects.

Problem Tree

Author	J.M. Chevalier

Acknowledgement   *P*roblem Tree is a SAS[2] adaptation of a technique widely used in the field of participatory research (see in particular FASID in *Readings and Links*).

Purpose   *Problem Tree* helps you analyze the first and second-level causes and effects of a core problem.

Guiding Principles

1. To deal with a problem you may need to understand what causes it and what the effects might be.

2. Understanding how different stakeholders view the causes and the effects of a problem may be important.

Process

1. Identify a **core problem** where you need to use *Problem Tree*. Define this problem as clearly as possible, and clarify the purpose of your analysis.

2. Ask "Why has this problem occurred?" Identify up to five or six existing factors that are directly responsible for the problem. These are the **first-level causes** of your core problem. Write (or draw) each first-level cause on its own card using a short sentence, with words that are clear and concrete (such as "The village population has grown" instead of "Higher population density"). *Timeline* may help you identify your core problem and its causes over time.

   When you write these short sentences, **make sure that you do not**:

   (a) Record more than one cause on a single card (such as "The lowland produces less than it used to, and good farmland is expensive");

   (b) Write down the cause and its effect(s) together (such as "The ranchers occupy a lot of land, which leads villagers to cut down the communal forest");

(c) Create different cards and sentences that describe the same cause (such as "The lowland produces less than it used to" and "Agricultural productivity has declined");

(d) Use words that emphasize the absence or lack of *a particular solution* to the problem at hand (such as "There are no regulations forbidding villagers from cutting forest trees"). Describe instead the consequence of what is lacking (such as "The forest is unprotected").

3. Place all the cards that show first-level causes in a row below the core problem, as in the following diagram:

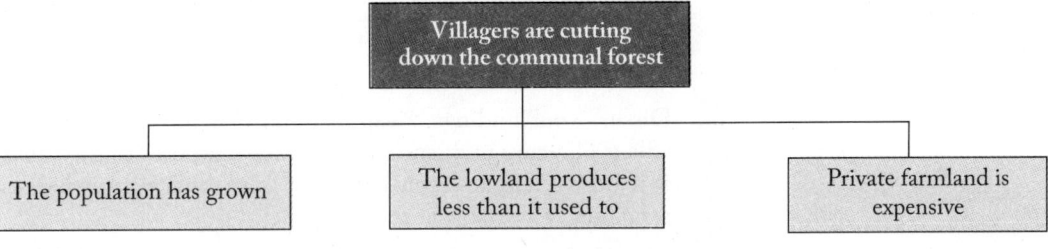

4. Use the method described in Step 2 to determine the factors that are directly responsible for each first-level cause. These are your **second-level causes**. Write (or draw) each second-level cause on its own card. Place the new cards in a row below the corresponding first-level causes.

5. Use the same method (Step 3) to determine the causes at the third level, directly responsible for each second-level cause, as in the following diagram:

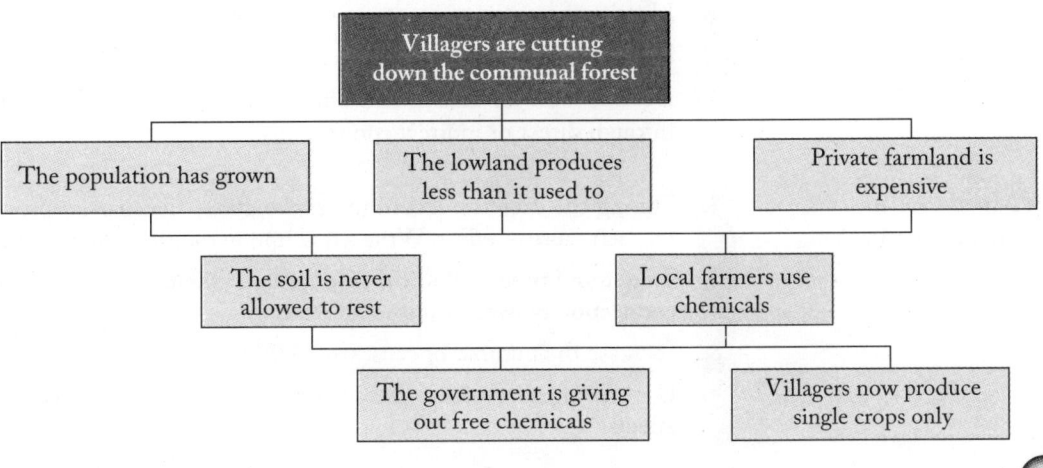

6. Go through the same steps (Steps 2 to 5) to determine the **first-level, second-level, and third-level effects** or implications of your core problem. These are effects that exist right now and that you can observe. Write (or draw) each effect on its own card, and place the new cards in rows above the core problem (see example below). Identification of fourth and fifth level causes and effects could be interesting to participants but may take the discussion too far from the core problem.

7. Look for causes and/or effects that reinforce each other through direct or indirect connections (such as "the land produces less over time because farmers use chemicals in response to poorer soils"). You will recognize these direct or indirect loops or "**vicious circles**" when you see that the same card fits into different parts of the diagram.

8. Discuss your findings. Keep in mind that the direct or indirect effects of a core problem may be active responses to the situation at hand (such as "villagers buy wood from other villages because it is no longer available at the local level").

9. Identify the causes that you believe are priorities, based on one of these factors: they are the most important, the most pressing, or the least difficult to handle.

Scaling Up or Down

For Simpler Versions

1. Draw a tree trunk to represent your core problem. Add roots and rootlets to represent the direct and indirect causes, and then branches and twigs to represent the direct and indirect effects (or implications) of your core problem.

2. Identify the *causes at one or several levels* but leave out the effects.

3. Restrict your analysis to major causes and effects only.

4. Do not look for causes and effects that strengthen each other through direct or indirect connections.

For More Advanced Versions

1. During the exercise, record the explanations that parties provide for each cause or effect. Write a description for each cause or effect.

2. Take more time to find the information you need to justify each connection between causes and effects.

3. Increase the number of causes and effects.

4. Use *Rating* to evaluate the importance of different causes and effects.

5. Include effects that may happen later and write them down on cards that are a different color.

6. For each cause, identify current factors that limit its actual impact and record the estimated time frame of each impact (see *Force Field*).

7. Do a *Problem Tree* analysis for each major event recorded in your *Timeline* analysis.

8. Enter your *Problem Tree* results in MindManager.

9. For a more advanced analysis of problems and their interaction, use *Problem Domain* or *Causal Dynamics*.

Readings and Links

FASID (Foundation for Advanced Studies of International Development). 2001. *Project Cycle Management: Management Tool for Development Assistance.* Tokyo, Japan: FASID.

IIRR (International Institute of Rural Reconstruction). 2001. *Recording and Using Indigenous Knowledge: A Manual.* Silang, Cavite, Philippines: IIRR.

Means, K.; C. Josayma; E. Nielsen; and V. Viriyasakultorn. 2002. *Community-Based Forest Resource Conflict Management: Training Package*, Volume 1, Section 3.2 and Volume 2, Activity 8, Rome, Italy: Food and Agriculture Organization. Available online at http://www.fao.org/DOCREP/005/Y4300E/Y4300E00.HTM and http://www.fao.org/DOCREP/005/Y4301E/Y4301E00.HTM, accessed on August 15, 2007.

Mind Tools. nd. 'Cause and effect diagrams'. Wimbledon, London, UK: Mind Tools.com. Available online at http://www.mindtools.com/pages/article/newTMC_03.htm, accessed on August 15, 2007.

———. nd. 'Drill Down'. Wimbledon, London, UK: Mind Tools.com. Available online at http://www.mindtools.com/pages/article/newTMC_02.htm, accessed on August 15, 2007.

Problem Tree: The Problem of not having Legal Title to Residential Lands in Siddeshwarwadi, Maharashtra, India

Key Words

Problem Tree, India, tribal people, Katkari, land tenure

Authors

D.J. Buckles, R. Khedkar, D. Patil, and B. Ghevde.

Context

Siddeshwarwadi is a hamlet of non-literate and very poor tribal people known as the *Katkari*. Most healthy men, women and children work as bonded labor at brick-making kilns in the region. They move from one place to another, from season to season, to find work, leaving their homes unattended for months at a time. The hamlet is located on parts of three properties owned by people in the nearby caste village (Siddeshwar) some 110 km southeast of Mumbai, Maharashtra. The *Katkari* do not have legal title to the land even though they have lived there for many generations and special clauses in Indian law affirm the rights of tribal people to residential lands (*Goathan*). Recently, *Katkari* in nearby hamlets living in similar circumstances have been forced to leave their homes by the landowners.

A non-governmental organization, SOBTI, has been working in Siddeshwarwadi and other *Katkari* communities for many years and was concerned that the residents' situation could worsen if they were also forced from their hamlet. When discussions began with residents they found that people in the hamlet did not consider legal title to their homesteads to be a pressing issue in their village. They had, however, heard of evictions and other problems with legal title in other Katkari villages and agreed to discuss the issue in detail with SOBTI.

Purpose

To identify the problems that arise from not having legal title to the residential lands (Goathan) of Siddeshwarwadi.

Process Summary

SOBTI convened an evening meeting of *Katkari* residents at a time when they were not traveling regularly to the brick-making kilns. A group of 12 residents (eight men and four women) joined in the assessment. After talking about the purpose of the meeting, participants were asked why the hamlet does not have legal title to the land. These reasons were labeled as the "parents" of the problem being discussed. After piling and sorting these reasons into several levels, the participants were asked to describe the result of not having legal title. These were labeled as the "children" of the problem being discussed. The multi-level relationships were displayed in a visual way using cards and discussed in detail.

The participants understood that a report would be prepared afterwards by the facilitators, and agreed to share their information.

Analysis

Figure 1 presents the reasons for and implications of not having legal title to the residential lands, as described by participants. The main **reasons for the problem** (parents) include: the legal status of the land-owners' claims, government inaction, and inaction and lack of concern by the *Katkari* themselves. The participants recognized that the landowners would not get very much for their land from a process of government expropriation, and that they were concerned that expansion of the village would not stop with legal recognition of the current village boundaries. Their power over government officials, including the police, is such that they can easily stall a legal process, and intimidate the *Katkari*. Villagers are largely unaware of their rights and lack the organization needed to demand them.

The main **results of the problem** (children) include: lack of access to basic amenities available to hamlets of tribal people through government programs, the *Katkari*'s lack of job options, constraints on access to education, and overcrowding. Collectively, these implications of the core problem refer to many aspects of *Katkari* day-to-day life.

Something that brought a lot of energy into the discussion was a recent decision by the landowners not to allow construction of a school in the hamlet. This forced the hamlet to locate their government-funded school in another village. Participants said they were concerned that their children were leaving school early or not going to school at all. The participants recognized that the children would lack full education, and as adults, they would have few job options or knowledge of legal rights and rules that could help them. Instead, they would most likely enter into bonded labor on brick kilns and move from place-to-place with their families in search of work. The utter lack of privacy in their homes and the poor health and high health costs caused by poor housing and sanitation were also linked, by the participants, to constraints flowing from the lack of legal title to land.

While the implications of the problem of their children's future were the focus of much of the discussion, participants concluded that the most pressing cause was the lack of concern of the *Katkari* themselves. Until and unless most of the residents see the problem as very important, group action cannot be imagined, government inaction is likely to remain, and landowners will continue to control the situation.

Interpretation

The initial indifference of the *Katkari* in Siddeshwarwadi over lack of legal title to the land reflects the fact that daily life is very difficult and unstable. They are used to living on the edge of survival. Participants

Figure 1: Reasons for and Implications of not having Legal Title to Residential Lands in Siddeshwarwadi, Maharashtra, India

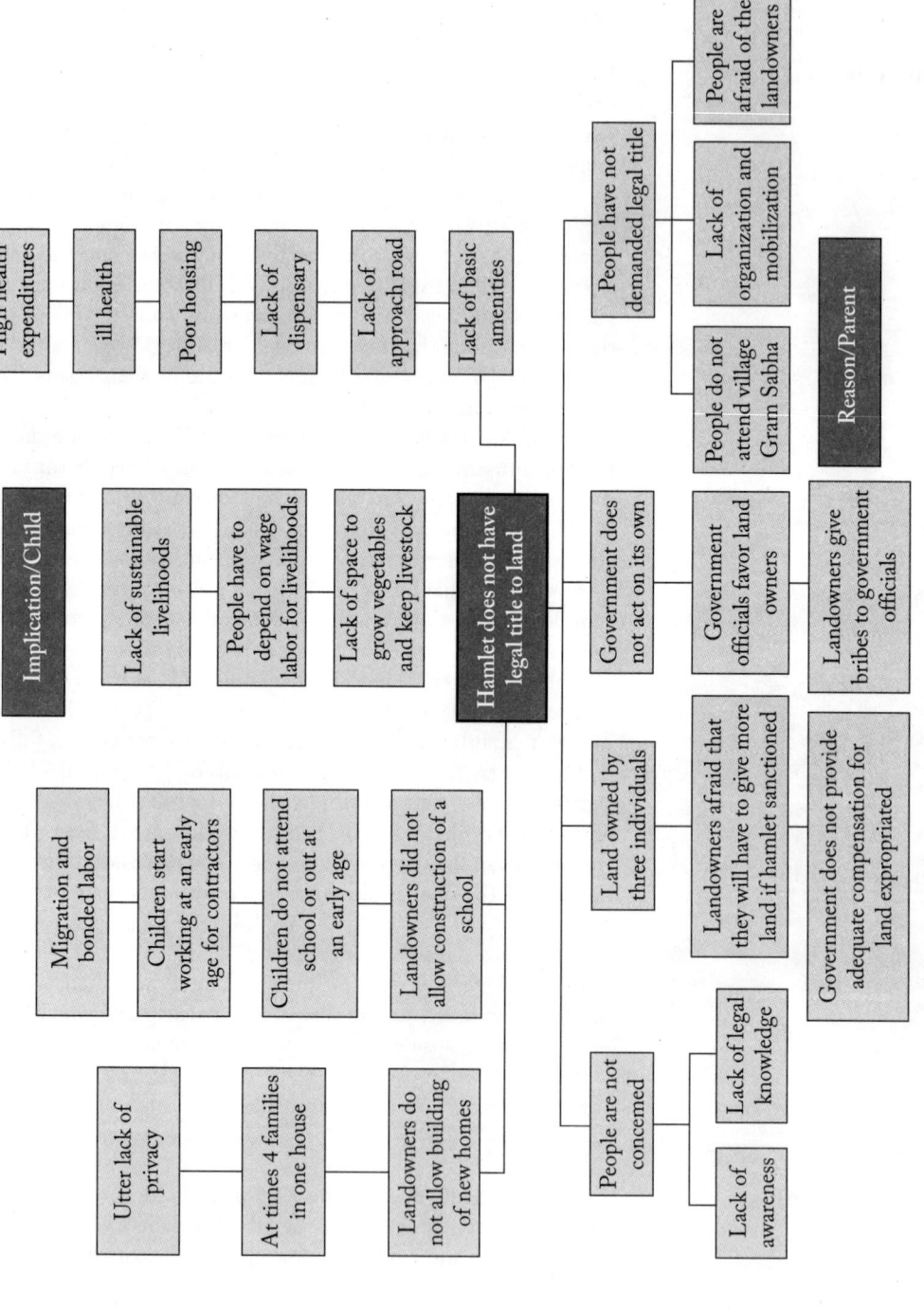

said that as there was no direct and immediate threat to their homes, not having legal title to the residential land seemed to be beyond their immediate concerns and capacities. Furthermore, they could not imagine what to do about it or how things could change. They said that the analysis of the causes and effects of not having legal title did change their assessment of the relevance of the issue to matters of more immediate importance to them. They recognized that they simply had not thought through the chain of causes and effects (parent and child) or compiled all the issues of concern to them in a single story.

Action

The participants decided to discuss their assessment of the situation with other residents, and to warn them of the possibility that landowners might decide to sell the land or use it for another end. They also decided to convene a meeting for the following week to try to develop a vision of the future that could inspire all residents to act collectively. (See Buckles, D. et al. The ideal scenario of Legal Title in Siddeshwarwadi, Maharashtra, India, The present Guide.)

Observations on the Process

At first, the discussion of causes and the implications of not having legal title to residential land confused participants, even though the ideas were carefully translated by a *Katkari* facilitator in the local language. The process caught on, however, once the facilitators started using the terms "parent" and "child" to mark these two aspects of the problem. The discussion also became much more engaging for the participants when the topic of the landowners' plan, to prevent building of a new school, arose. The final result was seen by the participants as an accurate description of their situation and useful to laying the groundwork for further discussions by them with other members of the community.

Force Field

Author

J.M. Chevalier

Acknowledgement

Force Field is a SAS[2] adaptation of a technique widely used in the field of participatory research (see in particular Mind Tools.com and Accel-Team.com in *Readings and links*).

Purpose

Force Field helps you understand people's views about the factors that cause a problem and those that counteract it and stop it from becoming worse.

Guiding Principles

1. To deal with a problem you need to understand the relationships between the factors that create or cause the problem and the counteracting factors that have opposite effects, and that stop things from getting worse.

2. People may have different views about the causes of a problem, and the factors that counteract it.

Process

1. Identify a **key problem** (such as deforestation in a certain region) where you need to use *Force Field*. Define the problem as clearly as possible, and clarify the purpose of your analysis.

2. Draw a **horizontal line**. At the end of this line, write (or draw) the core problem that you identified in Step 1 (see Step 5).

3. Identify the **causing factors** that create (or maintain) the problem. Write a description for each factor. Place a column or an arrow above the horizontal line to represent each causing factor. Note that causing factors (such as the construction boom in the example below) may have some positive implications (see Step 5).

4. Identify the **counteracting factors** that stop things from getting worse. Write a description for each factor. Place a column or an arrow below the horizontal line to represent each counteracting factor. Note that counteracting factors (such as migration in the example below) may have some negative implications (see Step 5).

5. Rate each cause and each counteracting factor using scores from 1 (weak) to 5 (strong). If you want this exercise to be more precise, identify **indicators** that define the meaning of each number on the scale. Show the **value of each factor** by making the size of each column (or arrow) bigger or smaller, as in the following diagram:

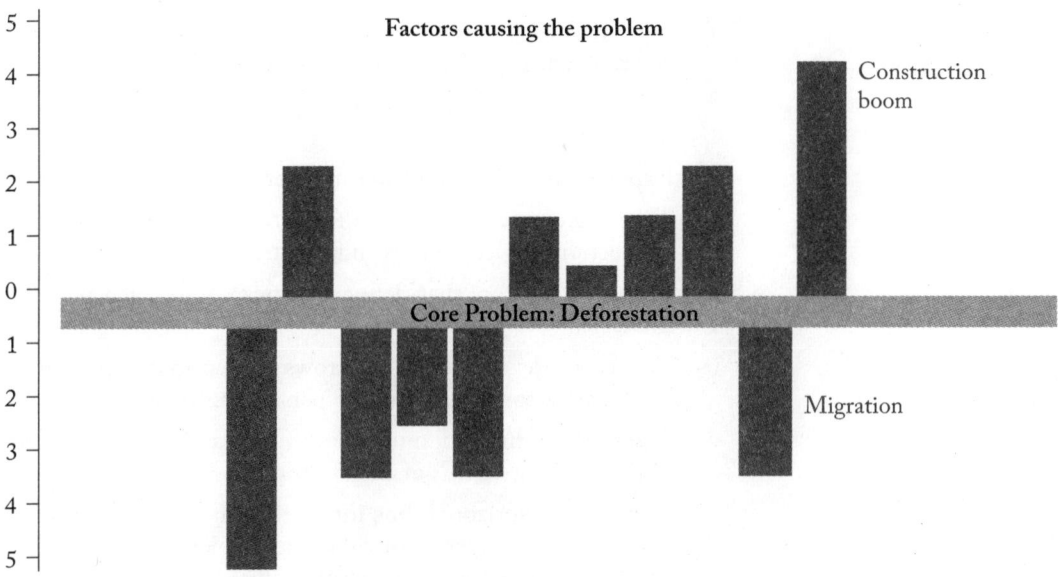

6. Identify the factors that you have some **control** over, and then those over which you have little or no control.

7. Each party (such as gender groups) may prepare its own *Force Field* analysis and then compare and discuss its findings with the other parties.

8. Discuss the results of your analysis and your priorities for action.

You can look for direct connections between causes and counteracting factors. A connection of this kind is called a **balancing loop**. It involves a factor that strengthens another factor, which in turn has a counteracting effect on its own cause. For instance, the construction boom may cause deforestation, which in turn causes the price of wood to go up, at some cost to the construction industry.

Scaling Up or Down

For Simpler Versions

1. Reduce the number of factors you will consider by removing those that have less impact on the problem.

2. Do not measure the value of each factor (as described in Step 5).

3. Leave out the analysis of balancing loops (Step 8).

For More Advanced Versions

1. Use *Freelisting* or *Timeline* to identify the factors that cause your key problem as well as those that counteract it.

2. During the exercise, record the explanations that parties provide for each factor.

3. Explore and include a greater number of factors.

4. Take more time to find the information you need to justify each connection between causes and effects.

5. Identify indicators that define the meaning of each number on the scale.

6. Use second-level columns or arrows to identify factors that cause first-level factors to exist and to persist over time.

7. Assess the estimated time frame (such as "short-term", "mid-term", or "long-term") of each factor.

8. Convert the horizontal line into a timeline of major events that have marked the history of your core problem. Then, define each event as either a causing factor (of conflict, for instance) or a counteracting factor (of peace, for instance).

Readings and Links

Accel-Team.com. 2005. *Force Field Analysis*. Cumbria, UK, Accel-Team. Available online at http://www.accel-team.com/techniques/force_field_analysis.html, accessed on August 15, 2007.

Mind Tools. nd. *Force Field Analysis—Understanding the Pressures For and Against Change*. Wimbledon, London, UK: Mind Tools.com. Available online at http://www.mindtools.com/pages/article/newTED_06.htm, accessed on August 15, 2007.

———. nd. Systems Diagrams—*Understanding How Factors Affect One Another*. Wimbledon, London, UK: Mind Tools.com. Available online at http://www.mindtools.com/pages/article/newTMC_04.htm, accessed on August 15, 2007.

SEAGA (Socioeconomic and Gender Analysis Programme). 2001. Intermediate Level Handbook, Section 7.1. Rome, Italy: Food and Agriculture Organization. Available online at http://www.fao.org/sd/seaga/4_en.htm, accessed on August 15, 2007.

Force Field: Factors Influencing the Fear of Eviction among the Katkari of Sarang Katkarwadi, Maharashtra, India

Key Words

Force Field, India, Katkari, tribal people, land tenure

Authors

D.J. Buckles, R. Khedkar, D. Patil, and B. Ghevde.

Context

Sarang Katkarwadi is a hamlet of 34 Katkari tribal families, located a few kilometres from a major highway between Mumbai and Pune. The hamlet has existed for more than 60 years on land owned by a non-tribal person in the nearby village of Sarang. Sarang is a prosperous agricultural community with access to a perennial water source for irrigation. A number of households lease agricultural lands from non-tribal villagers in Sarang but the vast majority work as bonded labor on brick-making units in the region. A few households work on a sand dredging operation for a contractor in Sarang village. All residents of Sarang Katkarwadi are listed by the government as Below the Poverty Line.

Recently, the local landowner sold nearly 10 acres of his land, including the land where the hamlet is located, to a person from Mumbai. This has created a great deal of uncertainty among the Katkari families regarding the future of their hamlet. They are afraid that sooner or later they will be evicted by the new landowner or that the land will be resold to another. The Academy of Development Science (ADS), a non-governmental organization working in the region for many years, has been encouraging the residents of Sarang Katkarwadi to press for their right to the land but the latter are reluctant to do so. The fear of eviction and open conflict prevented the Katkari from presenting a resolution regarding their land rights before the village council. Both ADS and villagers felt it was important to clarify why, so that they could continue to work together without putting the Katkari at risk.

Purpose

To develop a plan for responding to the situation that would not put the Katkari at risk.

Process Summary

The ADS convened a meeting of villagers in Sarang Katkarwadi that had participated in previous events concerning their legal rights to land. Six men from this group participated in the exercise, held in the home of one of the villagers. The group defined the key problem stopping them from pursuing their rights as fear of eviction by the landowner and listed the factors that drive or cause the problem and those that counteract it or stop it from getting worse. These were then rated on a scale of 1 (weak) to 5 (strong) and plotted as a graph on a large sheet of paper. Discussion focused on those factors they could control and actions that result from the assessment. The participants understood that a report would be prepared based on the exercise, and agreed to share their information.

Analysis

Graph 1 shows the balance of driving and counteracting forces, as identified and rated by the Katkari participants.

The forces driving the fear of eviction are:

1. The landowner has a legal title to the land;
2. Land prices are rising quickly;
3. The Katkari generally lack knowledge of their legal rights;
4. People in the hamlet are not organized;
5. There is a feeling of obligation toward the previous landowner due to past and ongoing favors; and
6. The livelihoods of most Katkari depend on others, including the non-tribal villagers.

The forces counteracting the fear of eviction are:

1. Families currently have *de facto* possession of the land;
2. Legal provisions (Government Circular dated May 1, 2000) proclaim housing rights;
3. The Katkari are classified as a Primitive Tribal Group with specific measures for legal protection of their rights;
4. There are provisions in the Integrated Tribal Development Project (ITDP) to compensate landowners in cases of expropriation; and
5. Leadership is emerging among the youth.

Graph 1: Factors that Drive or Counteract the Fear of Eviction

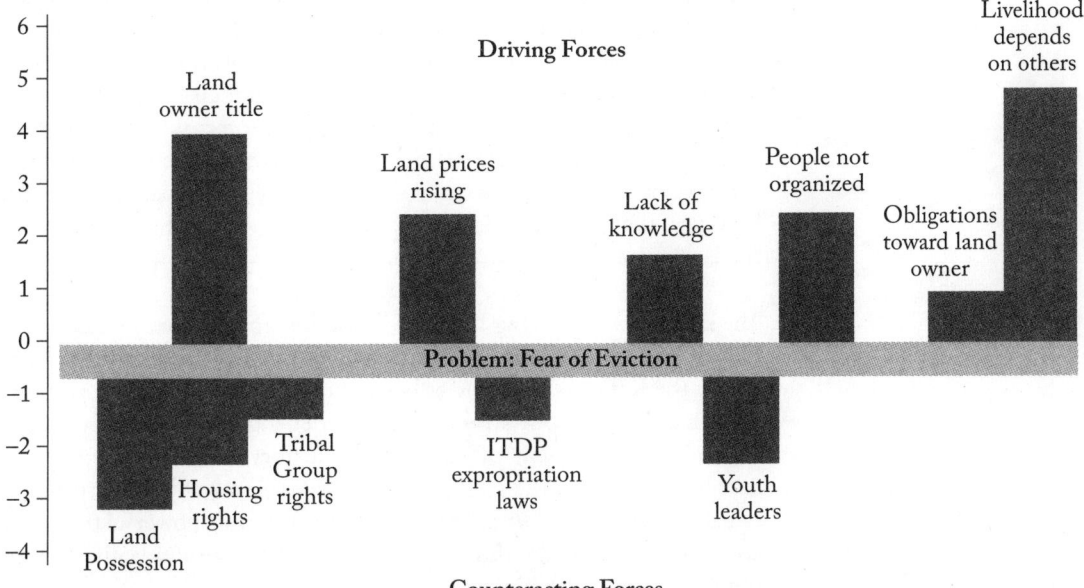

The forces driving the fear of eviction among the Katkari are seen by the participants as stronger overall than the counteracting or restraining forces. The landowner has legal title to the land, and can therefore count on the support of authorities to dispose of his land when and as he wishes. Land prices are rising rapidly, creating ever stronger fears that sellers and buyers will want to be sure the land is free of any encumbrance. The majority of residents in the hamlet remain unaware of their rights and the hamlet as a whole does not have the capacity to organize any collective resistance. Residents feel an obligation to the previous landowner and therefore some at least are more likely to go along with his wishes. Finally, a very strong driving factor unanticipated by ADS is the fact that the Katkari feel highly dependent on the non-tribal village and on non-Katkari employers generally for their livelihood.

The strongest counteracting or restraining force available to the Katkari is their current possession of the land: the Katkari live there while the landowner lives in Mumbai. This factor, along with the legal provisions that back up their tribal and housing rights to residence, helps allay their fears of eviction so long as they are there (and not migrating to work on brick kilns). The provisions of the ITPD for compensation of landowners in cases of conflict with tribal populations are not a strong counteracting force, especially considering that land prices are much higher than rates normally used by government agencies to expropriate landowners. The only other factor in their favor is the emergence of youth leadership in the hamlet keen to break free from their bondage, and able to call on legal protections available to them if the landowner actually begins to evict them. The participants indicated, however, that residents do not want to do anything that would force the landowner to act against them.

Interpretation

The strong forces driving the fear of eviction and relatively weak counteracting forces perceived by the participants reflect the extreme vulnerability the Katkari feel to forces beyond their control. Legal protections of various kinds, while strong on paper, depend almost entirely on the actions of government officials with a history of disinterest or even antagonism toward the plight of the Katkari. The Katkari fear eviction but also open conflict with actors that are much more powerful than they are and that can make things worse not only by uprooting them from their homes but also blocking their access to livelihood.

Action

The participants concluded from the analysis that they have no option but to live with the fear of eviction. Presentation of a resolution regarding their land rights before the village council seemed too risky at the present time. They appreciated, however, the importance of a continuous presence in the village as a factor stopping their fears from getting more intense. The emerging youth leadership in the community represented in the group resolved to keep track of family migration out of the community, as a means of monitoring when the hamlet is most vulnerable to eviction. They also decided to continue learning from ADS about their land rights, and to explore more actively the options for diversifying community livelihoods. ADS resolved not to press the Katkari to present a petition to village authorities.

Observations on the Process

The legal factors driving and counteracting the fear of eviction were difficult to score at first because a number of the participants were not very familiar with these provisions. This situation was managed by asking Katkari participants with more knowledge to explain to the others in detail, and revising the scores at various points in the discussion. The accuracy of the final result was confirmed by the participants, who also noted that it helped them understand the concerns of their neighbors. All participants felt that it was important for ADS to continue to provide them with access to information on land rights and that they could continue to do so quietly without putting either party at risk.

Timeline

Author	J.M. Chevalier
Acknowledgement	*Timeline* is a SAS² adaptation of a technique widely used in the field of participatory research (see in particular K. Means et al., 2002).
Purpose	*Timeline* helps you identify the events that have created a certain problem or situation. It explores people's views and knowledge about how a problem or situation has evolved over time, and changes that have occurred in the process.

Guiding Principles

1. In order to deal with a problem, you may need to understand the roots of the situation and events that led to it.
2. People may have different memories and interpretations of the events that created a certain problem.

Process

1. Identify the **core problem** or the **situation** where you need to use *Timeline*. Define this problem or situation as clearly as possible, and clarify the purpose of your analysis.
2. Record the name and the date of **one of the events or the changes** that led to the current problem or situation. Write (or draw) the event on its own card.
3. Add a **title** for the event (as in a book title) to the card. You can also add **basic facts** about the event, such as the date, the problems associated with the event, the names of key parties, and their actions. Record these facts on the reverse side of the card (or use a flipchart).
4. Use the same method (Steps 2 and 3) to list and describe **other events or changes** that led to the current problem or situation. Record each event or change on its own card. Add the related facts on the reverse side of each card (or use a flipchart for each event).

5. Continue until you have listed most of the important events or changes that you can remember.

6. Arrange all cards (or flipcharts) in **chronological order**. To simplify the analysis, treat minor events or changes as satellites of key events or changes.

7. Another option is to create a "**before-and-after**" table with six columns that describe the areas of change (Column 1), the changes from what used to be (Column 2) to the present situation (Column 3) for each area, how important these changes are (Column 4), and then the causes or reasons (Column 5) behind each change. In the last row, try to describe the overall difference between the past situation and the present. Here's an example of a "before-and-after" table:

Areas of Change	Before (10 years ago)	Now	Importance of Change (from 1 to 5)	Causes or Reasons
Jobs				
Environment				
Family				
Overall				

8. Each party (such as gender groups) may prepare its own timeline or "before-and-after" table, and then compare and discuss its findings and views with the other parties. Be aware that discussions about the past may bring back strong emotions.

Scaling Up or Down

For Simpler Versions

1. Reduce the number of events or changes appearing in your *Timeline*.

2. Do the *Timeline* diagram or the "before-and-after" table but not both.

For More Advanced Versions

1. During the exercise, record the explanations that parties provide for each event.

2. Take more time to find the information you need to complete the exercise.

3. Increase the number of events or move farther back into the past.

4. Use *Problem Tree* or *Force Field* to analyze each major event or change.

5. Place events of one kind (such as factors of peace) above the timeline and events of another kind (such as factors of conflict) below the timeline.

6. Use *Problem Domain* to list and compare events or changes and to assess how people view the meaning and impact of events over time.

Readings and Links

Borrini-Feyerabend, G.; M.T. Farvar; J. C. Nguinguiri; and V. A. Ndangang. 2000. *Co-management of Natural Resources: Organising, Negotiating and Learning-by-Doing*. Kasparek Verlag, Heidelberg, Germany: GTZ and IUCN. Available online at http://learningforsustainability.net/pubs/cmnr/cmnr.html, accessed on August 15, 2007.

Means, K.; C. Josayma; E. Nielsen; and V. Viriyasakultorn. 2002. *Community-Based Forest Resource Conflict Management: Training Package*, Volume 2, Activity 9. Rome, Italy: Food and Agricuture Organization. Available online at http://www.fao.org/DOCREP/005/Y4301E/Y4301E00.HTM, accessed on August 15, 2007.

Timeline: A History of Events and Actions that have Harmed or Protected Rupa Lake in the Pokhara Valley of Nepal

Key Words	*Timeline*, Nepal, Rupa Lake, watershed management
Authors	D. Poudel and D.J. Buckles

Context

Rupa Lake is one of eight lakes in the Pokhara valley of western Nepal. It is located about 15 kilometres east of the city of Pokhara and covers some 115 hectares, making it the third largest among these eight lakes, after Phewa and Begnas Lakes. Rupa Lake is fed by streams and rivers that descend from the mountain regions of the Himalaya's Annapurna Range. The lake, its wetlands, and a lower watershed are rich in flora and fauna due to the many micro-climates they create. More than 150 species of birds visit the lake and nearby forests. Fishers living around the lake depend on its aquatic resources for their livelihood, while other residents benefit from water and other resources that form part of the lake's wetlands. All are concerned about steady declines in the health of the lake and wetlands, and the threat of flooding and landslides near their settlements. The Nepali non-governmental organization LI-BIRD (Local Initiatives for Biodiversity, Research and Development) has worked for many years with residents surrounding the lake, and manages several community-based projects aimed at improving local livelihoods sustainably.

Purpose

To identify the events and actions that have harmed or protected the lake and its nearby wetlands.

Process Summary

The non-governmental organization LI-BIRD held a one-day meeting in a local hall, at the request of local authorities concerned about this problem. Some 21 people (12 men and nine women) attended from communities on the shores of the lake. Participants included representatives of local fishing cooperatives, local self-help groups (Community Based Organizations), schools, and local authorities. They were asked to describe past events or actions that had a major impact on the health of the lake and its wetlands. These were noted on cards and ordered chronologically on a wall. Discussion was encouraged throughout the process. Participants knew that notes taken during the event would be used to prepare a report, and agreed to share their information. The lead author of this report facilitated the exercise.

Analysis

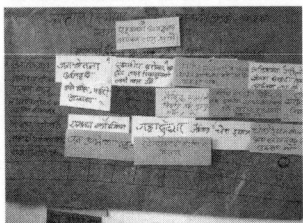

Participants identified 23 major events and actions affecting the health of the Rupa Lake and its wetlands between 1952 and 2005 (Table 1). In 1952, a major flood and series of landslides changed the watershed when large amounts of sediment entered the lake and surrounding wetlands. Participants said the landslides happened because of forest clearing in the lower watershed, which had been ongoing for a decade. Forest clearing became more intense after 1957 when local ownership and control of the forests was replaced by the Forest Nationalization Act. Slash-and-burn agriculture on national forest land became common, and was not controlled by government agencies. Major floods and landslides occurred again in 1962, 1972, and 1976. This created new agricultural areas in the wetlands and along the lakeshore. Government land surveys in 1962 and 1976 endorsed private claims to these new lands. Some local people diverted streams and rivers to cause new landslides and sedimentation so that they could claim new lands.

Permanent settlements began appearing in the lower watershed in 1979, increasing the amount of forest clearing. A major flood and landslide occurred in 1981, leading to more private claims to new land by local elites. The Begnas High School claimed a large piece of new land in a sensitive area near the shore of the lake.

In 1983 fish farms were set up. The waste from these farms, along with lake sedimentation, promoted the growth of harmful water plants (Water Chestnut and Water Hyacinth). The native species of Lotus were displaced. In 1984 gravel and sand were removed from the wetlands around the lake's main outlet, causing a drop in lake water levels.

In 1986 government officials and non-governmental organizations launched the first big effort to control flooding and landslides by building check dams in various places and by planting trees. They also set up a Community Forestry Program to support local ownership and control of forests. During this same time, new settlements in the watershed were set up or expanded and large pieces of forest were cleared. Non-government and poorly planned roads were built to link these settlements, causing soil erosion, landslides, and more sedimentation of the lake and wetlands.

In 1992 a landslide that would have happened near Bandre was prevented through the efforts of an outside agency. Several years later, check dams and tree planting at the place where the *Kalyangdi* and *Thulo Khola* rivers meet helped reduce the threat of flooding and landslides. This action was led by the same outside agency. Meanwhile, the growth of harmful water plants continued in the lake. The use of agricultural fertilizers on lands draining into the lake made the problem worse. Fishing with electric currents began in 1997, causing direct damage to aquatic life.

Major landslides occurred again in 2001. For the first time, these were a direct threat to settlements. Landslides in 2004 caused a lot of damage in many places and added more and more sediment to the lake and its nearby wetlands. In 2005 the Rupa Lake Fisheries Cooperative launched a major plan to clear the lake of harmful water plants.

Table 1: The Sequence of Events and Actions that Have Harmed or Protected Rupa Lake

	Before 1952 forest clearing in the lower watershed.
1952	A major flood and series of landslides flattened the lower Chaur and Talbesi rivers. Large amounts of sediment were deposited in and around the lake. This reduced the size and depth of the lake.
1957	Local ownership and control of forests was replaced by the Forest Nationalization Act. Forest clearing became more intense.
1962	Flooding and landslides filled parts of the lake and wetlands with sediment. A government land survey that year endorsed private claims to these new lands. Lake inlets were diverted by local people to promote sedimentation and create new lands on the lakeshore.
1972	Flooding and landslides in three areas (*Rupakot, Betayani* and *Hangshapur* wards) deposited sediment in the lake and its nearby wetlands.
1976	Flooding and landslides near *Hangshapur* ward added sediment to the lake and nearby wetlands. A government land survey upheld private claims to new lands, mainly by local elites.
1979	Various permanent settlements were set up in the nearby watershed, and forest clearing became more intense.
1981	Flooding and landslides added sediment to many parts of the wetlands and lakeshore. This land was then claimed by individuals. The Begnas High School claimed a large area near the lakeshore.
1983	Fish farms were set up. Waste from the farms, along with more sediment in the lake, displaced the lotus plant and promoted the growth of harmful water plants (Water Chestnut and Water Hyacinth).
1984	Gravel and sand extracted from the outlet increased water flow and reduced the depth of the lake.
1986	Check dams and community forestry programs were started by outside agencies and the government.
1988	New settlements were established or expanded.
1989	Forest clearing of 300 hectares and 54 hectares at *Lekhnath-11* and *Hangshapur-9* wards, respectively, provoked a major landslide. New lands were claimed by local elites.
1991	Construction of the *Begnas–Bhorletar* road eroded soils and caused sediment to enter the lake and wetlands.
1992	A potential landslide at *Bandre* was controlled with the help of an outside agency.
1994	Use of chemical fertilizers in agriculture increased, promoting the growth of harmful water plants in the lake.
1995	Check dams and reforestation programs were established by outside agencies at the place where the *Kalyangdi* and *Thulo Khola* rivers meet.

(Table 1 continued)

(*Table 1 continued*)

1997	Fishing with electric currents began.
2001	Flooding and landslides from the *Devisthan* river affected lower settlements.
2003	Road building at *Talbesi–Lipyani*, *Sourbas–Ramkot* and *Bhanjhyang–Begnas* eroded soil and allowed sediment to settle in the lake.
2004	Landslides in many areas (*Khada gaindo, Banskot, Hangshapur, Archalthar, Satdobato, Majhthana, Tallo Kahere, Lekhnath-10*) caused more sediment to enter the lake and wetlands.
2005	Harmful water plants were removed by the Rupa Fisheries Cooperative.
2005	Hailstorm damaged lake biodiversity.

Interpretation

Forest clearing in the lower and upper watershed has caused many floods and landslides over the past 50 years. As a result, the topography and ecosystem of the lake and its wetlands have changed a lot. Government policies that affect forest ownership and government endorsement of private claims to new lands added force to these events. Unplanned human settlements in the watershed increased the rate at which forest cover was lost. Non-government road building added more sediment to the lake and wetlands. More recently, uncontrolled dredging and pollution from land and fish farming caused more direct harm to the lake. Participants said that these events happened because neither they nor government officials had used foresight, planning and regulation. Most efforts to protect the lake were started by outside groups and offered few opportunities for community input. They also noted that local elites have benefited the most from government land policies that upheld private claims to new lands created by landslides and sedimentation. Only in recent years have local residents begun to see the direct threat to their settlements and the need to conserve sources of livelihood such as the lake fishery.

Action

The participants decided to make a formal petition to government to order a halt to cutting of those forests that remain in the lower and upper watershed. They also resolved to oppose government land surveys that endorse private claims to new lands created by landslides. At the end of the meeting the local authorities decided to develop a local action plan that would regulate and manage activities that might further harm the health of the lake and its wetlands.

Observations on the Process

The exercise used the Nepali calendar, which starts 56 years before the Western calendar. The dates were changed to the Western calendar for this report. Use of points of reference to major political events made it easy for participants to organize local events chronologically. The physical layout of the events on the floor also enhanced participation and allowed different people to work on the timeline simultaneously. The accuracy of the final result was confirmed by the participants, who noted that it was useful to their own thinking about the importance of different events in determining the current situation. The local authorities expressed appreciation for the value the analysis would add to the proposed local action plan.

Gaps and Conflicts

Author
J.M. Chevalier

Acknowledgement
Gaps and Conflicts is a SAS[2] adaptation of a technique used in the field of participatory research (see in particular K. Means et al., 2002).

Purpose
This technique helps you find out if your key problem is mostly about gaps or conflicts in power, interests (gains and losses), moral values, or information and communication.

Guiding Principles
1. You can understand a social problem by looking at whether it involves issues of power, interests (gains and losses), moral values (norms and principles), or information and communication.
2. These four kinds of issues may take one of these two forms:

   A gap involving a lack of resources; the absence of interest (gains or losses); a failure to appreciate the moral worth or value of something; a shortage of information and effective communication; or

   A conflict over who has the power to decide and how decisions are made; how gains and losses are distributed; the values that people believe in; the information that is given out and the ways that people communicate.

Process
1. Identify a **key problem** where you need to use *Gaps and Conflicts*. Define the problem as clearly as possible, and clarify the purpose of your analysis.
2. Identify the **main causes of your key problem**. Write (or draw) each cause on its own card. *Freelisting* or *Timeline* may help you identify these causes.
3. For each cause, ask what **kind of issue** it involves: one of power, interests (gains and losses), moral values, or information and communication. Use the definitions provided below. Discuss and clarify the definitions, using local examples and terms, if needed.

Power is your ability to achieve what you want by influencing others and using resources you control. These resources include:

(a) Economic wealth;

(b) Political authority (an office, position or role recognized by an institution or by local customs);

(c) The ability to use force or the threat of force;

(d) Information (including knowledge and skills), and the means to communicate.

Make sure that participants do not confuse the idea of "power" with the use of force only.

Interests are the gains and losses that you will experience based on the results of ongoing or proposed actions. These gains and losses affect the degree to which you control assets such as economic wealth, political authority, the use of force, information, the means to communicate, legitimacy, or social ties. Make sure that participants do not confuse the idea of "acting in one's *interest*" with "taking an *interest* in something".

Values are beliefs, judgments, norms or principles about what is important, and the degree to which something is good or bad, right or wrong. Make sure that participants do not confuse the idea of "value" with the price that something is worth on the market.

Information is what you know "for a fact" and believe to be true.

Communication is how you exchange information and make your views known to others.

4. On each card that describes a different cause, write the kind of issue it represents. Use a short sentence or key words (or drawings) that are concrete and clear to everyone. If the cause raises more than one issue (such as power *and* interests), write the same cause on two or more cards and record a different issue on each card.

5. Take each card and decide whether it involves a **gap or a conflict** (see definitions above). Record and explain your assessment on each card.

6. Create a *Gap and Conflict* table. Write the four kinds of issues in the first column. Write Gaps, Conflicts, and Ranking in the top row. Place each card in the appropriate column and row. Here's an example of a table showing gaps and conflicts associated with a proposal to privatize communal lands in an indigenous community.

Issues	Gaps	Conflicts	Ranking
Power	Those who want to privatize communal lands are not organized.	Ranchers occupy communal lands and control municipal politics.	1
Interests (gains and losses)	This is not important for the federal government and makes no difference to them.	The landless will gain, the ranchers will lose.	2
Moral values		Opposite values are used to justify communal and individual property systems.	4
Information & Communication	We do not know what the legal procedures are.	Municipal authorities refuse to let people speak when the village meets.	3

7. Use the last column to **rank the combined weight of row issues** according to the number and importance of the cards that appear in each row. Use a ranking scale of 1 to 4, from the greatest weight to the least.

8. Discuss the results of your analysis and your priorities for action.

   Be aware that the act of filling a *gap* (such as getting information on land ownership) can sometimes lead to a *conflict* between parties. Also participants often define as priorities those issues where they are already strong (such as filling information gaps, in the case of a non-governmental organization doing applied research).

Scaling Up or Down

For Simpler Versions

1. Focus on the most important causes only.
2. Leave out the distinction between gaps and conflicts.
3. Don't rank the causes.

For More Advanced Versions

1. During the exercise, record the explanations that parties provide when categorizing the causes.
2. Take more time to find the information you need to justify how you categorize each cause.
3. Increase the number of causes.
4. Use *Rating* to evaluate the importance of each issue.

Readings and Links

CRC (Conflict Research Consortium). 1998. *Problem List 1: Complicating Factors*. Boulder, CO, USA: CRC, University of Colorado. Available online at http://www.colorado.edu/conflict/peace/!overlay_problems.htm, accessed on August 15, 2007.

Means, K.; C. Josayma; E. Nielsen; V. Viriyasakultorn. 2002. *Community-Based Forest Resource Conflict Management: A Training Package*, Volume 1, Section 3.2, and Volume 2, Activity 12. Rome, Italy: Food and Agriculture Organization. Available online at http://www.fao.org/DOCREP/005/Y4300E/Y4300E00.HTM, and, http://www.fao.org/DOCREP/005/Y4301E/Y4301E00.HTM, accessed on August 15, 2007.

Mind Tools. nd. *Pareto Analysis—Selecting the Most Important Changes to Make*. Wimbledon, London, UK: Mind Tools.com. Available online at http://www.mindtools.com/pages/article/newTED_01.htm, accessed on August 15, 2007.

Gaps and Conflicts: Reasons for Neglect of Residential Land Issues in Navliwadi, Maharashtra, India

Key Words   *Gaps and Conflicts*, India, tribal people, land tenure

Authors   D.J. Buckles; R. Khedkar; D. Patil; and B. Ghevde.

Context   Navliwadi is a hamlet of tribal people known as the *Katkari*. All but one of 33 families in the hamlet are landless, and all live below the poverty line. The hamlet is on a hillock and does not have a drinking water source. Women from the hamlet have to carry water daily. Sometimes, two or three families live in the same house. There is no school in the hamlet and an approach road was built only a short time ago. The land on which the hamlet sits is owned by a distant descendent of a local royal family (*Bhor Sansthan*) who is well known in the field of education. Because of his social standing, the landowner does not want to appear to be opposed to the Katkari living on his land. However, he does not allow the *Katkari* to expand their homes or use land around the hamlet. The *Katkari* families are concerned about this and unhappy with the lack of interest by government officials and elected representatives in matters related to their hamlet. A non-governmental organization (SOBTI) has been working in Navliwadi and other *Katkari* communities for many years and has tried in the past to draw official attention to these kinds of problems.

Purpose   Determine whether the neglect of *Katkari* concerns by government officials and elected representatives is mostly due to **gaps** or **conflicts** in (*i*) power, (*ii*) interests (gains and losses), (*iii*) moral values (norms and principles), or (*iv*) information and communication.

Process Summary   SOBTI held a meeting of nine *Katkari* (six men, three women) at its Center near Navliwadi. Participants made a list of what they believed to be the reasons why their concerns have been neglected by government officials and elected representatives. They then stated what **kinds** of issues each cause involved, choosing between issues involving (*i*) power, (*ii*) interests, (*iii*) moral values, and (*iv*) information and communication. These were then further described by participants as either **a gap** or **a conflict**. The information was displayed on cards in a table format. Then, participants decided which issues were most important. SOBTI subsequently prepared a draft report on the assessment.

At the request of participants, no photographs were taken during the exercise. This was to reduce the risk of individuals being identified with the actions the group decided to take. The participants in the exercise understood that the results would be used in reports by SOBTI, and agreed to share the information they provided so long as it remained anonymous. The village name used in the report is fictitious.

Analysis

The issues that participants raised are as follows:

1. Government officials act in favor of the landowner because he holds political power and they do not want to oppose him. Participants said this reflects a power gap: *Katkari* lack the resources to influence government officials.

2. Government officials act in favor of the landowner because they believe he is the rightful owner. They do not recognize the moral claims of the *Katkari*, even though they have occupied the land for a long time. Government officials consider the *Katkari* good-for-nothings. Participants described this as a conflict in moral values: opposing judgments are made regarding rights and moral worth.

3. The *Katkari* do not press the issue with government officials or elected representatives because they are not aware of their rights as citizens or the laws that pertain to tribal lands and long-term occupancy of land. Participants described this as an information gap: *Katkari* do not know what rights they have.

4. Elected representatives are not aware of the legal rights of the *Katkari* and they do not believe the problem is serious or very important. Participants described this as an information and communication gap: information on *Katkari* rights is not communicated to elected representatives.

5. Elected representatives and government officials see no gain from helping to solve the *Katkari's* problems, and they do gain financially from their relationship with the powerful landowner. Participants described this as a conflict of interests: elected representatives and government officials gain from the neglect and the *Katkari* lose.

The ranking of the issues that cause government and elected officials to neglect the *Katkari* are presented in Table 1. A conflict in interests (gains and losses) between the *Katkari*, on the one hand, and both government officials and elected representatives, on the other, was considered by the participants to have the greatest overall weight in causing the problem. Government officials and elected representatives gain financially from the current situation, and see no gain from helping to solve the *Katkari's* problems.

Table 1: Ranking of Issues that Result in Neglect of Katkari Concerns

Type of issue	Gaps	Conflicts	Ranking
Power	*Katkari* lack resources to influence government officials.		2
Interests		Elected representatives and government officials gain and the *Katkari* lose.	1
Values		There are opposing judgments regarding rights.	4
Information/ Communication	*Katkari* do not know what rights they have. Information is not communicated to elected representatives.		3

A gap in the power of the Katkari to influence was seen as the second most significant overall reason for the neglect, followed closely by gaps in information and communication affecting both the *Katkari* and elected representatives. While judgments on the part of government officials regarding the moral worth of the *Katkari's* land claim play a role, this was considered an issue of lesser weight overall compared to the others.

Interpretation

The **conflict of interests** reflects the fact that patronage plays an important and well-known role in Indian society. Participants agreed that success in government jobs and politics depends on keeping and adding to the networks of people who have power, such as the landowner. The participants also recognized that the **gaps in information and communication** related to the *Katkari's* legal rights make the situation worse by keeping from public view the illegal advantage that the landowner has.

Action

Towards the end of the assessment, the participants decided to present a land petition at the village assembly (*Gram Sabha*) and with officials of the revenue department (*Tehsildar*), in an attempt to broaden their network of support and draw attention to their rights.

Observations on the Process

Differences within the group appeared when two *Katkari* men said they did not agree with the arguments made against the landowner, whom they believed to be an ally in the situation. This tension was managed by reminding participants that the focus of the assessment was neglect of government officials, a concern shared by all. The arguments of women in the group for ranking the **conflict of interests** as the main reason for neglect also helped manage the differences by keeping attention on the main topic.

Causal Dynamics

Author

J.M. Chevalier

Acknowledgement

Causal Dynamics is a SAS[2] adaptation and development of input-output analysis, a well-known technique used in economics, and economic policy and planning throughout the world for the past half-century.

Purpose

Causal Dynamics helps you assess the causes of a key problem and the way each cause interacts with other causes.

Guiding Principles

1. To resolve a key problem, you must look at how key **factors** interact—how your key problem interacts with its causes and how each cause interacts with other causes.

2. The **apparent weight** of a factor is your initial estimate of its overall importance in relation to a core problem. The **real weight** of a factor is your estimate of how important the factor is when its causes and effects (other than the core problem) are put aside—by doing as if these factors that cause it or result from it did not exist (for instance, illiteracy would still have some weight even if poverty did not exist).

3. To reduce the *apparent weight* of a factor, you must reduce its real weight or the real weight of its causes. To reduce the *real weight* of a factor, you must act on it directly.

Process

Creating a Causal
Dynamics Table

1. Identify a **key problem in a situation** where you need to use *Causal Dynamics*. Define the problem of situation as clearly as possible, and clarify the purpose of your analysis. Write (or draw) the key problem on a card and a short description on the reverse side of the card. Make a copy of this card. For instance, your organization feels that the way it manages knowledge is of little use to

its members, which is a problem if it is to implement a learning approach to project activities. See this example in Step 12.

2. Make a list of the **causes** that contribute to your key problem. Write (or draw) each cause on two separate cards and describe it on the reverse side of one card. This gives you two sets of cards showing the same causes. For instance, your organization's lack of innovation may be a factor that contributes to its knowledge management problem described in Step 1. See this example in Step 12.

The key problem and its causes should be concrete, distinct from each other, and clearly defined. If they are too general, use the *Laddering Down* technique to make them more meaningful and detailed. Ask "What do you mean by this?" or "Can you give an example of this?" You can also use description and storytelling to explore your topic area (such as describing the key events and difficulties of a knowledge management project), and then use this information to identify the key problem and its causes.

3. Create a table. Place one set of factor cards in the top row of your table. Then place the other set of factor cards in the first column. See example in Step 12.

If you prefer to use a **simple version of** *Causal Dynamics*, follow only the steps that are underlined (Steps 4, 7 to 10, 13 to 17, 20 to 22, 24 and 25) and ignore all the instructions regarding the real and apparent weights of each factor.

4. Evaluate the degree to which each factor **causes** or contributes to the factor represented by Column 2. Ask which of the row factors contribute to that column factor, and to what degree in each case. For instance, "Which of the row factors (listed in Step 12) contribute to poor knowledge management in your organization, and to what degree in each case?" Clarify the question if necessary. Use a rating scale of 0 to 10. Do not insert a score in the square that combines the same column and row factor ("Poor Knowledge Management" by "Poor Knowledge Management" for instance).

Record each score on a new card. To help you interpret the results of this exercise, write the reason given for each score on the reverse side of its card. Place the resulting score cards in the appropriate rows in Column 2. See example in Step 12.

If you want this exercise to be more precise, identify **indicators** (using simple statements) that define the meaning of each number on the scale. If you don't want to use written numbers when rating the factor, use simple phrases first and then convert the phrases into measurable objects (from 0 to 5 twigs, stones, noodles or seeds, for instance). Or you can score each factor with the help of five cards colored white (value 0), light grey (value 1), medium grey (value 2), dark grey (value 3), and black (value 4). Another option is to draw a tree trunk with five roots of different sizes; the larger the root is, the more important it is as a root cause that feeds the trunk. You place a column card on the trunk, and then you place each row card on a root that reflects its importance as a "root cause". Test your scale with the group to make sure that the exercise, the scale, and the indicators are clear to everyone.

You can give the same score to two or several factors. Don't use **averages** when people have disagreements about scores. Instead discuss the issue until you reach an agreement based on consensus or a majority vote.

When asked how Factor A contributes to Factor B, participants may invert the question and indicate how B contributes to A. When this happens, you can insert the score in the B (row)– A (column) square, and then come back to your initial question about how A contributes to B.

If you prefer not to use a table, make only one set of factor cards and place these in a column in plain view of all participants. When discussing the factors, move the top card to one side and begin by asking to what extent do the remaining column cards cause the factor set to one side. Continue this line of questioning down the column, always referring to the isolated factor card. Once these relationships have been scored, and duly recorded on paper, return the top card to the column and pull out the next factor card. All cards remaining in the column can then be discussed as causes of the isolated factor card. Continue until all interactions have been assessed and recorded by a note-taker in table form. This procedure lends itself to a direct conversational style of facilitation focusing on the factors rather than the construction of a table. It also makes it easier to use pictures or objects instead of factor cards, and work in a smaller space.

5. Evaluate the **apparent weight** of each factor using a rating scale of 1 to 10. The apparent weight of a factor is your initial estimate of how important each factor is in relation to the key problem identified in Step 1. Since factors with apparent weights of less than 3 are very weak, they should not be included in the analysis. Write the apparent weight of each factor in the top left corner of the corresponding card in the top row.

6. Once you have inserted all scores in Column 2, evaluate the **real weight** of the column factor. This is your estimate of how important the factor would be *if all the other factors did not exist* (for instance, "Poor Knowledge Management" would still have some weight even if "Lack of innovation" and other factors did not exist). Use a rating scale from 1 to 10. The score for the real weight of a factor must be the same or less than the factor's apparent weight identified in Step 5. Write the score on the corresponding factor card in the top row, in the bottom right corner of the card.

7. Repeat Steps 4 and 6 for all other columns. See example in Step 12.

   If you prefer to focus less attention on the table, use a **flipchart to represent each column factor**. On each flipchart place the other factor cards and the degree to which each of them causes or contributes to the factor represented by the flipchart. On each flipchart indicate the apparent weight and the real weight of the flipchart factor. Once the flipcharts are completed, use the table created in Step 4 to compile the scores.

   If you have to do the ratings in a short time, place the most important factors in the first rows and the first columns (in the top left) of your table and rate them first. Or you can group the factors, name each group, and then rate the groups instead of the factors. You can also reduce the number of factors by eliminating those that are less important (with lower apparent weights). Another option is to divide all participants into smaller groups, and then ask each group to choose one or a few columns and do the corresponding ratings. Use this option only if the participants don't need to be involved in all the ratings.

8. Calculate how much each factor contributes to other factors. To calculate this **Cause Index** for each row, total all scores in each row and write the result on a card. Indicate on the same card (in parentheses) the maximum total and the average score for each row (the total score divided by the number of column scores). Create a last column to the right, and insert your Cause Index cards in this column, in the corresponding rows. Write **Cause Index** on a card, and insert the card at the top of the column. See example in Step 12.

9. Calculate how much each factor is the effect of other factors. To calculate this **Effect Index** for each column, total all scores in each column and write the result on a card. Indicate on the same card (in parentheses) the maximum total and the average score for

the column (the total score divided by the number of row scores). Create a last row at the bottom, and insert your Effect Index cards in this row, in the corresponding columns. Write **Effect Index** on a card, and insert the card at the beginning of your last row. See example in Step 12.

10. Calculate the sum of all Cause Index scores and insert the result at the bottom of the last column. Divide this number by the sum of all maximum Cause Index scores (shown in parentheses in your last column). This gives you the **Total Cause Index percentage.** Insert this percentage at the bottom of the last column.

   To verify your calculations, total all scores in your last row and divide the result by the sum of all maximum scores. This should give you the same result as your Total Cause Index percentage. See example in Step 12.

11. Calculate the sum of all apparent weight scores shown in the top row (in the top left corner of each factor card). Write the result in the top left corner of your Cause Index card (at the top of your last column). Then, calculate the sum of all real weight scores shown in the top row (in the bottom right corner of each factor card). Write the result in the bottom right corner of your Cause Index card.

12. Identify the **scores that contradict** the main tendencies of your table. To do this, identify the columns where the real weight of a factor is very different from its apparent weight; these weights are indicated in the corners of the card inserted at the top of each column. Compare each score in these columns with its average column score to see if they are on the same lower side or upper side of the middle point of your scale (5 in a scale of 0 to 10, for instance). If a score is *not* on the same side as the average column score, compare the score with its average row score to see if they are on the same lower side or upper side of the middle point of your scale. If the score is *not* on the same side again, draw a circle around the score. For instance, in the following table the Poor HRM Strategy column shows a real weight (3) that is significantly lower compared with its apparent weight (8). In this column, the score for the lack of innovation's contribution to poor HRM strategy (4) is on the lower side of the middle point (5); this contradicts the average column score (5.3) as well as the average row score (5.7), which are on the upper side of the middle point.

   Here's an example of a *Causal Dynamics* table involving seven factors using a causal scale of 0 to 10:

	10 Poor KM 2	7 Lack of innovation 4	7 Quantitative approach 4	6 RBM 4	7 Weak partnering 6	8 Poor HRM strategy 3	6 Donor dependency 5	51 Cause Index 28
Poor KM	x	0	8	8	8	2	2	28 (60) 4.7
Lack of innovation	10	x	6	8	4	(4)	2	34 (60) 5.7
Quantitative approach	10	10	x	4	4	10	0	38 (60) 6.3
RBM	8	2	2	x	4	4	0	20 (60) 3.3
Weak partnering	8	8	8	0	x	8	0	32 (60) 5.3
Poor HRM strategy	8	10	10	4	8	x	6	46 (60) 7.7
Donor dependency	6	(4)	6	10	4	6	x	36 (60) 6.0
Effect Index	50 (60) 8.3	34 (60) 5.7	40 (60) 6.7	34 (60) 5.7	32 (60) 5.3	34 (60) 5.7	10 (60) 1.7	234/420 56%

Note: KM: Knowledge Management. RBM: Result-Based Management. HRM: Human Resource Management. See interpretation in Step 25. Values in upper left are apparent weights, and lower right are real weights.

Creating a Causal Dynamics Diagram

13. Create a **diagram** by drawing a vertical line that crosses a horizontal line. This creates a cross within a square. Write the situation and the problem (identified in Step 1) above the diagram using key words or a drawing. See example in Step 20.

14. Write the number that represents your **middle score** where the lines cross. To calculate the middle score, total the maximum Cause Index scores in any row and divide the result by two. In the table shown in Step 12, the maximum Cause Index in any row is 60; the middle score is therefore 30. See example in Step 20.

15. Write the minimum and the maximum Cause Index for any row (0 and 60 in the table shown in Step 12) at opposite ends of the vertical and horizontal lines. Use the **vertical line** to represent the Cause Index of each factor (using the last column scores from your table in Step 12). Use the **horizontal line** to represent the Effect Index of each factor (using the last row scores from your table in Step 12). See example in Step 20.

16. In each corner of the diagram, write (or draw) the **type of factor** that you obtain when you combine the possible outcomes. The diagram gives you four types of factors: causes and effects in the top right; causes in the top left; effects in the bottom right; and independent factors in the bottom left. See example in Step 20.

17. To place each factor in the diagram, mark where the factor is located on both the vertical line (using its Cause Index) and the horizontal line (using its Effect Index). Draw a line from each location and use a **dot** (•) to mark the place where the two lines intersect. Write the name of the factor close to the dot. See example in Step 20.

18. Adjust the size of each dot to indicate the **real weight** of each factor in relation to its apparent weight (see Steps 5 and 7). Use bigger dots when the real weight of a factor is close to its apparent weight. See example in Step 20.

19. Use arrows to indicate relationships that **contradict the main tendencies** of your diagram. To identify these relationships, use the scores encircled in Step 12. Use **continuous arrows** for scores above the middle point of your scale, and **broken arrows** for scores below the middle point. The continuous arrows indicate bottom-side factors that contribute to factors located on the left side of your diagram. The broken arrows indicate upper-side factors that do *not* contribute to factors located on the right side of your diagram. See example in Step 20.

20. Include in the diagram any **other information** that may be useful, using your own code. For instance, use numbers to indicate the **length of time** you need to reduce the weight of each factor, and then colors to indicate the **degree of control** that you have over each factor. For instance, use green dots for factors over which you have some control, and red dots for factors that you do not control).

Here is an example of a *Causal Dynamics* diagram using the scores from the table shown in Step 12. The problem or situation assessed is that the way the organization manages knowledge tends to be limited (see Summary on page 150).

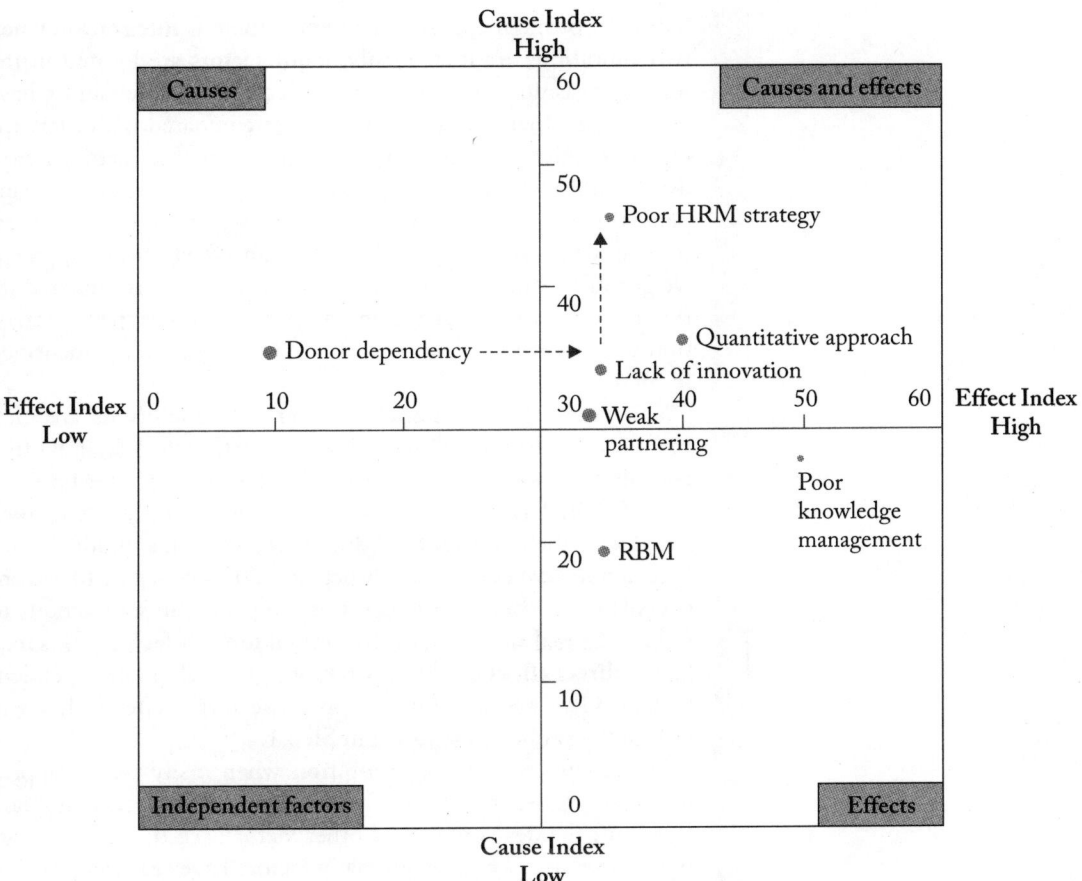

Cause Index
High

| Causes | 60 | Causes and effects |

50

● Poor HRM strategy

40

● Donor dependency ------- ▶ ● Quantitative approach

● Lack of innovation

Effect Index
Low

| 0 | 10 | 20 | 30 | 40 | 50 | 60 |

● Weak
partnering

Effect Index
High

●
Poor
knowledge
management

20 ● RBM

10

| Independent factors | 0 | Effects |

Cause Index
Low

**Interpreting
the Results**

21. To interpret your *Causal Dynamics* analysis, start with a review of the **process** itself, including the way that participants interacted and reached decisions at each step of the process. You can also review the **substance** of the exercise, including the problem that participants selected, their purpose in doing the exercise, the causes they identified, the kind of information or knowledge they used to rate the factors, the apparent weight and the real weight of each factor, the contradictions and information added in Steps 19 and 20, and so on. Summarize all the main points of your review.

22. Assess the overall level of interaction of your factors. A *Causal Dynamics* analysis can produce three possible results: integration,

hierarchy or fragmentation. You know there is **integration** when two conditions are met. Firstly, many factors are located in the top-right section of your diagram. Secondly, many factors have real weights that are significantly lower compared with their apparent weights. This gives you a high Factor Interaction Level, usually above 40 percent (calculated in Step 23). When this happens, think of actions to reduce the real weight of one or several top-right factors. This may have a **chain effect** on the apparent weight of all other dependent factors, which in turn may reduce the apparent weight of the initial factor(s). Give special attention to those chain effects that will reduce the problem identified in Step 1.

You know there is **hierarchy** when two conditions are met. Firstly, your diagram shows mostly top-left factors (causes) that contribute to bottom-right factors (effects). Secondly, the bottom-right factors have real weights that are significantly lower compared with their apparent weights. This gives you a middle Factor Interaction Level score, usually between 20 percent and 40 percent (calculated in Step 23). When this happens, think of actions to reduce the real weight of one or several top-left factors. This may have a **direct effect** on the apparent weight of all other dependent factors. Give special attention to those direct effects that will reduce the problem identified in Step 1.

You know there is **fragmentation** when many factors appear in the bottom-left section of your diagram (or when many factors limit the development of other factors; see tips later). Fragmentation also occurs when many factors have real weights that are almost the same compared with their apparent weights. Both situations give you a low Factor Interaction Level score, usually below 20 percent (calculated in Step 23). Fragmentation means there is little interaction among the factors. Thus changing the real weight of one factor will not cause the apparent weight of many other factors to change. When this happens, think of **various actions** to reduce the real weight of several bottom-left factors that will reduce the problem identified in Step 1.

23. To calculate the Factor Interaction Level (FIL), multiply the Total Cause Index percentage (the percentage figure at the bottom of the last column) by the **Total Real Weight Reduction**. The Total Real Weight Reduction is the Total Apparent Weight (the number in the top left corner of your Cause Index card, at the top of your last column) minus the Total Real Weight (the number in the bottom right corner of your Cause Index card, at the top of

your last column), which you then divide by the Total Apparent Weight. In short:

$$\text{FIL} = \text{Total Cause Index \%} \quad \times \quad \frac{\text{Total Apparent Weight} - \text{Total Real Weight}}{\text{Total Apparent Weight}}$$

For instance, in the table shown in Step 12, the Total Cause Index percentage is 55.7 percent, or 234/420. The Real Weight Reduction is 45.1 percent, or (51–28)/51. Thus the Factor Interaction Level is about 25 percent, or 55.7 percent × 45.1 percent.

Keep in mind that factors that limit the **Factor Interaction Level** (FIL) include independent factors (in the bottom left of your diagram) as well as factors with real weights that differ little from their apparent weights (marked by bigger dots in your diagram).

Acting on Your Key Problem and Its Causes

24. Discuss how you can act on your key problem directly or through its main causes and the factors affecting them. Discuss the causal links between the key factors that you want to act on, including the relationships (marked by arrows) that contradict the main tendencies of your diagram. These actions should take into account the degree of control you have over key factors and the time you need to reduce their weight.

Keep in mind that actions to reduce the real weight of causes (factors in the top of your diagram) may create **a chain effect** on all other factors affected by it. This chain effect may also have an impact on the initial factor itself.

By contrast, actions to reduce the real weight of effects (in the bottom of your diagram) will have limited impact on other factors. These bottom factors may be important in relation to your key problem. However, to reduce their weight, you need to **act directly** on them (or through causes not identified in your analysis).

In the case of factors that have scores for apparent weight and real weight that are nearly the same (**bigger dots** mark their location in the diagram in Step 20), you also need to act directly on them (or through causes not identified in your analysis) in order to reduce their weight.

25. Discuss the order in which you should act on certain factors. Include this information in your diagram by inserting a number in superscript at the end of each factor. For instance, write *Poor HRM Strategy[1]* if this is the first cause you should act on (see Step 20).

Here is an example of a full *Causal Dynamics* diagram and its summary interpretation:

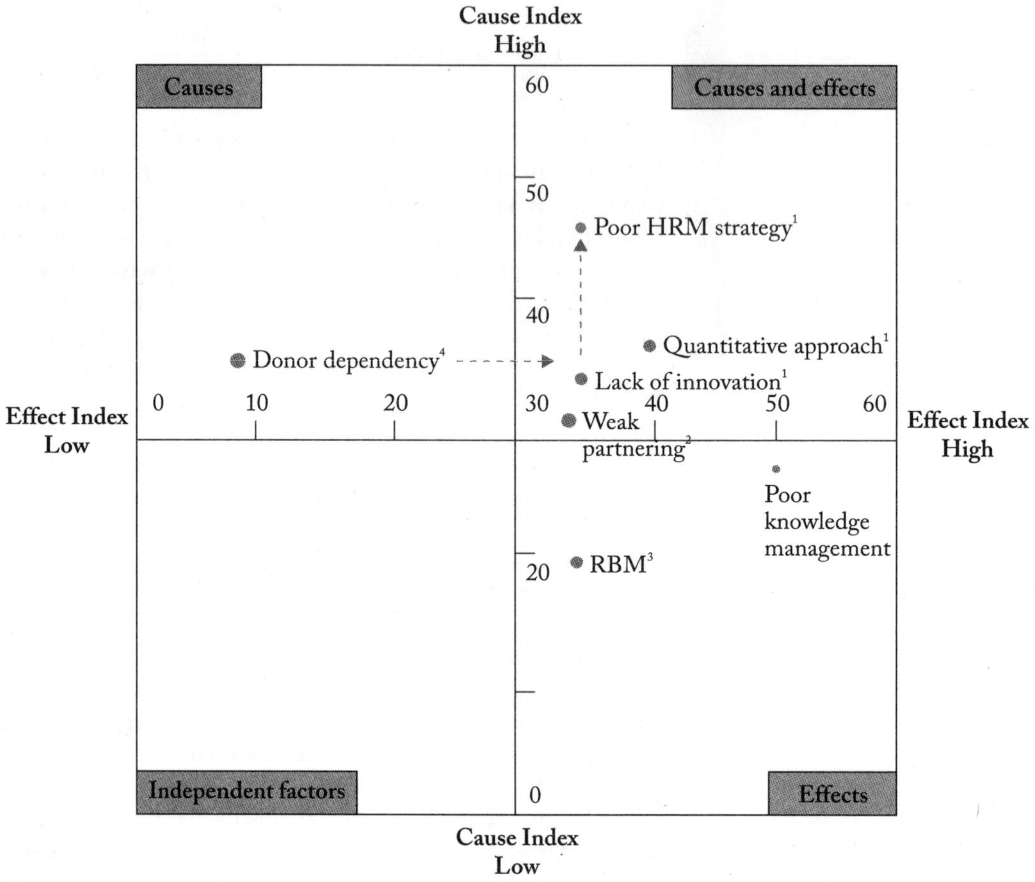

Cause Index
High

| Causes | | 60 | | Causes and effects |

50

● Poor HRM strategy[1]

40

Effect Index
Low   ● Donor dependency[4] - - - - →   ● Quantitative approach[1]

0   10   20   30   40   50   60   **Effect Index**
High

● Lack of innovation[1]

● Weak
partnering[2]

● Poor
knowledge
management

20   ● RBM[3]

| Independent factors | | 0 | | Effects |

Cause Index
Low

Summary of this example: This organization feels that the way it manages knowledge is not as useful to its members as it should be. This is a problem if it is to implement a proposed learning approach to KM (Knowledge Management). Using the *Causal Dynamics* technique, the team members choose to focus on the key factors in the top right of the diagram labeled with a 1 in superscript—factors that are both causes and effects of the problem. They discover that their non-strategic management of human resources (Poor HRM Strategy) is a major contributing factor. Since they have some control over this factor, they decide to free up some resources and use them to innovate in the field of KM. To innovate they must move away from the main cause of this factor—their donor's technological approach to KM and the organization's overemphasis on quantitative measurement of results. Once these actions are taken, the organization will explore better ways to involve their partners in KM activities, a goal that will take longer. If successful on all these fronts, the real weight of poor knowledge management will drop (smaller dot). Other objectives, such as rethinking the organization's dependence on a single donor, and Results Based Management (RBM), are less urgent. In the long run, the organization might want to act on these factors directly or through causes not identified in this analysis.

Scaling Up or Down

For Simpler Versions

1. Ignore all the instructions regarding the real and apparent weights of each factor, and do the following steps only: 4, 7 to 10, 13 to 17, 20 to 22, 24 and 25.

2. Work with one or two people or with small groups of people who have many common characteristics.

3. Use no more than four factors. Reduce the number of factors by eliminating some or through the *Freelisting* technique.

4. Use drawings or pictures to represent each factor.

5. Don't use indicators to define the meaning of each number in your rating scale.

6. Use a flipchart to represent each factor and to describe and rate the contributions that other factors make to the flipchart factor (see Step 4). Then, discuss how you can act on your key problem directly or though the factors affecting them.

For More Advanced Versions

1. Take more time to gather the information you need to complete the exercise.

2. During the exercise, discuss and record the views that participants express.

3. Work with a greater number of people or groups.

4. Use more than four factors.

5. Identify criteria to justify each rating exercise. Write a description for each indicator and each contribution score.

6. Use surveys to find out how people characterize and rate the factors in a topic area.

7. Add more information in Step 20.

8. Use Excel to create your cross-shaped diagram (Step 20).

9. Use *Problem Domain* to produce a detailed description of all factors.

10. Compare the effects of actions to reduce the weights of different factors.

11. Include factors that limit the development of your key problem. You will then need a rating scale of −10 to +10 to assess the apparent weight and the real weight of each factor and its impact on other factors. When you calculate total maximum scores, use

+10 as the maximum score and −10 as the lowest. Modify your *Causal Dynamics* diagram to include negative scores and possible outcomes (see Step 15). Keep in mind that when using a rating scale of −10 to +10, a low FIL (see Step 21) may indicate that factors interact a lot by contributing to other factors in some cases and limiting their development in other cases.

Readings and Links

EVALSED (Evaluation of Socio-Economic Development). 2004. 'Input/Output Analysis' in *The GUIDE, Methods and Techniques*. Brussels, Belgium: European Commission. Available online at http://www.evalsed.info/page.aspx?id=mth112, accessed on August 15, 2007.

Heussen, H.; and Jung, D. 2003. 'SINFONIE'. Denkmodell, Berlin, Germany. Available online at http://www.denkmodell.de/WebObjects wwwDenk modell.woa/wa/CMSshow/1063038, accessed on August 15, 2007.

Krumme, G. 2003. *Analysis of Interdependence Structures: Input-Output*. Seattle, WA: University of Washington. Available online at http://faculty.washington.edu/krumme/207/inputoutput.html#ionet, accessed on August 15, 2007.

Leontief, W.W. 1986. *Input-Output Economics*. 2nd edition. NY, USA: Oxford University Press.

Causal Dynamics: Reasons for Growing Tobacco in Daulatpur, Bangladesh

Key Words

Causal Dynamics, Bangladesh, agriculture, environment, tobacco

Authors and Acknowledgement

D.J. Buckles and J.M. Chevalier. The authors wish to acknowledge the efforts of Farida Akhter of UBINIG, who helped to facilitate the assessment.

Context

Although Daulatpur in Kushtia district, Bangladesh, was once an important food growing area, tobacco has been its main crop for more than 20 years. The British American Tobacco Company (BATC) has operations in various parts of the country. It promotes tobacco as a large-scale monocrop. Currently, tobacco accounts for the highest use per hectare of both fertilizers and pesticides of any major crop grown in Bangladesh. Despite these inputs, weeds infest many fields and soil quality is declining. The women and children who tend the fire when curing tobacco suffer ill health from inhaling the smoke. Farmers in Daulatpur are working with UBINIG, a Bangladeshi non-governmental organization active in the region for many years. The farmers say they want to stop growing tobacco but feel they can't do so. The meeting with farmers was convened as a first step in finding ways to support their desire to shift out of tobacco production.

For more information on this project, see Akhter, F. and D. Buckles, 2006, *From Tobacco to Food Production: Assessing Constraints and Transition Strategies in Bangladesh*, First Interim Technical Progress Report to IDRC, International Development Research Centre, Ottawa, ON, Canada, 18 pp.

Purpose

To assess why farmers continue to grow tobacco, despite their concerns.

Process Summary

UBINIG hosted the assessment at its Centre in Pabna near Daulatpur. A group of 10 tobacco farmers (seven men and three women) participated. After talking about the purpose of the exercise, farmers stated their reasons for growing tobacco. These reasons were piled and sorted, with agreement from all, into a list of six. A large drawing, on a whiteboard, of a tree with roots and branches was used to depict the relationships among all six factors. Each factor was scored on a scale of 1 to 5 by asking farmers to state the extent to which one factor (shown as a root of the tree) contributes to another (shown as a fruit on the branches of the tree). A double entry matrix was created from these ratings, with totals tallied by row and column. Farmers then rated on a scale of 1 to 7 the importance or weight of each factor as it relates to growing tobacco (apparent weight), and the importance that would remain if other factors did not exist (real weight). The participants discussed a summary figure (Graph 1) showing how various factors interact, and they decided on next steps. The lead author facilitated the exercise, and received permission from the participants to share their information.

Analysis

Table 1 shows the factors assessed, and the ratings generated during the discussion. Farmer descriptions and explanations of the factors are:

- Tobacco production can pay well. The price for the highest grade of cured tobacco set by the BATC is high, but drops a lot for lesser quality leaf. Farmers hope that they will get the top price, even though most do not. Farmers also tend to underestimate the costs of inputs and losses due to poor harvests and curing problems.

- Some farmers have a card from the BATC, which provides them with credit to buy fertilizers, pesticides and seed. It also gives them an exclusive right to sell cured tobacco to the Company. They can use the rights of the card to buy cured tobacco from other farmers, thereby setting themselves up as tobacco traders as well as producers. The BATC only provides a card to people with whom they have an established relationship.

- Tobacco farmers can receive a single payment for their entire crop. This is attractive because it provides a way to amass large sums for things like debt repayment, new land, houses, marriages or social obligations. It also provides the cash needed by those who have a BATC Card so they can be part of the tobacco trade.

- There are currently no alternative cash crops to consider or compare with.

- Most farmers in Daulatpur grow only tobacco. This creates social pressure to farm this way and increases the scale and efficiency of the BATC operations.

- Tobacco curing creates jobs, especially for women and children at home.

Table 1: Reasons Why Daulatpur Farmers Continue to Grow a Tobacco Monoculture

Factors	Can pay well	BATC Card facilities	Single payment	No alternate cash crops	Jobs created	Most grow tobacco	Cause Index Average rating (total score)
Can pay well	x	2	4	3	3	4	2.8 (14)
BATC Card facilities	3	x	4	4	3	3	3.8 (19)
Single payment	4	2	x	4	3	4	3.0 (15)
No alternative cash crops	4	2	3	x	1	5	2.6 (13)
Jobs created	3	0	0	2	x	3	1.8 (9)
Most grow tobacco	4	2	3	5	3	x	2.8 (14)
Effect Index Average rating (total score)	3.6 (18)	1.6 (8)	2.8 (14)	3.6 (18)	2.6 (13)	3.8 (19)	60% (90/150)
Apparent Weight	6	6	7	7	4	5	
Real Weight	3	4	4	6	1	3	

The last column in the table shows how much each factor causes or contributes to other factors (Cause Index), and the seventh row shows how much each factor is the effect of other factors (Effect Index). The Total Cause Index (60 percent), shown at the intersection of the two indices, provides an overall measure of the extent to which factors interact as causes and effects of each other. The apparent and real weights for each factor are shown in the last two rows of the table. Graph 1 shows the same factors when their cause index is plotted in combination with their effect index. The size of the square representing each factor (or its real weight) is larger for factors that would retain much of their weight even if other factors did not exist.

Four of six factors fall in the upper-right quadrant, reflecting factors that relate to other factors as both causes and effects. This result points to a situation of **integration** among the reasons for growing tobacco: farmers receive a single payment, it can pay well, most farmers in the area grow tobacco, and there are no alternative cash crops. These factors reinforce each other, which in turn helps farmers decide to continue to grow tobacco. The lack of other cash crops and the single payment would continue to be important factors (high real weight) even if other factors did not exist.

The BATC card (and other kinds of credit), a factor located in the upper left quadrant, contributes to other factors but does not depend on them. Participants noted that it has a strong impact on all other factors (values of 3 and 4 in the table), but is not itself affected much by them (values of 2 and 0). Participants also said that the real weight of this factor would persist even if other factors did not exist.

Participants noted that the jobs created by growing tobacco, a factor located in the lower right quadrant, is primarily an effect of other factors. The real weight of this factor would be low if other factors did not exist.

Graph 1: Reasons Why Daulatpur Farmers Continue to Grow Tobacco

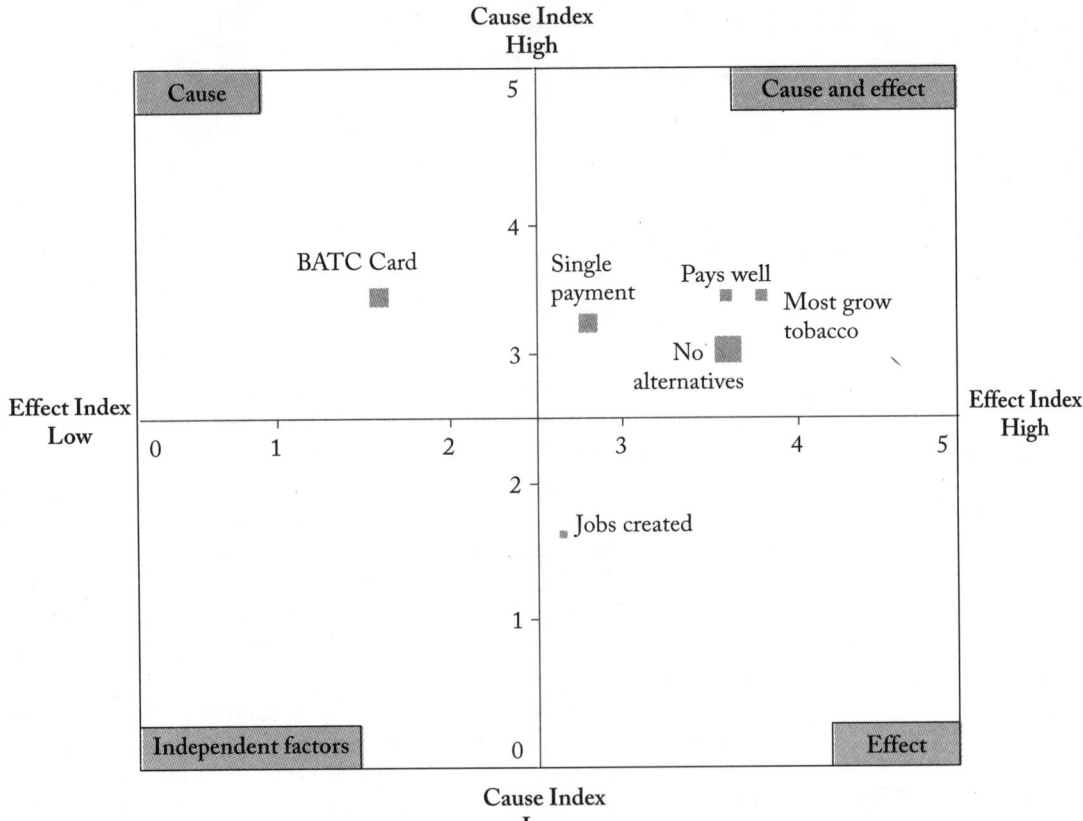

Interpretation

Farmers are trapped in a vicious circle of interacting factors that reinforce the decision to continue to grow a tobacco. This reflects the entrenched nature of tobacco farming in Daulatpur. Participants remarked that farmers have invested in developing a relationship with the BATC.

They have also come to value the single payment for an entire crop and easy access to the inputs they need to produce tobacco (provided by the BATC card). Experimenting with new crops and other production systems, normally a feature of Bangladeshi agriculture, has stopped. Over time, the technology (seed and knowledge) and markets for traditional crops and livestock systems withered away. Tobacco farmers have become prisoners to their own investments in the crop. Farmers said that the various problems created by growing tobacco have become apparent to all, and concern has increased to a point where they now recognize the need for change.

Action

The course of action that emerged from the analysis was to start experimenting on a small scale with alternative cash crops. Participants argued that the lack of other cash crops is a persistent and important reason why they continue to grow tobacco. Talk within the group focused on crops such as peanuts, jute, mustard seed, lentils, and pulses that can be grown in mixed farming systems, require few purchased inputs, store well and can be sold as needed at local and regional markets. Such crops also require a lot of labor. Participants concluded that if they start investing actively in tobacco alternatives with these characteristics it might create a chain effect on the other factors affected by it: tobacco may not pay as well when compared to the lower costs of alternative crops; the benefits of a single payment may not seem as compelling compared to a steady stream of income; and fewer farmers may grow tobacco, encouraging others to make the shift as well.

While the real weight of the single payment and BATC card would persist, even if other factors did not exist, participants concluded that there was nothing they could do directly about either of these factors.

The meeting ended with farmers deciding to experiment with other crop systems, and for UBINIG to help by providing access to seed, identifying markets, and working with farmers to broaden and deepen the criteria they use to assess the economic returns of these crops.

Observations on the Process

The main question "To what extent does A cause or contribute to B" was initially confused with "To what extent does B cause or contribute to A". This problem was managed by using the tree metaphor and drawing. The analysis generated a lot of enthusiasm for experiments and provided some direction regarding what crop features to consider. The result of the exercise was considered a turning point for participants interested in pursuing alternatives to tobacco. They noted that it provided them with a clear explanation of their situation which was useful to their discussions with other farmers who were not yet convinced of the kinds of investments they needed to make, to shift out of tobacco.

Validation

Author	J.M. Chevalier

Purpose

This technique helps you validate the results of an assessment using two criteria. The criteria are: the extent to which the assessment is based on evidence (sound and sufficient information and analysis), and the extent to which it achieves consensus through collaborative thinking.

Guiding Principles

1. An assessment is any careful investigation of a situation in fields of knowledge and action ranging from daily livelihoods (such as farming or fishing) to professional disciplines (such as medicine or agronomy) and scientific research.

2. How valid an assessment is, depends on the extent to which it is based on evidence, using sound and sufficient information and analysis.

3. How valid an assessment is also depends on the extent to which it achieves consensus through collaborative thinking. When stakeholders contribute to an assessment and reach a common understanding of a situation, they may be in a better position to decide on what should be done to achieve their goals.

4. The extent to which an assessment should be based on evidence and consensus depends on various factors, such as how well the stakeholders understand the issue being analyzed, how much time and information is available, the urgency to act, the impact the assessment has on stakeholder activities, how much stakeholder approval and involvement is required, and so on.

Process

1. Identify an **assessment** you have done or need to do as part of your project or program activities. Clarify the purpose of your analysis.

2. Create a diagram by drawing a vertical line that crosses a horizontal line (see example in Step 5). This creates a cross inside a square. Write 0 and 10 at opposite ends of the horizontal line. The value 10 indicates that the assessment is based on **evidence** (very sound and sufficient information and analysis). The value 0 shows the opposite (the evidence is unreliable and insufficient). If you want this exercise to be more precise, identify **indicators** that define the meaning of each number on the scale.

3. Write 0 and 10 at opposite ends of the vertical line. The value 10 indicates a strong **consensus** achieved through collaborative thinking. The value 0 shows the opposite (no consensus at all or strong disagreement). If you want this exercise to be more precise, identify indicators that define the meaning of each number on the scale.

4. Discuss the extent to which the assessment identified in Step 1 is based on evidence and stakeholder consensus. Plot the level of **evidence** used on the horizontal line, and the level of **consensus** obtained on the vertical line. Connect the values from the two lines, using the letter "X" to mark the place where they meet. See example in Step 5.

5. Use the same diagram to plot the level of evidence and consensus that you need in order to reach a decision or make plans. Using another "X" to mark the place where the two values that you're aiming for meet. Draw an arrow from the first "X" to the second.

   Before you decide how much evidence and consensus you need, discuss the factors that should influence your decision, such as how well the stakeholders understand the issue being analyzed, how much time and information is available, the urgency to act, the impact the assessment has on stakeholder activities, how much stakeholder approval and involvement is required, and so on.

   Here is an example of a *Validation* diagram that shows the actual and the desired levels of evidence and consensus associated with an assessment:

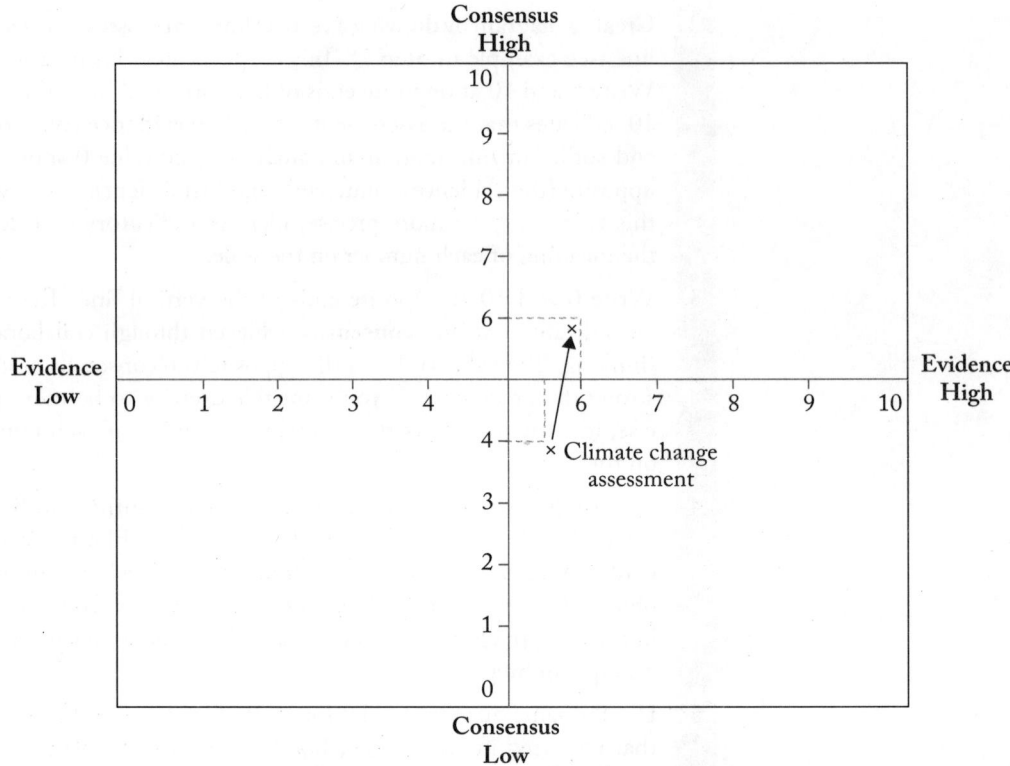

Consensus
High

Evidence
Low

Evidence
High

× Climate change
assessment

Consensus
Low

6. Use the results of your analysis to identify what it is you're ready to plan or decide. Then, identify what you can do to obtain the **best available evidence** or the **best possible consensus** that you need before you can make other plans or reach other decisions.

7. Each party (such as gender groups) may do its own *Validation* exercise and then discuss its results with other parties.

Scaling Up or Down

For Simpler Versions

1. Do not use indicators to define the meaning of each number on your scales (for levels of evidence and consensus).

For More Advanced Versions

1. During the exercise, discuss and record the views that participants express.

2. Use indicators for levels of evidence and for levels of consensus.

3. Take more time to discuss the factors that determine how much evidence and consensus you need (Step 5).

Validation: Validation of a Timeline Assessment by a Milk-Producers' Cooperative in Honduras

Key Words

Validation, Timeline, Community Economic Development, Cooperatives, Honduras

Authors

L. Suazo-Gallardo and D.J. Buckles.

Context

The Jamastrán Valley and Highlands of Danlí are farming and ranching areas in the Department of El Paraíso near the border Honduras shares with Nicaragua. Most ranchers raise cattle for two reasons. They sell some male animals for meat while the milk from cows is sold to cheese-makers in the region. Over the years, the owners of livestock have tried to organize themselves to negotiate milk prices, develop regional and export markets for their products, and address technical problems that arise. These attempts to organize have had uneven results. Many of the producers' organizations failed a few years after they got started.

The Board of Directors of the United Producers Agricultural Co-operative (COAPUL), the largest cooperative in the region, decided to assess the history of these organizations. The purpose of the assessment was to identify the events and actions that had helped or hindered their development. They planned to use this information to write a proposal for new funding. At the request of COAPUL, the lead author of this report used the *Timeline* technique to do the assessment. The group also validated the result, as reported here. They felt that it was important to do so before using the information in the project proposal.

Purpose

To validate a *Timeline* assessment by a milk producers' cooperative in Honduras.

Process Summary

The *Timeline* and *Validation* assessments were conducted during a half-day meeting with 10 people that knew about the origins and evolution of COAPUL. The meeting was convened by COAPUL's Board of Directors. Participants identified the organizations from which COAPUL had emerged and the key events and actions that led to both success and failure over the years. When the assessment was complete, the group reviewed its plans and how it might use the results of *Timeline*. They then validated the results and discussed whether or not they were "good enough" to meet their needs. Participants agreed to have their information used in this report.

Analysis

A key conclusion of the *Timeline* assessment was that having a large and committed membership improves the organization's capacity to negotiate milk prices and attract the investment needed to improve production methods. In the past, producers would sell part of their production on their own and part of it through the cooperative. This made it difficult for organizations to present a united front to buyers. Membership would decline after a few years when it became clear that the cooperative could not offer members better prices for milk than the open market. Participants said that COAPUL's investments in improving the sanitation and storage of milk made it possible to offer a better quality product to cheese-makers in the region. An effective membership drive in 2001 and commitment by members to sell their milk collectively also enhanced COAPUL's negotiating power. These developments happened thanks to INCADE's technical and financial help and members' technical and administrative skills, acquired in previous organizations.

Participants validated the *Timeline* result using two criteria (Figure 1):

- The extent to which the assessment was based on **evidence** (sound information and analysis), and
- The extent to which it achieved **consensus** among stakeholders through collaborative thinking.

The group rated the current *Timeline* result at level 6 for evidence (using a scale of 0 to 10 where 0 would show that the evidence was not reliable and 10 would show that the evidence was very sound and in-depth). This reflected the group's view that the *Timeline* exercise had identified the most important events in the life of various organizations, and that they were still unsure about some of the local and national events that contributed to their development.

The group rated the current *Timeline* result at level 5 for consensus, also using a scale of 0 to 10. They noted that a 0 would show that there was disagreement within the group or that key actors had not been consulted. A level of 10 would show complete agreement among key stakeholders. The level 5 rating for consensus reflected the group's view that many other people who had been part of producer organizations had not been consulted, and that the group did not agree on the main reasons why some of the prior organizations had failed.

Participants concluded that the *Timeline* result was good but not good enough for their purpose. The *Timeline* assessment had helped the group understand links among the many different organizations that had existed and the different legal structures and names they had used. However, some confusion remained. They also said that more

Figure 1: Validation of a Timeline Assessment by COAPUL

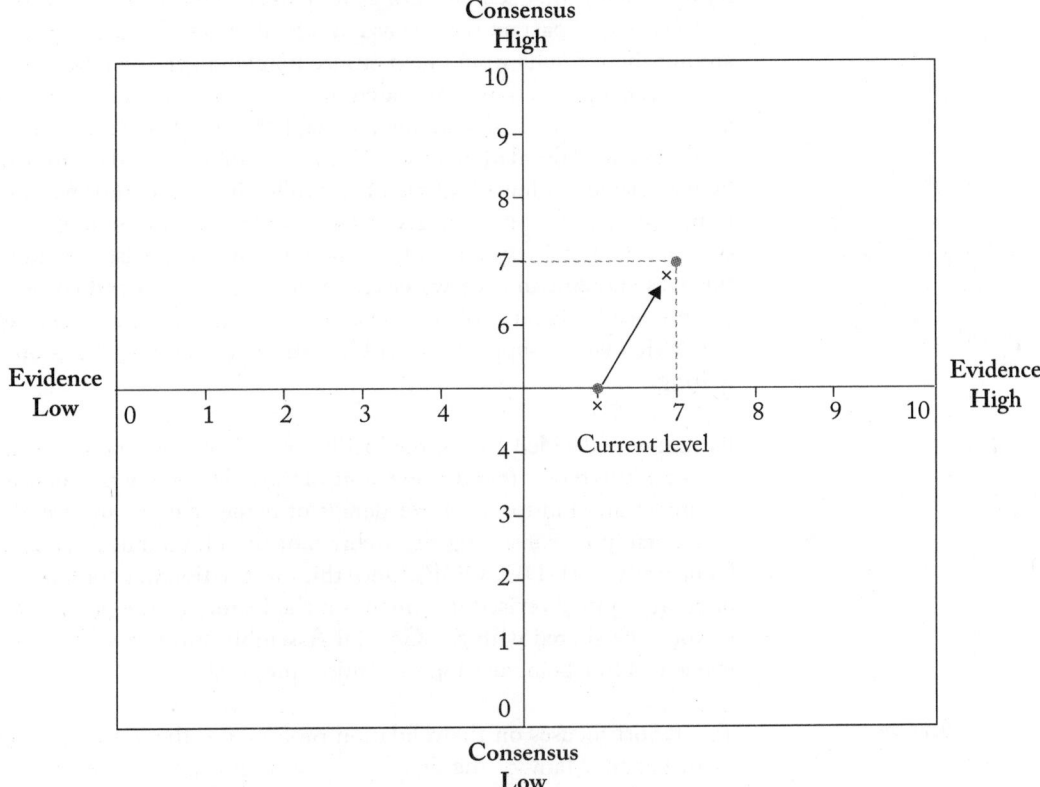

documentation of the factors that affected membership in the organization would greatly improve their proposal for new funding. Based on these observations, they decided that more information was needed. They also felt that greater consensus was needed to ensure that most members would support the conclusions and implications of the *Timeline* assessment. A level of 7 on both evidence and consensus was considered by the group enough to support plans for use of the *Timeline* results in the funding proposal.

Interpretation

Validation of the results of the *Timeline* assessment showed that more evidence and consensus was needed before they could proceed with plans to use the results in a proposal. More details on the names and dates of registration of related organizations would strengthen claims in the proposal about the long-standing legitimacy of COAPUL. They also noted that more analysis of the factors that affected their evolution would bolster a key argument about the importance of member solidarity, namely, that selling milk as individuals rather than collectively had a strong impact on the survival of organizations. Greater consensus around these results would help ensure that younger and newer members of the organization appreciated the struggles of older members and that a sense of belonging among all members would be enhanced.

Participants decided that the *Timeline* assessment could be improved by interviewing a few older members, collecting more information on trends in membership from secondary sources, and presenting the results at a General Assembly of the membership. They also agreed that this was enough; an even wider search for information and consensus was not needed because plans were already in place to make other assessments that would support COAPUL's strategic planning and proposal writing.

Actions

Participants decided to ask the facilitator of the assessment and lead author of this report to interview more of the older members of producer organizations and to search for details of name changes and trends in membership by consulting the archives of the Honduran Institute for Cooperatives (IHDECOOP). Once this information was compiled and integrated into a revised document on the history of the organization, it would be shared with the General Assembly and revised further, as needed, before being used in the project proposal.

Observations on the Process

This report focuses on the validation process, not the *Timeline* assessment per se. Many of the details on the origins and evolution of the organization are presented elsewhere (see SAS[2] Technique Report #22 at www.sas2.net). Participants felt that the proposed improvements in the *Timeline* assessment would give them the best available evidence and the best possible consensus, considering the time available and proposed use of the result. They also noted that validation of the result made the value of the *Timeline* assessment clear, and gave them new ideas for creating a booklet on the history of the organization.

Stakeholder Identification

Author	J.M. Chevalier
Acknowledgement	*Stakeholder Identification* is a SAS[2] adaptation of techniques used in the field of participatory research (Mayers, 2005; Attachments).
Purpose	*Stakeholder Identification* helps you choose the method that you need to identify the key actors or stakeholders involved in a core problem or action. You can also use this technique to visualize the differences between stakeholders who may affect a situation or course of action and stakeholders who may be affected by it.

Guiding Principles

1. Stakeholders are actors that can influence or be affected by a certain problem or action.

2. People may be members of different stakeholder groups. This is true of leaders and public officials who have their own stakeholder profile at the same time as they belong to broader groups (for whom they act or speak).

Process

1. Identify a **core problem or action** where you need to identify the stakeholders. Define the problem or action as clearly as possible, and clarify the purpose of this exercise.

2. From the list below, choose the method(s) that will help you identify the **key actors or stakeholders** that can influence or be affected by the problem or action identified in Step 1. Modify the methods according to your needs. The methods are:

   (a) *Identification by experts*

   Use staff, key agencies (such as non-governmental organizations), local people, or academics who have a lot of knowledge about the situation to identify stakeholders.

   (b) *Identification by self-selection*

   Use announcements at meetings, in newspapers, on local radio or other media to invite stakeholders to come forward.

This will attract those who believe they will gain from communicating their views and are able to do so.

(c) *Identification by other stakeholders*

Identify one or two key stakeholders. Ask them to suggest other key stakeholders who share their views and interests, as well as those who may have a different way of looking at the issues.

(d) *Identification using written records and population data*

Census and population data may provide useful information about the numbers of people by age, gender, religion, residence, and so on (see *Stakeholder Sampling*). You may also obtain stakeholder information from directories, organizational charts, surveys, reports or written records issued by local authorities, donor agencies, government bodies, experts, academics, non-governmental organizations, business and industry, and so on.

(e) *Identification using oral or written accounts of major events*

You can identify key stakeholders by asking some of them to describe the major events in the history of a problem and the people who were involved in these events (see *Timeline*).

(f) *Identification using checklists*

You can identify stakeholders by using the checklists provided in Attachments A and B. Modify the checklists according to your needs.

You may include yourself and those who are doing the analysis in your list. You may define the *representatives of a group* as a stakeholder distinct from those they represent. Also, you may include in your list the community of all stakeholders, as a group with its own profile.

You may need to come back to this exercise in the future so that you can identify stakeholders that you left out or did not involve at earlier stages of your project.

When identifying stakeholders, be aware that some people may accept ancestors, future generations, spirits, and non-human species as legitimate parties to the situation.

3. Write (or draw) the name of each stakeholder on its own card. If your list of stakeholders is too long, use *Sorting* to organize them into stakeholder groups and then write each group on its own card.

4. Create a **rainbow diagram** by drawing a horizontal line with half a circle around it. Draw two semicircles inside the chart using the middle point of the horizontal line as their center. Also divide the rainbow into three equal parts: one part to the left, one in the middle, and one to the right. See example in Step 6.

5. Insert cards that represent stakeholders that are **the most affected** by the problem or action in the small semicircle. In the middle semicircle, insert cards of stakeholders *moderately* affected by the problem or action. In the large semicircle, insert cards of stakeholders who are the *least* affected by the problem or action. See example in Step 6.

6. On the left side of your diagram, place the cards that represent stakeholders who influence your core problem or action the *most*. In the middle, place those who *moderately* influence the problem or action. On the right side, place those who influence the *least*.

Here's an example of a rainbow diagram:

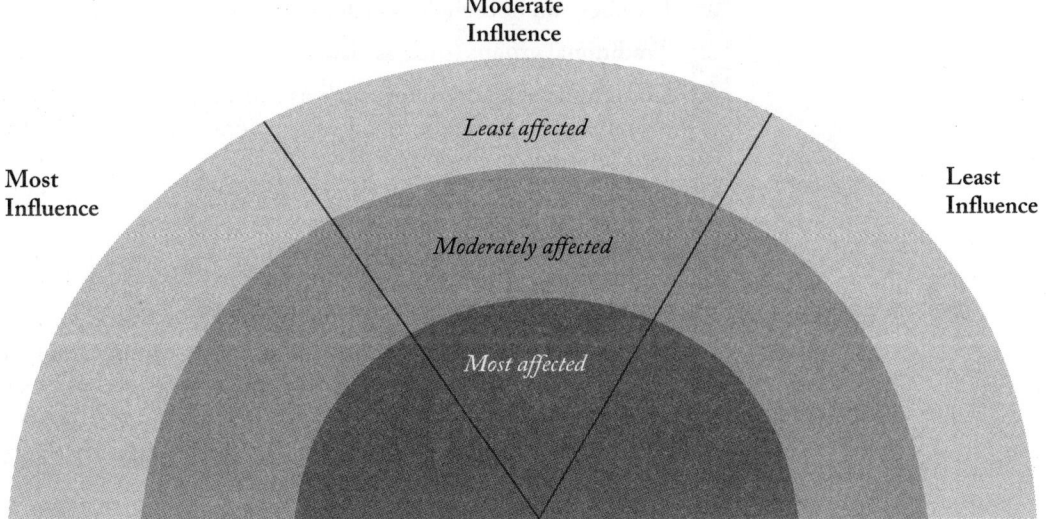

You can adapt this diagram by using other characteristics that better describe the main differences between your key stakeholders. For instance, you can use the semicircles to identify stakeholders working at the local, the regional, and the national levels. Also you can use a single vertical line to separate private sector from public sector stakeholders.

Scaling Up or Down

For Simpler Versions

1. Use one identification method only.
2. Do not use the rainbow diagram (Steps 4 to 6).

For More Advanced Versions

1. Use several identification methods.
2. Repeat the exercise later.

Reading and Link

Mayers, J. 2005. *Stakeholder power analysis.* Power tools series. London, UK: International Institute for Environment and Development. Available online at http://www.policy-powertools.org/Tools/Understanding/SPA.html, accessed on August 16, 2007.

Attachment A: Checklist for Stakeholder Identification

1. Individuals (such as company owners)
2. Families and households (such as long-term local residents)
3. Traditional groups (such as clans)
4. Community-based groups (such as self-interest organizations of resource users, neighborhood associations, gender or age-based associations)
5. Local traditional authorities (such as a village council of elders, a traditional chief)
6. Political authorities recognized by national laws (such as elected representatives at the village or district levels)
7. Non-governmental bodies that link different communities (such as a council of village representatives, a district-level association of fishermen)
8. Local governance structures (administration, police, the judicial system)
9. Agencies with legal jurisdiction over natural resources (such as a state park agency)
10. Local governmental services in the area of education, health, forestry and agriculture, etc.
11. Relevant non-governmental organizations at the local, national or international levels

12. Political party structures (at various levels)

13. Religious bodies (at various levels)

14. National interest organizations (such as a workers' union—also called people's associations)

15. National service organizations (such as the Lions Club)

16. Cultural and voluntary associations (such as a club for the study of unique national landscapes, an association of tourists)

17. Businesses and commercial enterprises (from local cooperatives to international corporations)

18. Universities and research organizations

19. Local banks and credit institutions

20. Government authorities at the district and regional levels

21. National governments

22. Foreign aid agencies

23. Staff and consultants of relevant projects and programs

24. International government bodies (such as UNICEF, FAO, UNEP)

25. International unions (such as IUCN)

Source: Borrini-Feyerabend, G.; and M. Brown. 1997. "Social Actors and Stake-Holders" (edited version) in Borrini-Feyerabend, G. (ed.), *Beyond Fences: Seeking Social Sustainability in Conservation.* Gland, Switzerland: IUCN. Available online at http://www.iucn.org/themes/spg/Files/beyond_fences/bf_section4_1.html, accessed on August 16, 2007.

Attachment B: Checklist of Questions for Stakeholder Identification

1. Are there communities, groups or individuals who may be **affected** by the management decisions? Are there historic occupants (such as indigenous communities or nomads) or traditional resource users with customary rights of ownership or use of the lands? Are there recent arrivals? Non-resident users of resources? Absentee landlords? Major secondary users of local resources (such as buyers of products or tourists)? Are there local non-profit organizations concerned with natural resources? Are there business people or industries that might be negatively affected by natural resource management decisions? Are there research, development

or conservation projects in the area? How many employees (national and international) live in the area because of such projects? Are these people active in natural resource management?

2. Who are the main traditional **authorities** in the area? Are there government agencies officially responsible for the resources at stake? Are there respected institutions that people rely on in the area?

3. Who has **access** to the land, area or resources at stake? Who is using the natural resources now? In what ways? Has this changed over time?

4. Which communities, groups and individuals are most **dependent** on the resources? Is this because of livelihood or economic advantage? Can these resources be replaced by others that are less ecologically valuable or fragile?

5. Who is responsible for **claims**, including customary rights and legal jurisdiction, in the territory or area where the resources are located? Are there communities with historic and/or other types of acquired rights? Are various government sectors and ministry departments involved? Are there national and/or international bodies involved because of specific laws or treaties?

6. Which communities, groups or individuals are most **knowledgeable** about, and capable of dealing with, the territories or resources? So far, who has a direct experience in managing them?

7. How does use of the resources **change** depending on the seasons, the geography and the interests of the users? Are there seasonal migration patterns? Are there major events or trends (such as development projects, land reforms, migration, natural increase or decrease in the population) affecting local communities and other interested parties?

8. Are there other **co-management projects** in the region? If so, to what extent are they succeeding? Who are their main partners?

Source: Borrini-Feyerabend, G.; M.T. Farvar; J.C. Nguinguiri; and V.A. Ndangang. 2000. *Co-management of Natural Resources: Organising, Negotiating and Learning-by-Doing* (edited version). Kasparek Verlag, Heidelberg, Germany: GTZ and IUCN. Available online at http://learningforsustainability.net/pubs/cmnr/cmnr.html, accessed on August 16, 2007.

Stakeholder Identification: Identifying Stakeholders in a Project to Prevent and Reduce the Impacts of Floods and Landslides in Nepal

Key Words

Stakeholder Identification, natural disasters, risk reduction and mitigation, Nepal, Chitwan

Authors

T.B. Sapkota, D. Poudel, D. J. Buckles.

Context

Chitwan district in central Nepal is often affected by floods and landslides. Various government and non-governmental organizations (NGOs) provide disaster relief efforts but few focus on preventing or reducing the impacts of natural events. Practical Action (PA) is an NGO that has been active in the region for several years. It provides disaster relief and has been planning a project that would support more stable livelihood options in communities affected by disasters. Linking disaster management to the development of livelihoods that reduce the risk and impacts of floods and landslides had not been done in this part of Nepal before. Given this new approach, PA wants to ensure that it develops its project goals and plans with the right institutions and people.

Purpose

To identify the stakeholders likely to be *affected by* or likely to have an *influence on* project goals, project design, and activities.

Process Summary

Practical Action convened a meeting at its office in Chitwan. Representatives of several institutions with knowledge of the flood and landslide problems in the area, or the livelihood options open to the rural poor, were invited to attend. The group included two members of PA's own staff, one professional from LI-BIRD (a research NGO that specializes in rural livelihoods), two representatives of the District Development Office (DDO) of Chitwan responsible for coordinating and monitoring government and NGO projects in the district, and two representatives from the NGO Coordination Committee of Chitwan (NGOCC) which coordinates NGO development activities. Together, they identified organizations with knowledge about disaster relief or knowledge about livelihood options in the region.

Practical Action held a second meeting a month later with representatives of communities where it planned to implement activities and where other potential stakeholders lived. This meeting included representatives of community-based organizations, local NGOs, and local leaders.

In both meetings, groups discussed the problems created by floods and landslides, their experience with efforts to create or support livelihoods that could reduce the risks and impacts of floods and landslides, and project goals and plans. They then identified stakeholders that are or should be involved in the project and mapped their relationships to the project. This was done by placing cards for each stakeholder on a rainbow figure on the floor. The three bands of the rainbow represented the degree to which stakeholders would be affected by the success or failure of the project (from most affected to least affected). The bands were divided into three sections or pie shapes representing stakeholders that influence the project to various degrees (from most to least influence). Cards for each stakeholder were then placed in the middle section of the figure, depending on the degree to which they are or could be affected by the project. After all cards were set down in the middle section, they were then moved to the left side, right side or allowed to remain in the middle section, depending on how much they influence the project (from most to least influence). The map that emerged was then discussed and the groups decided as to which stakeholders are key to the project and what kind of relationship they have or could have with other stakeholders. Tek Sapkota facilitated the assessment. Participants were aware that the results of the exercise would be used in reports, and agreed to share their information.

Analysis

The first group meeting identified 17 stakeholders with many degrees and types of potential relationships (actual or potential) to the project (Figure 1). They described Practical Action and The Water Induced Disaster Management Office in Chitwan (WIDMO) as the stakeholders that would be most affected and also have the most influence over the project. The project is a major initiative for Practical Action and the focus on livelihoods represents a new approach for the organization. Project success or failure would certainly affect PA's future direction and strength. It also has a very high degree of influence on the project because of its leadership role. WIDMO, a specialized government agency that monitors and assesses disasters in the district and coordinates relief efforts, was also assessed by the group as a stakeholder that would be strongly affected if the project were successful. It can also strongly influence the project through its official guidelines for disaster relief, and through recommendations it might make about future projects of this type.

The first group noted that communities vulnerable to disasters would be highly affected by the project, but only if their communities are included in project activities. Since no communities had been selected at that time, the group included "vulnerable communities" as a general description of an affected stakeholder. Participants also recognized that communities currently had little influence on the project (least influence), a situation they resolved to address later.

The District Development Office (DDO) and the District Administration Office (DAO) are government institutions that approve projects in the region, enforce development policies, and monitor and evaluate project activities. Participants felt that DDO and DAO policies and activities would be moderately affected by a successful experience with a livelihood options project because such an approach would have an impact on their current disaster relief practices. Participants also recognized that these two government bodies could strongly influence the project, and even block it if they wanted to. As a result, they identified the DDO and DAO as key stakeholders with whom the project needs to establish a close working relationship.

An NGO network called the Common Forum of NGOs working for Disaster Management (CFNDM) was identified as both moderately affected by, and with moderate influence on the project. Participants pointed out that the CFNDM can influence the project by bringing relevant information from its members into goal-setting and planning, and would then benefit from access to information on the livelihood options approach proposed by the project. The NGO network NGOCC, by contrast, has less direct experience with disaster management, compared to the CFNDM. While it would be moderately affected by the project, it would be somewhat less influential in goal-setting and planning. A number of NGOs that PA is considering as potential partners for the project were also identified and assessed as stakeholders that would be moderately affected by the project while currently having little influence (for example, Forward, Ecocenter, Sahabhagi, Multidimensional Agriculture for Development [MADE], in Figure 1).

Participants identified some government agencies (DADO, DLSO, DFO) and the NGO, LIBIRD, as stakeholders least affected by the project but with a moderate capacity to influence it because they have special knowledge of livelihood options, or are responsible for certain development activities in the region. Two special interest organizations (the Jwalamukhi Club or JMC and the Bird Education Society or BES) were identified as least affected and least influencing stakeholders. The Jwalamukhi Club is a district NGO that promotes peace among political and rebel groups in Nepal; the Bird Education Society is mostly concerned with conserving bird and other fauna habitats. Both organizations, like all others in the district, are drawn into relief efforts when a major flood or landslide occurs in the district. They have very little to offer directly to the project (least influence) and their relief work might benefit somewhat from the livelihood approach developed by the project (least affected).

Figure 1: Relationship of Different Stakeholders to the Practical Action Project

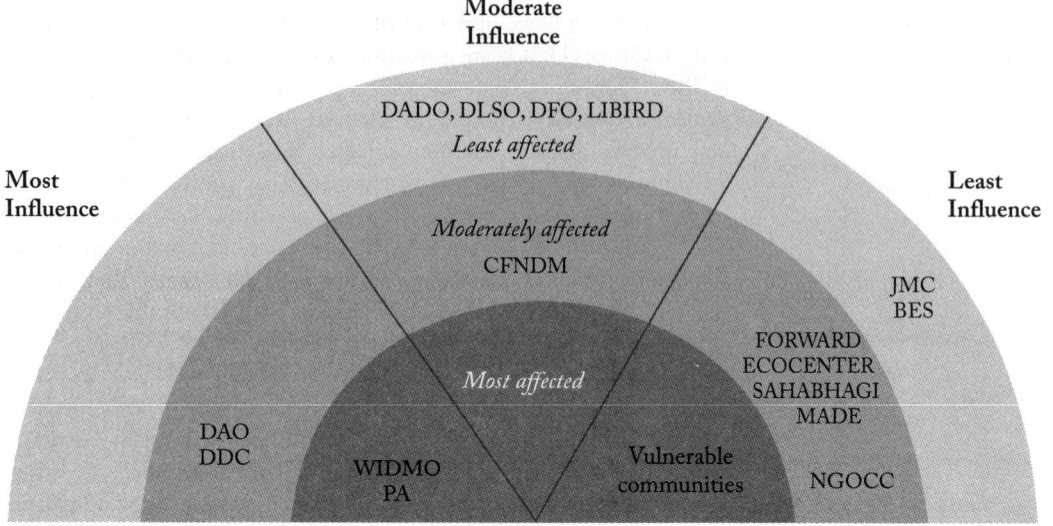

Note: DADO-District Agriculture Development Office; DLSO-District Livestock Service Office; LI-BIRD-Local Initiatives for Biodiversity, Research and Development; DFO-District Forest Office; NGOCC-Non-Governmental Organization Coordination Committee; FORWARD-Forum for Rural Welfare and Agricultural Reform for Development; ECOCENTER-Ecological Service Center; MADE-Multidimensional Agriculture for Development; NRUSEC-Nepal Rural Self-reliance Campaign; JMC-Jwalamukhi Club; BES-Bird Education Society; DAO-District Administration Office; DDC-District Development Office; WIDMO-Water Induced Disaster Management Office; CFNDM-Common Forum of NGOs working for Disaster management; PA-Practical Action.

As a result of the analysis by the first group, PA invited other stakeholders to a second meeting to review and revise the stakeholder map. PA selected the communities to be invited and included the NGO that it had chosen to implement the project (MADE). The assessment by the second group showed several adjustments. First, MADE now occupied a similar position to PA and WIDMO except that its influence over the project would be relatively moderate given its role as a contractor. Its future activities would, however, be strongly affected by the project's success or failure.

Second, participants made several distinctions that clarified and modified the relationship of vulnerable communities to the project. They argued that local community leaders are stakeholders who are distinct from the general community. Their knowledge of the history of both disaster impacts and development initiatives across communities, as well as their political and administrative roles, make them stake-holders that can moderately influence project goals and plans. Participants assessed the extent to which local leaders would be affected by the project as moderate, reflecting the fact that they have many other interests and roles within their communities, and are not directly involved in or benefiting from project activities. Participants also argued that representatives of the selected communities should be directly involved in goal-setting and project planning. This degree of influence would create a shift to moderately affecting the project while also being strongly affected (same position as MADE). Specific ways to achieve this shift within the project were discussed, as noted below. Participants also created a separate category of communities not targeted by the project—that would be affected by and influence the project to a much lesser extent, possibly through the work of other NGOs.

Figure 2: Relationship of Different Stakeholders to the Practical Action Project

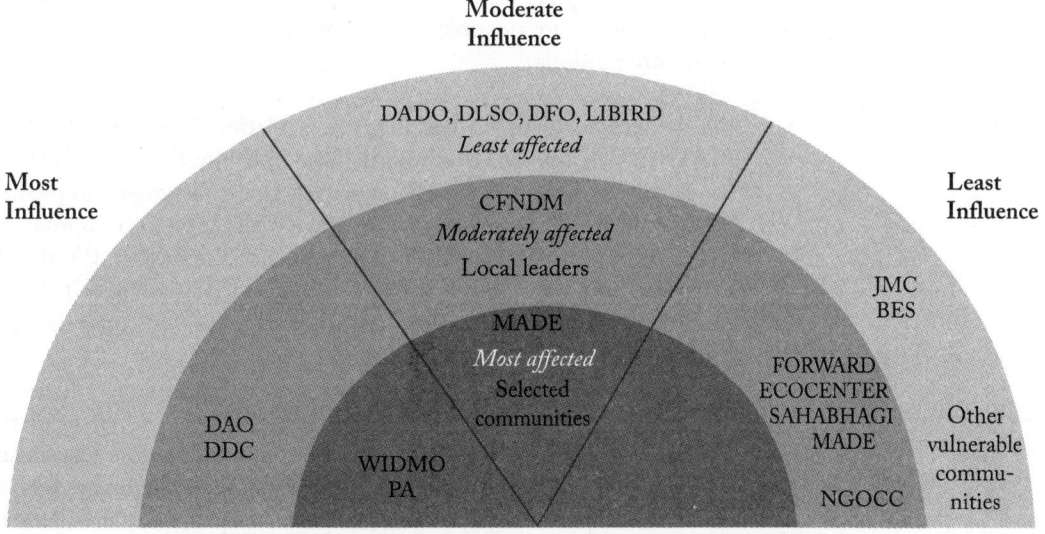

Note: DADO-District Agriculture Development Office; DLSO-District Livestock Service Office; LI-BIRD-Local Initiatives for Biodiversity, Research and Development; DFO-District Forest Office; NGOCC-Non-Governmental Organization Coordination Committee; FORWARD-Forum for Rural Welfare and Agricultural Reform for Development; ECOCENTER-Ecological Service Center; MADE-Multidimensional Agriculture for Development; NRUSEC-Nepal Rural Self-reliance Campaign; JMC-Jwalamukhi Club; BES-Bird Education Society; DAO-District Administration Office; DDC-District Development Office; WIDMO-Water Induced Disaster Management Office; CFNDM-Common Forum of NGOs working for Disaster Management; PA-Practical Action.

Interpretation

Participants in the first exercise, while few in number, had a lot of knowledge about the organizations that respond to disasters and work on improving community livelihoods. This made it possible to develop a comprehensive list, including candidate implementing organizations and communities. Further consultation with these other stakeholders was needed, however, to assess their views on the project. The changes to the stakeholder map made by the second group of participants reflect their view that communities are not only "beneficiaries" of the project but also actors in their own right with knowledge and views that can and should influence project directions. The total number of key stakeholders in the project remains low because few organizations have experience with livelihood options as a way to prevent or reduce the social impacts of disasters. While many organizations with knowledge and experience on disaster relief exist, they have less to offer or gain from this new focus. Because they are stakeholders that also represent other stakeholders as well as their own interests, the Common Forum of NGOs working for Disaster Management (CFNDM) and local community leaders are possible sources of information on the project for these other groups.

Action

PA decided to focus on building close relationships with WIDMO, MADE, some selected communities and both the DAO and DDO by consulting with them regularly on project goals, design and implementation. Specific plans were made to engage with the chosen communities to ensure that they have a chance to influence the project. PA also decided to meet once in a while with CFNDM and local community leaders to update them on the project and provide them with materials they could share with other stakeholders.

Observations on the Process

The first group of participants knew a lot about disaster relief and district level development policies, but they could not address the relationship of NGOs and communities to the project because the project was still choosing its partners. They were, however, very comfortable with the task of listing relevant groups and discussing their possible roles within the project. Participants were satisfied with the final list and distinctions made among stakeholders. They recognized, however, that they needed to discuss the project more with other stakeholders they had identified. The second meeting gave participants a chance to learn the views of other stakeholders, and to integrate the perspectives of the NGOs, representatives of selected communities, and local leaders. Participants agreed on the final analysis and said that it clarified the relationships among stakeholders and with the project. They noted that the results of the exercise showed why there should be certain lines of communication among key stakeholders and between the key stakeholders and other groups. They also said they were satisfied with the commitment by PA to engage communities in ways that enhance their influence in the project.

Social Analysis CLIP
(Collaboration, Conflict, Legitimacy, Interests, Power)

Author   J.M. Chevalier

Purpose   *Social Analysis CLIP* helps you create profiles of the parties involved in a core problem or action. These profiles are based on four factors: (*i*) power, (*ii*) interests, (*iii*) legitimacy, and (*iv*) existing relations of collaboration and conflict. The technique allows you to describe the characteristics and relationships of key stakeholders in a concrete situation (such as a conflict of interests among powerful stakeholders) and to explore ways to resolve social problems (such as building trust or empowering marginalized groups).

Guiding Principles

1. **Stakeholders** are the parties whose **interests** may be affected by a problem or action. They also include those who can influence the problem or action, using means at their disposal, such as **power**, **legitimacy**, and existing **ties of collaboration and conflict**.

2. **Interests** are the gains and losses that you will experience based on the results of existing or proposed actions. These gains and losses affect your access to power, legitimacy, or social relationships (including group memberships).

3. **Power** is your ability to influence others and use the resources you control to achieve your goals. These resources include economic wealth, political authority, ability to use force or threats of force, access to information (knowledge and skills), and the means to communicate.

4. **Legitimacy** is when other parties recognize by law or by local customs your rights and responsibilities, and the resolve you show when exercising them.

5. **Social relations** involve existing ties of collaboration and conflict (including group memberships) that affect you in a certain

situation and that you can use to influence a problem or an action.

6. The way that power, interests, legitimacy, and social relations are distributed in each situation determines the **stakeholder structure** and possible **strategies** to manage social problems or actions.

7. People may be members of different stakeholder groups. This is true of leaders and public officials: they have their own stakeholder profile and at the same time they belong to broader groups (for whom they act or speak) that have other profiles. Thus you can use *Social Analysis CLIP* to examine the relationship between representatives and the stakeholder groups they represent.

8. Stakeholders use their own **ideas and words** to define social categories and relations (including terms of "representation") within a context that is familiar to them.

Process

1. Identify a **situation** or **proposed action** that requires stakeholder analysis. Define the situation or proposed action as clearly as possible so that the participants can identify the precise interests at stake, the resources and forms of power that people can use to attain their goals, and the relevant rights and responsibilities they can exercise with resolve. Clarify the purpose of your analysis.

2. Identify all the **stakeholders** who may influence or be affected by this situation or proposed action (see *Stakeholder Identification*). Note that you may include yourself and those who are doing the analysis in your list. You may define the representatives of a group as a stakeholder different from those they represent. Also you may include the community of all stakeholders in your list, as a group with its own profile. Put the name (or a picture) of each stakeholder on its own card.

3. Identify and describe the level of **power or resources that each stakeholder can use** to oppose or promote the situation or action defined in Step 1. Exclude forms of power that stakeholders would not normally or realistically apply to the situation or proposed action (for example, it is highly unlikely a stakeholder would use force to promote a green manure project). Power can take four different forms:

(a) Economic wealth;

(b) Political authority (an office, position or role recognized by an institution or by local customs);

(c) The ability to use force or threats of force; and

(d) Access to information (including knowledge and skills) and the means to communicate.

Discuss and clarify these definitions of power, and replace them with the stakeholders' social categories and terms if necessary. Then, record the level of power on each stakeholder's card using one of three values: **high, middle, or low/no power**. On the same card, record the form and the level of power that the stakeholder can apply to the situation or proposed action.

4. Identify and describe the **net interests** of each stakeholder—the gains that each makes from the situation or proposed action minus the estimated losses. These net gains or losses include the degree to which a stakeholder gains or loses controls over important assets, such as economic wealth, political authority, the use of force, access to information, the means to communicate, legitimacy, or social relationships (including group memberships). Record and describe briefly the net interests on each stakeholder card, using one of five values: high gains (++), middle gains (+), low/no interests (0), middle losses (–), or high losses (– –).

Discuss and clarify these definitions of interests, and replace them with the stakeholders' own categories and terms if necessary. Make sure that participants do not confuse the idea of "net gains and losses" with "taking an interest in" or "being interested in something".

5. Identify and describe each stakeholder's level of **legitimacy** based on law or local customs. Legitimacy is the degree to which other parties recognize the stakeholder's rights and responsibilities (exercised with resolve). Focus on the rights and responsibilities that relate to the situation or proposed action identified in Step 1. Briefly describe and record the kind and the level of legitimacy on the stakeholder's card using one of three values: **high, middle, or low/no legitimacy**. If a stakeholder's legitimacy is in dispute, assign the "middle" value and note the dispute on your card.

Discuss and clarify this definition of legitimacy, and replace the definition with the stakeholders' own category and terms if necessary.

Here's an example of a stakeholder profile card:

Situation or proposed action: ....

Stakeholder individual or group: ....

Ⓟ OWER   High ▪   Middle ▪   Low/None ▪

Description: ....

Ⓛ EGITIMACY   High ▪   Middle ▪   Low/None ▪

Description: ....

Ⓘ NTERESTS   High + ▪   Middle + ▪   Low/None ▪
                      High − ▪   Middle − ▪

Description: ....

To help you categorize each stakeholder and transfer the information to the following table, give the stakeholder the letter P, the letter I or the letter L only if the corresponding score is "high" or "middle".

6. Create a table (see example in Step 9). In Column 1 list the following **stakeholder categories**:

Categories	High/Middle Ratings ☐		Low/No Ratings ☐
UPPER			
Dominant	PIL	Power, Interest (+ or −), Legitimacy	
Forceful	PI	Power, Interest (+ or −)	Legitimacy
MIDDLE			
Influential	PL	Power, Legitimacy	Interest (+ or −)
Dormant	P	Power	Legitimacy, Interest (+ or −)
Respected	L	Legitimacy	Power, Interest (+ or −)
LOWER			
Vulnerable	IL	Interest (+ or −), Legitimacy	Power
Marginalized	I	Interest (+ or −)	Power, Legitimacy

You can also represent these categories in a Venn diagram:

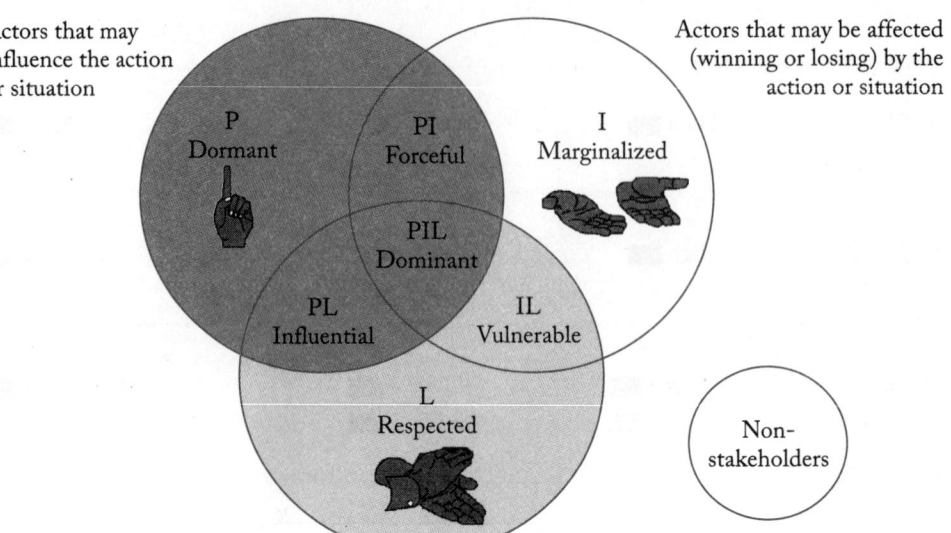

Actors that may influence the action or situation

Actors that may be affected (winning or losing) by the action or situation

P Dormant

PI Forceful

I Marginalized

PIL Dominant

PL Influential

IL Vulnerable

L Respected

Non-stakeholders

Actors that have recognized rights, responsibilities, and resolve

The stakeholder categories are ranked vertically, based on the following factors, **in order of importance** (according to the weight that each factor generally carries in social history). The first, is the power that stakeholders can exercise (see the four sources of power in Step 3). The second, is their interests as affected by the situation or proposed action. The third, is legitimacy—whether other parties recognize a stakeholder's rights and responsibilities and its resolve to exercise them. *Discuss and revise these assumptions and change the concepts and terms to ones that participants prefer, if needed.* You may want to use symbols or drawings to represent each concept, such as raising a fist or finger (for power), holding out the hands (for interests), and clapping hands (for legitimacy).

7. Insert the five categories of net **gains and losses** in the top row: high net losses (− −), middle net losses (−), low/no interests (0), middle net gains (+), and high net gains (++).

8. Place each stakeholder card in the square that corresponds to its profile. Use bold letters (or any other code) to identify the stakeholders who are participating in the analysis (such as a regional non-governmental organization). Don't place cards in the squares

that combine contradictory attributes (such as "dominant" stake-holders with "low/no" interests). These squares are marked with the letter "x" in the example presented in Step 9.

9. Identify the ties of **collaboration or conflict** (including relevant group memberships) that each stakeholder has with other stake-holders. Note that stakeholders may collaborate in some areas and be in conflict in other areas. Include ties that may be unrelated to the situation or action identified in Step 1.

Use **your own code** (such as colors) to identify these ties. For example, draw squares or circles around stakeholders who have collaborative ties with each other. Draw red arrows between those who have a history of conflict. You may use thinner and thicker lines to indicate levels or types of conflict, and broken lines to show relations that are likely to develop over time. Here's an example of a full CLIP table:

Proposed Action: Privatization of Communal Lands

Stakeholder categories		High net losses	Middle net losses	Low/no interests	Middle net gains	High net gains
PIL	Dominant	Local authorities		x		State oil company Federal State
PI	Forceful	Ranchers Merchants		x		
PL	Influential	x	x		x	x
P	Dormant	x	x		x	x
L	Respected	x	x	NGO	x	x
IL	Vulnerable	Small farmers		x		
I	Marginalized			x		Landless workers

Summary of this example: The national government wants to privatize the communal lands. New landowners would then be allowed to sell their land to a state-owned oil industry that needs land and labor. Local workers that do not own land could be hired if communal lands were sold to the State. But the local ranchers, some of whom are also merchants holding key positions in local politics, would lose a lot. So would the small farmers. The regional non-governmental organization facilitating this analysis is defending the interests of the small farmers by fighting the proposal. But they are aware that ties between themselves and the local authorities and also between small farmers and ranchers are not particularly good.

10. Discuss the results of your CLIP analysis. From the following list, select the stakeholder scenario or the combination of scenarios that best describes your situation (see the legend below the list):

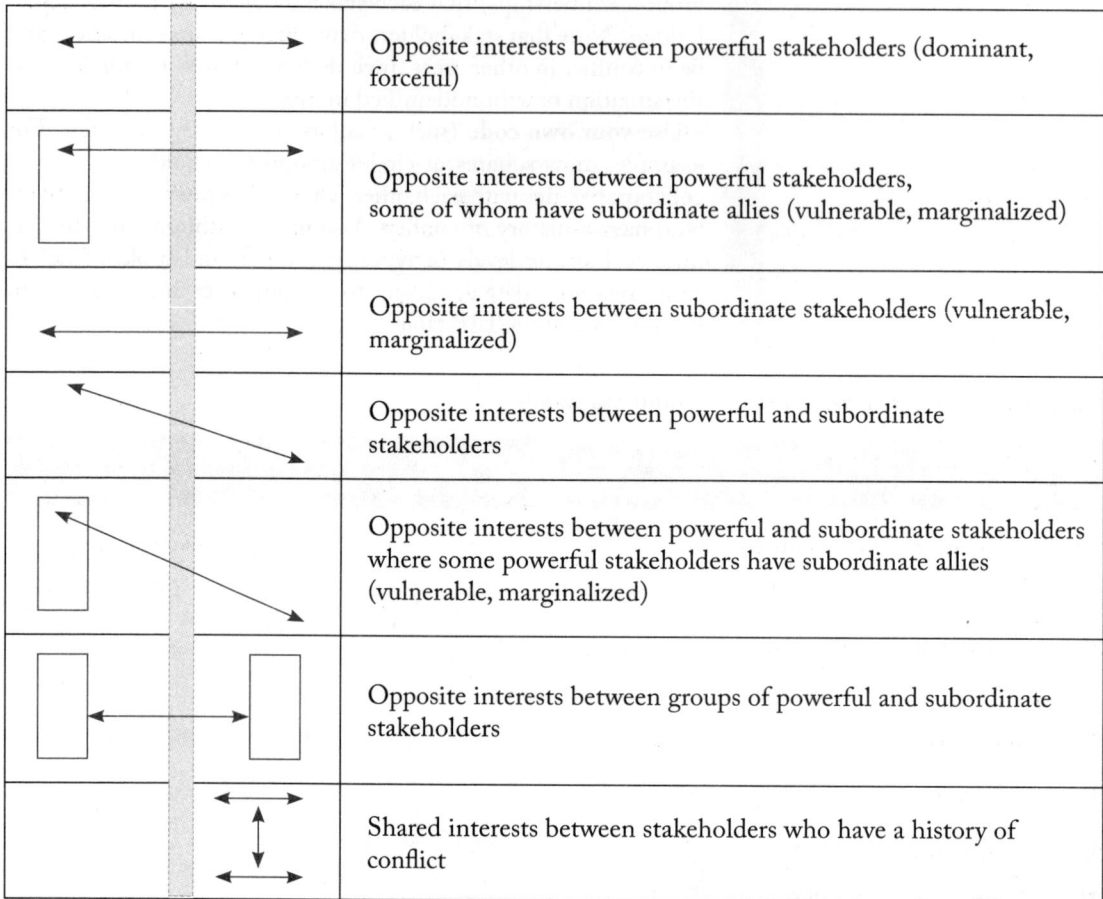

	Opposite interests between powerful stakeholders (dominant, forceful)
	Opposite interests between powerful stakeholders, some of whom have subordinate allies (vulnerable, marginalized)
	Opposite interests between subordinate stakeholders (vulnerable, marginalized)
	Opposite interests between powerful and subordinate stakeholders
	Opposite interests between powerful and subordinate stakeholders where some powerful stakeholders have subordinate allies (vulnerable, marginalized)
	Opposite interests between groups of powerful and subordinate stakeholders
	Shared interests between stakeholders who have a history of conflict

Note: *Arrows* indicate conflicts. *Boxes* indicate stakeholder alliances based on shared interests. Note that the description for each scenario also applies to its mirror image—arrows on the left hand side instead of the right in the last scenario, for instance.

11. Discuss the actions and the **first steps** that stakeholders can take to achieve their goals while dealing with the opposite interests recorded in your CLIP analysis. Include steps to modify existing stakeholder relations, such as actions to **empower the vulnerable and marginalized groups** that have pressing needs or interests. These steps may alter the profiles you obtained in your CLIP

analysis, and produce greater fairness and more effective responses to the problem or action identified in Step 1.

Focus on steps to overcome key problems relating to issues of power, interests, and legitimacy as identified in your analysis. Here are some examples of possible steps:

Power: increasing the resources available to some stakeholders; strengthening local organizations; making the process more democratic; creating opportunities for leadership; organizing a public demonstration; and so on.

Interests: developing a common vision of shared interests and goals; assessing the impact or the costs and benefits of an action; creating new incentives or mecahnisms of redistribution; and so on.

Legitimacy: using the legal system; upholding local norms; educating people about their rights and responsibilities; increasing public awareness; and so forth.

12. Some of the stakeholders you identified in Step 2 will not appear in your table if they are not significantly affected by the situation or action you identified in Step 1 and if they do not have the power or legitimacy to intervene. If this is the case, leave them out from your analysis or discuss what you can do to involve them.

13. Assess how existing ties of **collaboration or conflict** make the situation easier or more difficult to manage. This is important in situations where all key stakeholders may benefit from a proposed action but have a history of poor collaboration or open conflict (see last scenario in Step 10). Discuss the actions and the first steps that you can take to reduce conflict or to improve relations of collaboration, including developing new coalitions, seeking third party mediation, and building trust.

If you choose to **build trust** among stakeholders, discuss how you will achieve this and what indicators of trust you will use. To facilitate the discussion, participants may think of two stakeholders they trust, the reasons they trust them, and what people have done to create that trust. The same can be done with the stakeholders that participants do not trust.

Scaling Up or Down

For Simpler Versions

1. Limit the number of stakeholders by excluding those who are least involved or by regrouping stakeholders who share many characteristics. To organize your list of stakeholders into stakeholder categories, use *Sorting*.

2. Use only three values to determine the stakeholder interests: high net losses, low/no interests, or high net gains.

3. Identify stakeholder profiles using the Venn diagram only (see Step 6; indicate net losses with an *I*– sign and net gains with an *I*+).

4. Use *The Wheel* to represent and compare the levels of power, interests (net gains or losses), and legitimacy for each stakeholder.

For More Advanced Versions

1. Do many stakeholder profiles.

2. Take more time to gather the information you need to complete the exercise.

3. During the exercise, discuss and record the views that participants express.

4. Do a more detailed analysis of types and levels of collaboration and conflict using *Social Domain*.

5. Do a more detailed analysis of interests using *Interests* or *Internal Dialog*.

6. Do a more detailed analysis of power using *Power*.

7. Do a more detailed analysis of legitimacy using *Legitimacy*.

8. If you are drawing more detailed stakeholder profiles using *Power*, *Interests*, or *Legitimacy* techniques, create a CLIP table that incorporates the scales and the results from each technique.

9. Revise the definitions and ranking of power, interests, and legitimacy, or use your own criteria to create each stakeholder profile.

Readings and Links

Callens, K.; B. Seiffert; and S. Sontheimer. 2000. *Conducting a PRA Training and Modifying PRA Tools to Your Needs. An Example from a Participatory Household Food Security and Nutrition Project in Ethiopia*. Rome, Italy: FAO. Available online at http://www.fao.org/docrep/003/X5996E/X5996E00.htm, accessed on August 17, 2007.

Howlett, D.; R. Bond; P. Woodhouse; and D. Rigby. 2000. *Stakeholder Analysis and Local Identification of Indicators of the Success and Sustainability of Farming Based Livelihood Systems*. Working Paper No. 5. Manchester, United Kingdom: Centre for Agricultural Food and Resource Economics, University of Manchester. Available online at http://les.man.ac.uk/ses/research/CAFRE/indicators/wpaper5.htm, accessed on August 16, 2007.

Means, K.; C. Josayma; E. Nielsen; and V. Viriyasakultorn. 2002. *Community-Based Forest Resource Conflict Management: Training Package*, Volume 1,

Section 3.3, and Volume 2, Activity, 13-15. Rome: FAO. Available on-line at http://www.fao.org/DOCREP/005/Y4300E/Y4300E00.HTM, and http://www.fao.org/DOCREP/005/Y4301E/Y4301E00.HTM, accessed on August 16, 2007.

Mitchell, R.K.; B.R. Agle; and D.J. Wood. 1997. "Towards a theory of stakeholder identification: defining the principle of who and what really counts." *Academy of Management Review*, 22(4): 853–886.

To do Venn diagram analyses of social relations online, go to http://www.venndiagram.com/, accessed on August 17, 2007.

Social Analysis CLIP: Creating Strategic Alliances in the Tobacco Farming Areas of Southern Bangladesh

Key Words

Social Analysis CLIP, Bangladesh, agriculture, tribal people, stakeholder analysis

Author and Acknowledgement

D.J. Buckles. The author wishes to acknowledge the efforts of Rafiqul Huq Titu who helped to design and facilitate the assessment.

Context

Lama is a township of tribal people and Bengali settlers in Bandarban District of the Chittagong Hill Tracts (CHT) of southern Bangladesh. It straddles the banks of the Matamuhuri river and is close to lush forests. The British American Tobacco Company (BATC) and other tobacco buyers have been promoting the production of tobacco in the villages of the township since 1984. Currently, tobacco farming uses fertile river valley soils during the main growing season. Each year, a lot of wood must be cut in order to cure the tobacco leaves (using smoke). Problems that stem from tobacco production include a decline in food farming, ill health from exposure to the pesticides and smoke used in the production process, deforestation, soil erosion, and high debt loads among small and marginal farmers. UBINIG, a non-governmental organization that supports ecological farming in a nearby township, has recently contacted a few farmers in Lama that want to stop tobacco farming. UBINIG wonders whether it should launch a broad campaign to promote ecological farming in this region.

For more information on this project, see UBINIG, Carleton University, 2006, *From Tobacco to Food Production: Assessing Constraints and Transition Strategies in Bangladesh*, First Interim Technical Progress Report to IDRC, 18 pp.

Purpose

To identify the strategic alliances that UBINIG might use to support farmers who want to stop tobacco farming.

Process Summary

UBINIG invited two male farmers from Lama to their Cox's Bazaar Centre for a meeting. One of the farmers had been working with UBINIG for a year and had already stopped tobacco farming, in favor of horticulture. He identified and invited to the meeting two tobacco farmers who were open to doing the same. The merits of shifting out of tobacco into horticulture and other forms of agriculture were discussed, along with the challenges that both they and UBINIG have in the region. The farmers created a list of stakeholders and discussed terminology and ratings for each stakeholder until there was a common understanding. This information was recorded on cards and a table was drawn on a flip-chart to represent the stakeholder structure. The group then discussed the history of conflict and collaboration among stakeholders, followed by actions UBINIG could take to mobilize support for a shift to ecological farming. The process was facilitated by Daniel Buckles, the report author, with permission to report on the findings given by the participants.

Analysis

The profile of 15 different stakeholders is based on ratings of three factors that can affect the proposed action: interests, power, and legitimacy (Table 1). The two columns on the left show stakeholders whose interests would be affected negatively by the shift to ecological farming (– – and –). The two columns on the right are stakeholders whose interests would be affected positively (+ and ++). The middle column shows stakeholders whose interests are neutral. The higher the stakeholders are in the Table, the greater is their power to oppose or support the shift to ecological farming.

The effect of legitimacy on a stakeholder's profile is shown by the presence or absence of "L" in the pie chart in the column on the far left. Alignment with "I" and "P" in the pie chart indicate interests and power, respectively. Each stakeholder group is aligned horizontally with these letters to show how these factors combine to create each profile. The broken red line shows a history of conflict between the tobacco farmers and the BATC. The solid lines show histories of collaboration among those stakeholders. Highlighting indicates the three stakeholders who were part of the assessment (UBINIG, Food Farmers, and Tobacco Farmers).

The stakeholder structure shows that powerful stakeholders have opposing interests, and that some also have subordinate allies. A large block of forceful stakeholders (labeled BATC, Company Employees, Wood Dealers, Pesticide Dealers and Tobacco Traders) would be strongly opposed to the proposed shift from tobacco to ecological farming. Some support for their position comes from Lease Owners, Money Lenders, and Irrigation Pump Owners. An opposing block of three stakeholders holds similar power to this group, and they support the shift to ecological farming (Irrigation Scheme, CHT Council, UBINIG). Between these two blocks lies a block of three vulnerable or marginalized stakeholders (labeled Tobacco Farmers, Laborers, and Food Farmers) whose interests would be negatively affected by or neutral to the proposed action. One cannot conclude, however, that they are allies of the powerful stakeholders opposed to the shift, because there is a history of conflict between them. Nor can they be counted on to support the shift to ecological agriculture; collaboration between food farmers and UBINIG is recent and still weak. Both groups have a relationship with the CHT Council, a forum that can bring them together. One stakeholder (Zone commander) is an influential and neutral party, making him a potential mediator.

Table 1: Stakeholder Structure in Lama as it Relates to a Shift to Ecological Agriculture

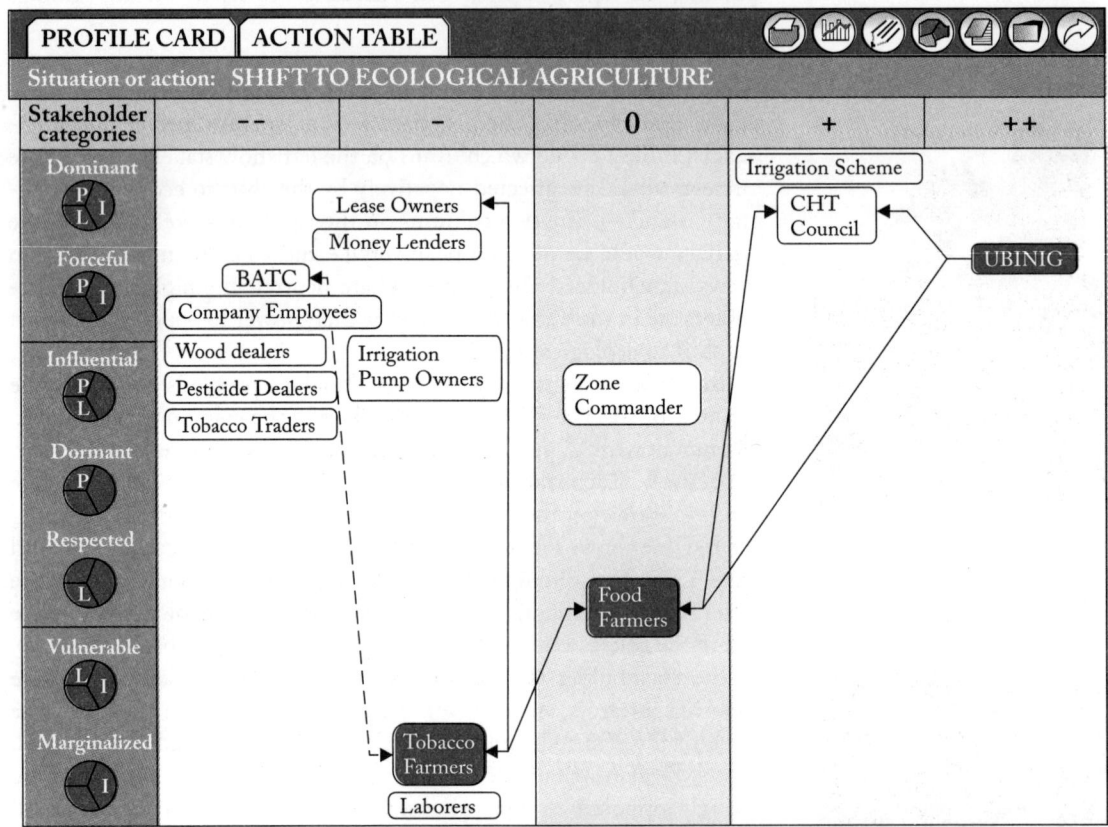

PROFILE CARD	ACTION TABLE				
Situation or action: SHIFT TO ECOLOGICAL AGRICULTURE					
Stakeholder categories	– –	–	0	+	+ +

Interpretation

The scenario is a challenging one for UBINIG because, according to the participants, most tobacco farmers will not believe their interests would be served by the proposed action, and food farmers will be neutral at best.

Action

Despite the challenges, several actions were identified as a result of the exercise. UBINIG decided it could try to indirectly influence tobacco farmers through its recent, positive link with food farmers who have close

ties with tobacco farmers. The two farmers who took part in the assessment noted that the connection between them had already followed this path: one of the farmers had made the shift from tobacco to ecological farming after being exposed to that option through UBINIG, and invited the other farmer to think about doing the same. They noted, however, that this action would have little influence on the majority of tobacco farmers unless the campaign was supported by new information on the net economic benefits of ecological farming. The participants encouraged UBINIG to support or undertake research on the economic gains and losses from tobacco farming from the point of view of men and women, and to compare these to various forms of ecological farming. UBINIG agreed and also decided to study the impact on prices of more local food supplies and whether it is feasible to market horticulture products outside the township. Finally, the participants discussed building closer relations between UBINIG, the Chittagong Hill Tracts Regional Council and the government Irrigation Scheme as a way to create support for the shift both from the Zone Commander and the marginal stakeholders. They decided, however, that this action should come later, once the perceived interests of tobacco farmers and food farmers change in ways that show more support for the proposed action.

Observations on the Process

The farmer participants provided all of the information used to rate the various stakeholders, while the UBINIG staff added information on the history of collaboration and conflict that it was aware of. The facilitator asked for confirmation of results at each stage in the exercise, and encouraged the farmers to actively record their views on the cards provided. These were visually recorded using words, pictures and objects representing the various factors and stakeholders. Both parties (farmers and UBINIG) discussed and agreed on the strategy that would be most useful as a result of the exercise. They were very surprised and enthused with the final table pulling together the information they had generated as it accurately expressed for them the key dynamics in the situation and the path ahead. They also noted that the exercise had made them more clearly aware of the challenge they faced, and that this was useful to their planning.

Social Domain

Author J.M. Chevalier

Acknowledgement *Social Domain* is a SAS² adaptation and development of the concepts and techniques of Personal Construct Psychology (see in particular the works of G.A. Kelly, http://repgrid.com/pcp/; Jankowicz, 2004; and Gaines and Shaw, 2004).

Purpose *Social Domain* examines how people view actors and relations between them using words and characteristics that participants themselves choose and define. It also shows how people negotiate their views of actors across social and cultural boundaries. The technique may be used to test people's views against experience, solve problems, and learn in the process.

Guiding Principles

1. People make constant efforts to understand and influence other people's views, beliefs and expectations in life. They do this through role interaction, communications, and strategic action. People's views and knowledge of reality are thus products of social behavior developed across cultural and social boundaries.

2. Your knowledge and understanding of actors involved in a core problem or action is based on how you create and organize relations between actors and their characteristics. You can thus use *Social Domain* to examine:

   (a) A domain or **topic area** (such as managing natural resources in a certain area);

   (b) **Actors** involved in a domain or topic area (such as people influencing and affected by a project to manage natural resources in a certain area);

   (c) **Characteristics** that you organize into continua from one pole to its opposite and that you apply to actors (such as describing some actors as being more affected by a project than others);

(d) **Relations** consisting of degrees of similarity or difference between actors or characteristics (such as describing actors that are more affected by a certain project as having also less power to intervene).

3. *Social Domain* is an application of Domain Analysis, a general technique that you can also use to analyze existing problems or actions (see *Problem Domain*), value systems (see *Value Domain*), options for action (see *Option Domain*), and elements in Nature (*Domain Analysis*).

4. Your views and knowledge of actors and their characteristics may be logical and coherent. At the same time your views may be flexible and may change according to context. These levels of **coherence** and **flexibility** will vary from one topic or situation to another.

5. You can test your knowledge and views against your experience of reality and develop **new relationships** among actors and their characteristics. *Social Domain* may thus reveal **learning opportunities** such as overcoming convergence, polarization, fragmentation, vagueness, disagreement, misunderstanding, confusion, instability, resistance to change, and failure to predict.

Process

Identifying the Actors and their Characteristics

1. Identify a **core problem or action** where you need to use *Social Domain*. Define the problem or action as clearly as possible, and clarify the purpose of your analysis.

2. Identify all the **key actors** (individuals or groups) who may affect or be affected by this problem or action (see *Stakeholder Identification*). Note that you may include yourself the way you are (**actual self**) or would like to be (**ideal self**) and those who are doing the analysis. You may define the representatives of a group as an actor different from those they represent. Also you may include the community of all actors in your list, as a group with its own profile. Write (or draw) the name of each actor on a separate card.

The minimum number of actors is usually six and the maximum is 12. You can **supply** or **negotiate** some or all of these names or simply **ask** the participants to identify them, depending on the purpose of the exercise and your role as facilitator.

3. Create a table. Begin the table by writing **"Characteristics"** at the top of Column 1. Then, place all the actors' cards in the top row (see Step 6). To do the analysis without using a table, go to Step 10.

4. To focus the discussion, you may choose a **key aspect or question** that you can use to compare the actors and that clearly relates to the action or problem identified in Step 1. For instance, you may focus on:

   (a) The forms and levels of **interests** that actors have in a project;

   (b) The **forms and levels of organization** or **power** that actors can apply to a situation;

   (c) The degrees and the ways in which different actors are **trusted** or viewed as **legitimate**;

   (d) Differences in **institutional characteristics**;

   (e) The **actions or positions** that actors take in a project or a conflict;

   (f) The **information, skills or learning styles** that actors might apply to a situation; and

   (g) The **kinds of conflicts** or **relations of collaboration** that exist between actors. If you select this topic, you should use Step 2 to list all one-to-one relations between actors (such as yourself and Actor A, yourself and Actor B, and so on), as opposed to listing all the actors separately.

5. Choose **three actors** from the top row at random. Identify two of them (a pair) that are the same in some way, and different from the third. Then, identify what it is these two have in common, something that is relevant to your topic, the key question you identified in Step 4, and the purpose of your exercise. Write down the characteristic they share (such as both hold "positions of authority") on a new card and give the characteristic a score of 1. Place the card in the first column, below the second row.

   Then, identify what makes the **third actor different from the pair**. Write down this opposite characteristic (such as this actor is "just a citizen") on the same card that you used to write the pair characteristic, and give it a score of 5. If you don't want middle scores that may have ambiguous meanings, use a rating scale with an even number of points (such as 1 to 4 or 1 to 6). Write down a clear definition of the characteristic and its opposite on the reverse side of the card.

Here are some tips to help you identify a characteristic and its opposite:

(a) You can **supply** or **negotiate** each characteristic and its opposite or **ask** the participants to identify them.

(b) The characteristics you identify should be **relevant** to your topic area. They should also be **focused** and **clear,** consisting of **concrete** adjectives, nouns, actions or verbs ending in "–ing" rather than abstract terms, qualities or ideas.

(c) If the characteristics are vague or sound like clichés, use the *Laddering Down* technique to make them more meaningful and detailed. Ask "What do you mean by this?", "Can you give an example of this?", "How can you tell this?", or "In what way is this true?" (for instance, "In what way is this actor more powerful compared with other actors?").

(d) When identifying the opposite of a characteristic, don't use **negative phrases**, such as "not local" to describe the opposite of "local". Negative phrases tend to be vague and meaningless. Use *Laddering Down* questions (such as "What do you mean by this?") to get a precise expression of an opposite which may vary according to the situation or topic. For instance, the opposite of "local" could be either "regional" or "national", depending on the context.

(e) When using characteristics to describe each actor, do not interpret the descriptions as statements of facts that are either right or wrong. *Social Domain* statements should be **accurate** only in the sense of truly reflecting people's views and knowledge of social reality.

(f) If a characteristic and its opposite **do not apply** to several actors, try rewording them or eliminate the characteristic and its opposite.

(g) For other means to identify characteristics and their opposites, see Step 7.

6. Use the characteristic and it opposite created in Step 5 to **rate all the actors**, from 1 to 5. Ask each actor to rate itself, or discuss the score for each actor until participants reach an agreement. You can give the same score to two or several actors. Record each score on its own card. To help you interpret the results at the end of this exercise, write the reason given for a score on the reverse side of its card. If the characteristic and its opposite do not apply to an actor, don't write anything on the card. If the scores are nearly

the same for all actors, redefine the characteristic and its opposite or eliminate them.

Place each score card in the second row, below the corresponding actor. Here is an example of a table with a list of six actors and scores that reflect a distinction between actors in "positions of authority" and those who are "just citizens".

Characteristics	Actor A	Actor B	Actor C	Actor D	Actor E	Actor F
Authority (1)	1	4	2	1	5	5
Citizens (5)						

This first distinction may be something you want to explain (such as the level of support that each actor expresses for an existing action). If this is the case, reorganize all of your actors' cards (row 1) and score cards (row 2), arranging the cards from the highest score to the lowest. This will help you interpret the table and explain what you want to explain (such as why certain actors support a certain course of action while others do not).

Don't use **averages** when people have disagreements about scores. Instead discuss the issue until you reach an agreement based on consensus or a majority vote.

If you want this exercise to be more precise, identify **indicators** that define the meaning of each number on the scale. If you don't want to use written numbers when rating the actors, use simple **phrases** first and then convert the phrases into measurable objects (from 1 to 5 twigs, stones, noodles or seeds). For instance, scores 1 and 5 will mean that "the actor has one characteristic or its opposite only"; score 3 will mean that the actor combines the two characteristics evenly; and scores 2 and 4 will mean that the actor combines the two characteristics unevenly, with one being more important than the other. Another option is to score each actor with the help of 5 cards colored white (value 1), light grey (value 2), medium grey (value 3), dark grey (value 4), and black (value 5).

Another rating technique (see *Tree Mapping*) consists in creating a new set of cards for all the actors and dividing the cards into two **piles** of any size: one pile that best represents the characteristic, and the other pile that best represents its opposite. Repeat the same exercise with each pile by dividing the actors into those that best represent the pile characteristic and those that fall somewhere between the characteristic and its opposite. Do this several times until you have rated all the actors along the continuum from one characteristic to its opposite.

7. Repeat the process described in Step 5 to identify **other characteristics and their opposites**.

   You cannot use a characteristic together with its opposite more than once, but you can use a characteristic *or* its opposite separately more than once (such as "wealthy" as opposed to "poor" in one case, and then "wealthy" as opposed to "respected" in the other case).

   If the participants cannot identify what it is that two actors have in common or what makes the third actor different from the pair, ask the question in another way, apply the *Laddering Down* technique (see Step 5), choose another three actors at random or choose two cards instead of three.

   You can use other participatory techniques to identify characteristics and their opposites, without comparing actors chosen at random. A simple technique consists in asking the **catch-all question**: "Can you think of some new, different characteristic and its opposite?" Another option is the **full context** procedure where you look at all actors and find out two that are the most similar and why, and then the actor that is the most different from these and ask again why. You can also use **description and storytelling** to explore your topic area (such as describing the history of a conflict over natural resources in a region), and then use this information to identify the actors and their characteristics, with the help of the *Laddering Down* technique (see Step 5).

   To identify several characteristics and their opposites in a **short time**, divide all participants into groups of two or three. Ask each group to choose three actors' cards at random and to identify a relevant characteristic and its opposite (using the process described in Step 5). Collect these new characteristics and their opposites, discuss and clarify their meaning, and group together those that are the same.

8. Repeat the process described in Step 6 to **rate all the actors** again using the new characteristics and their opposites. Add a new row for each characteristic and its opposite and record each score and the reason given for it on the corresponding card. Place each score card in its row, below the corresponding actor.

   To do the ratings in a **short time**, ask each actor participating in the exercise to rate itself for each characteristic and its opposite. You can also divide all participants into smaller groups. Then, ask each group to choose a different characteristic and its opposite and to use these to rate all the actors. Use this technique only if the participants do not need to be involved in all the ratings.

Here is an example of a table that shows the scores for six actors, using five characteristics:

Characteristics		Actor A	Actor B	Actor C	Actor D	Actor E	Actor F
Authority	(1)	1	4	2	1	5	5
Citizens	(5)						
Landowners	(1)	5	1	4	4	4	3
Landless	(5)						
Old	(1)	4	2	3	3	2	1
Young	(5)						
Business	(1)	5	5	2	4	4	2
Labor	(5)						
Locals	(1)	4	1	3	4	1	2
Outsiders	(5)						

9. If you have many characteristics, you can group them into the appropriate **categories** supplied by the facilitator or created and defined by the participants (such as characteristics that concern the kind of power that actors can apply to a situation, those that concern their interests, and so on; see *Sorting*). You can rank the characteristics and their opposites within each category by order of importance. This will help you interpret the table at the end of the exercise.

Doing the Analysis without Using a Table

10. If all the actors are present, you can use the *Social Domain* technique without having to record all scores in one table. Instead of creating a table, use the following method:

(a) Divide all participants into random groups of three. Ask each group of three to identify two of them (a pair) that are the same in some way, and different from the third. Find a characteristic that is shared by the pair, and then the characteristic that makes the third person different (see tips in Step 5).

(b) Make a list of the distinctions between characteristics and their opposites that you obtain from all the groups. Discuss and clarify the meaning of each distinction. Group together the distinctions that are the same. Reduce the list to four to six distinctions that matter the most in relation to the problem or action identified in Step 1. To help you interpret the results of your analysis, you may rank the characteristics by order of importance.

(c) Ask each participant to rate itself for each characteristic and its opposite, from one to five (see tips in Step 6). Ensure that participants have a common understanding of what the scale numbers mean for each characteristic and its opposite. Each actor should record its ratings on a card named after itself. All actors' cards should show the same characteristics, in the same order, and with the same format. Here's an example of an actor's card that corresponds to Actor A in the table presented in Step 8:

Card for Actor A

Characteristics	1	2	3	4	5	Characteristics
Authority		X				Citizens
Landowners					X	Landless
Old				X		Young
Business					X	Labor
Locals				X		Outsiders

(d) Ask each participant to find others that have cards with many row scores that are identical or similar (only one point apart) to theirs. Give special attention to similarities in the first rows, those that describe the most important characteristics.

(e) Each group formed around similar cards should then prepare and present a brief description of the *characteristics* group members have *in common*. When a group presents itself, other groups may come closer to the group if they feel they are similar in significant ways or distance themselves if the differences are more important than the similarities. Following this, all participants should discuss the *main differences* observed between groups. For a more advanced interpretation of your results, see Steps 11 to 17.

When using this method, be aware that participants may miss some important similarities or differences. They may also use implicit characteristics that are relevant to the exercise without being recorded on the cards.

Interpreting the Results

11. To interpret your *Social Domain* analysis, start with a **review** of the **process** itself, including the way that participants interacted and reached decisions at each step of the process. You can also review the **substance** of the exercise, including the topic that participants selected, their purpose in doing the exercise, the actors and the characteristics they identified, the kind of information or knowledge they used to rate the actors, and so on. Summarize all the main points of your review.

12. To interpret the final table (see Step 8), start with a **snapshot** discussion of column scores that describe the actors. Look for things that are obvious about the **actors**, such as: the way each of them is characterized; whether the scores tend to be in the middle or closer to the poles; if some actors have the same scores as others or come close to the ideal self (see Step 2); and so on.

    You can then look at row ratings to see if there's anything obvious about the **characteristics**, such as: the fact that some characteristics have scores that vary little and others a lot; some characteristics are more meaningful compared with others that are repetitive or descriptive; the ratings for one row coincide with the ratings for another row or they are nearly the opposite; and so on.

    Summarize all the main points of your snapshot discussion.

13. To interpret the column scores in greater detail, look for the **actors that are similar** and summarize the characteristics they share. You can **group together** these actors by moving the columns around and placing them side by side (use masking tape to stick the column cards together). You will know that two or more actors are alike when they have similar row scores for most characteristics, including the most important ones. In the table shown in Step 8, actors A and D are alike. They hold positions of authority and do not own land, operate businesses or live in the area.

    To calculate the level of difference between two columns, calculate the sum of differences (SD) between same-row scores (leave out rows that have empty squares). You then calculate the total maximum difference for all scores (this is MS, the maximum score, minus 1, multiplied by C, the number of row characteristics that got ratings). The level of difference between two actors is SD divided by the total maximum difference for all scores, multiplied by 100. To turn this level of difference into a percentage similarity score, subtract it from 100. In other words:

$$100 - \frac{SD \times 100}{(MS - 1) \times C}$$

Define the points where you consider levels of similarities between actors to be high or low.

Using the table in Step 8 as an example, the sum of differences (SD) between the recorded scores for actors A and D is 3 and the total maximum difference is 20 $[(5-1) \times 5]$. This results in a difference of 15 percent ($3/20 \times 100$). Looking at it another way, the two actors are similar at a level of 85 percent.

When comparing several actors, you can focus on those row characteristics that are more important or interesting. If you focus on **two characteristics** only, you can create a diagram by drawing a vertical line that crosses a horizontal line. This creates a cross inside a square. If your scale is 1 to 5, write 1 and 5 at opposite ends of both the horizontal line and the vertical line; indicate what these minimum and maximum scores actually mean. Write 3 where the two lines cross. Place each actor in the diagram by locating its score on the horizontal line and then its score on the vertical line. Connect the marks from the two lines, using the letter "x" to mark the place where they meet. The closer two actors are in the diagram, the more similar they are. Here is an example of this cross-shaped diagram:

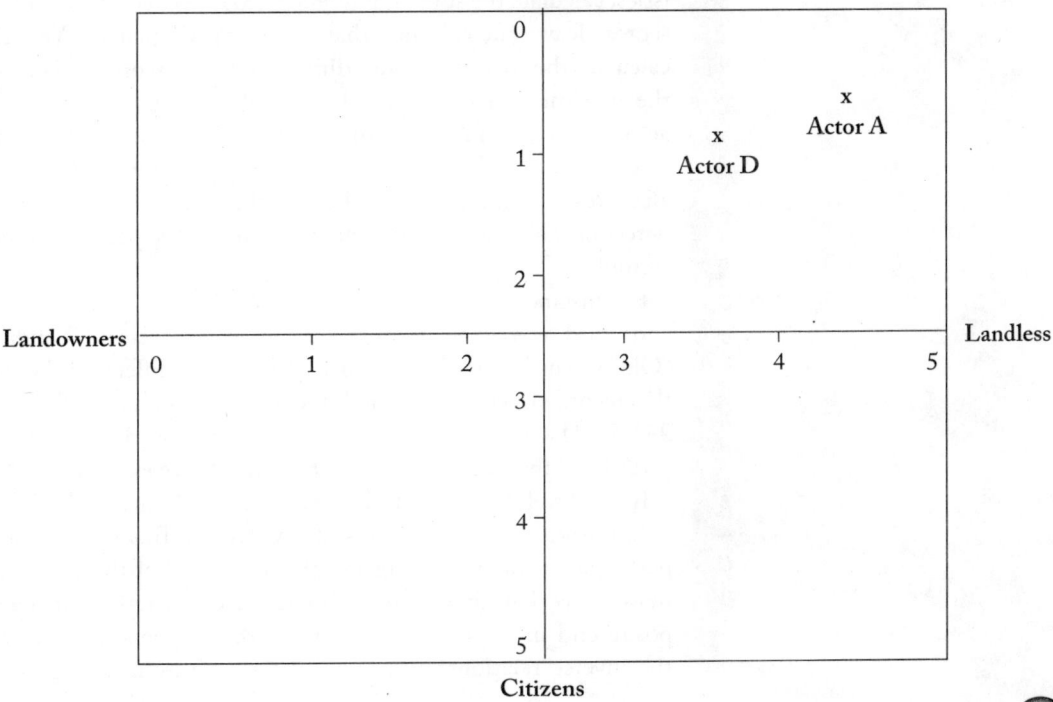

14. Now that you have identified actors with similar profiles, you can interpret the row characteristics in greater detail and look for **matching characteristics**. You can **group together** these matching characteristics by moving the rows around and placing them side by side (use masking tape to stick the row cards together). You will know that there is a **match** between two or more characteristics when you realize that "if participants say score x in one row then they tend to say score y in the other row". In the table shown in Step 8, people in positions of authority (with low scores in the first row) tend to be outsiders (with high scores in the last row). By contrast, those that are "just citizens" are locals. Note that matching characteristics may help answer a key aspect of your topic area (such as the level of support that each actor expresses for an existing action; see Step 6).

To help people participate in the analysis, divide the participants into smaller groups, and ask each group to choose a different characteristic and its opposite. Then, each group should find other row characteristics with scores that are very similar or that are nearly the opposite (see explanation below).

To calculate the level of difference between two row characteristics, calculate the sum of differences (SD) between same-column scores (leave out columns that have empty squares). You then calculate the total maximum difference for all scores (this is MS, the maximum score, minus 1, multiplied by E, the number of actors that got ratings). The level of difference between two characteristics is SD divided by the total maximum difference for all scores, multiplied by 100. To turn this level of difference into a percentage similarity score, subtract it from (see page 200 for the formula).

For instance, the table created in Step 8 shows that the second and third row characteristics ("Landowners" versus "Landless", "Old" versus "Young") are similar. The sum of differences between the recorded scores is 8 and the total maximum difference is $24 [(5-1) \times 6]$. The level of difference is therefore 33 percent ($8/24 \times 100$) and the level of similarity, 67 percent. See example below.

If the level of similarity is very low, this indicates an inverse relationship between two sets of row scores. This means that "if participants choose a characteristic at one end of the continuum in one row then they tend to choose the characteristic at the opposite end in the other row". When this happens you can turn the inverse relationship into a positive one by reversing all the scores in one row (from 2 to 4 or from 5 to 1, in a scale from 1 to 5, for instance). Positive relationships are easier to interpret. For instance, the following table reverses the scores for the last row of the table created in Step 8. Using these reverse scores, the level of similarity between the first and last rows ("Authority" versus "Citizens", "Locals" versus "Outsiders") is 79 percent.

Characteristics		Actor A	Actor B	Actor C	Actor D	Actor E	Actor F
Authority	(1)	1	4	2	1	5	5
Citizens	(5)						
Locals	(1) now 5	(4) now 2	(1) now 5	(3) now 3	(4) now 2	(1) now 5	(2) now 4
Outsiders	(5) now 1						

Define the points where you consider levels of similarities between characteristics to be high or low. Where you find high matches between row scores, discuss whether these characteristics and their opposites have the same **meaning** or the same cause, or if some are **examples** or **causes** of others.

When looking for matching characteristics, focus on those characteristics and relationships that are of interest to the participants, and no more. Do not over-interpret these relationships, and let the participants play an active role in the analysis.

15. You can look at similarities and differences between some actors and their characteristics during the rating process (Step 8), before the table is completed. At the end of the exercise you can enter your actors, your characteristics, and your ratings in RepGrid (http://repgrid.com/SAS/) and use the Focus and PrinGrid commands to perform the calculations described in Steps 13 and 14. The Focus command creates a table where actors that have the most similar ratings are placed side by side. Characteristics that have the most similar ratings also appear side by side, with negative matches converted into positive relationships. A diagram with lines meeting at various points (outside the table) indicates the levels of similarity between actors and between characteristics. This is called **cluster analysis**.

The PrinGrid command creates a graph with calculations based on **principal component analysis**. The graph shows the location of each actor in relation to other actors (dots). It also shows the location of actors in relation to a number of straight lines representing the characteristics (the longer the line is, the more the characteristic varies in its ratings). Closer distances reflect closer relationships between actors (dots), between characteristics (lines), and between actors and their characteristics. To interpret the graph, focus on the characteristics that are grouped near two imaginary lines, one vertical and the other horizontal; these principal components show percentage figures that indicate the extent to which each component explains all relationships (see example below).

Rethinking Your Analysis

16. You can modify your list of actors, your characteristics and opposites, and your scores at any time during the process.

You may want to look for a **new characteristic** and opposite if you need to split two actors that are closely matched. To do this, find the difference between the two actors that are almost the same (such as actors A and D in the table created in Step 8). Use the new characteristic and its opposite to rate all the actors and record your scores in a new row.

You may want to look for a **new actor** if you need to split two characteristics that are closely matched. To do this, find an actor that brings together the characteristics that are rarely matched (for instance, in the table created in Step 8, a local person that holds a position of authority). Insert the new actor in a new column and rate it for each characteristic and its opposite.

Learning from Your Analysis

17. *Social Domain* can help you identify **learning opportunities** that are structural (such as convergence, polarization, fragmentation, or vagueness), communicational (such as disagreement, misunderstanding, or confusion), temporal (such as instability or resistance to change) or adaptive (such as the failure to predict).

Structural Learning Opportunities

Convergence

You know there is convergence in your table when the row scores you recorded are closely matched. It will be clear that you can re-group most characteristics into two categories that are opposite each other, with the actors falling somewhere along the continuum from one set of opposites to another. For instance, in the table presented in Step 8, the younger the actors are, the more often they are outsiders that have no land and hold positions of authority.

If convergence is a problem, search for other actors that may combine the characteristics in new ways (such as younger actors that own land and don't hold positions of authority).

Polarization

You know there is social polarization in your table when you can regroup most actors into two categories that are opposite each other. One group of actors has one set of characteristics, and the other group is opposite in all respects. For instance, in the table shown in Step 8, actors A, C, and D are young outsiders that have no land and hold positions of authority. By contrast, actors B, E, and F are older, "just citizens" and locals that own land.

If polarization is a problem, look for ways to reduce social divisions. In the example above, the suggestion might be: "Can we imagine ways of having locals in positions of authority?"

Fragmentation

You know there is social fragmentation in your table when few actors and few characteristics are closely matched. There is no pattern in the system. Each actor is entirely different. For instance, there may be so many actors and they may be so different from each other that no explanation can be found as to why certain actors support an existing action and others do not.

If fragmentation is a problem, search for other actors or characteristics that may reveal some meaningful pattern in the system. For instance, if each actor has a unique combination of characteristics, the suggestion might be: "Can we ask men and women to form two groups and for each group to propose a new way to manage the forest park?"

Vagueness

You know there is vagueness in your table when the scores for the actors do not vary much. If this is a problem, search for the likely cause. Some likely reasons include: participants have very different views of the actors and will negotiate them through average scores; they see mostly the relationships between the actors, not the differences; they have limited knowledge of the topic area; or the actors they chose are too broadly defined.

Communicational Learning Opportunities

Disagreement

You know there is disagreement (between the tables that different people make) when people give very different scores to the actorsusing the same characteristics. To measure levels of agreement and disagreement between two sets of scores, total the differences between same-square scores and divide this number by the total maximum difference between all squares (this is MS, the maximum score, minus 1, multiplied by E, the number of actors that got ratings).

Here is an example of a disagreement at a 63 percent level (15/24) between two groups who rate the same actors using the same characteristic and its opposite (the power to intervene, either economic or political):

Characteristic and its Opposite: Power to Intervene, either Economic (1) or Political (5)

Parties	Actor A	Actor B	Actor C	Actor D	Actor E	Actor F
Group 1	2	1	4	3	5	3
Group 2	5	4	1	3	1	5
Difference	3	3	3	0	4	2

If disagreement is a problem, identify the key area(s) of disagreement (such as how to characterize Actor E in the table shown above) and discuss the scores until they reflect a common assessment of the situation.

There may be cases where you want to *compare many characteristics and tables* representing the views of different individuals or groups. To do this, reorder the row characteristics in each table from top to bottom, with *those at the top matching the ratings of a key characteristic* (such as the level of support for an existing action). These top matching characteristics represent what each individual or group has in mind when thinking about important aspects of the topic. Then, look for top matching characteristics that participants agree or disagree with across your sample. If the tables contain many characteristics, you can group them into categories (see Step 9), reorder the characteristics from top to bottom within each category, and then look for top match agreements and disagreements across your sample within each category.

Misunderstanding

You know there is misunderstanding when a party (such as men) fails to predict how the other party (such as women) will rate certain actors. To measure levels of misunderstanding, each party must try to guess how the other party will rate the same actors using the same characteristic(s). Then, total the differences between the original scores and the scores each group predicted for the other. Divide this number by the total maximum difference for all squares (this is the maximum score minus 1, multiplied by the number of actors). As an example, the following table shows a high level of misunderstanding between two parties. Although both think they share similar views about the benefits that several actors derive from a project, their views are different.

Characteristic and its Opposite: Estimated Benefits, Low (1) or High (5)

Parties	Actor A	Actor B	Actor C	Actor D	Actor E	Actor F
Party 1	2	1	4	3	5	3
Party 1 viewed by party 2	5	4	1	4	1	5
Difference	3	3	3	1	4	2
Party 2	5	4	1	5	1	5
Party 2 viewed by party 1	2	1	2	3	5	3
Difference	3	3	1	2	4	2

If misunderstanding is a problem, identify the key area(s) and the likely causes of misunderstanding (such as the perceived benefits for Actor E in the table shown above). Compare and discuss your scores until you gain a better understanding of each other's views.

Levels of agreement may be combined with levels of understanding to produce *six possible scenarios*:

	Misunderstanding		Understanding
Agreement	Scenario 1 The parties agree but do not know it	Scenario 2 The parties agree but one does not know it	Scenario 3 The parties agree and both know it
Disagreement	Scenario 4 The parties disagree but do not know it	Scenario 5 The parties disagree but one does not know it	Scenario 6 The parties disagree and both know it

Confusion

You know there is confusion (between the tables that different people make) when the parties describe the same situation using a different list of actors or characteristics. If confusion is a problem, search for common actors and/or shared characteristics to create some basis for mutual understanding and agreement.

Temporal Learning Opportunities

Instability

You know there is instability (in the same table over time) when the way that you view a topic and characterize actors changes quickly or frequently over time, without any clear justification. If instability is an issue, identify the factors that may explain this (see other techniques in the *Problems* module). You can look for a list of actors and characteristics that are more meaningful. You can also take more time to discuss the ratings or to gather the information you need to complete the exercise.

Resistance to Change

You know there is resistance to change (in the same table over time) when you're aware of learning opportunities and prefer to maintain the existing problems of convergence, polarization, fragmentation, vagueness, disagreement, misunderstanding, confusion, instability or failure to predict. If resistance to change is an issue, identify the factors that may explain this (see other techniques in the *Problems* module) or take more time to discuss the topic, the actors, and their characteristics. Note that the list of actors and their characteristics you identify in a certain situation (which reflects *how* people think) is generally more difficult to change as compared to the actors' ratings (which reflect *what* people think).

Adaptive Learning Opportunities

Failure to Predict

You know there is a failure to predict when real events do not confirm the characteristics and the ratings you applied to the actors in your analysis. To assess the predictive value of your analysis, select key characteristics and their opposites, and then identify outcome indicators that define the meaning of each number on your rating scale (involving the actors' levels of commitment to a project, for instance). Collect reliable information on these indicators in relation to each actor to see if the characteristics are relevant and the ratings are confirmed.

If the failure to predict is an issue, change your ratings or look for characteristics that have better predictive value.

Scaling Up or Down

For Simpler Versions

1. Work with one or two people or with small groups of people who have many common characteristics.

2. Use no more than six actors and no more than six characteristics. Reduce the number of actors by eliminating some or through the *Freelisting* technique. Exclude actors who are least involved or by regrouping actors who clearly share many characteristics.

3. Use drawings or pictures to represent each actor and each characteristic.

4. Describe the actors using a limited set of key characteristics.

5. Do not group the characteristics into categories (Step 9).

6. Rate the actors with a simple scale (using + or – signs, scores from 1 to 3, or simple phrases).

7. To calculate the level of similarity between two sets of scores, divide the number of SAME scores (include scores that are identical or only one point apart) by the TOTAL number of scores (SAME + DIFFERENT).

8. Do the qualitative interpretation described in Steps 11 and 12 and leave out all mathematical calculations and comparisons.

9. Do not discuss the learning opportunities described in Step 17.

For More Advanced Versions

1. Take more time to gather the information you need to complete the exercise.

2. During the exercise, discuss and record the views that participants express.

3. Work with a greater number of people or groups.

4. Use more than six actors and more than six characteristics.

5. Use surveys to find out how people characterize and rate the actors in a topic area.

6. Rate the actors using a scale of 1 to 7 or 1 to 9.

7. Write a detailed description for each actor and for each characteristic.

8. Identify indicators to justify each rating exercise.

9. Do advanced calculations and graphics using RepGrid (http://repgrid.com/SAS/). Do a Focus Analysis to measure the level of similarity between actors and between characteristics. Do a Principal Component Analysis to identify the main connections within a *Social Domain* table or a "Socio Analysis" to measure the similarities between two or more tables.

10. Use *Role Dynamics*, *Network Dynamics* or *Social Dynamics* to understand the interaction between actors.

Readings and Links

Blowers, G.H.; and K.P. O'Connor. 1996. *Personal Construct Psychology in the Clinical Context.* Ottawa, ON, Canada: University of Ottawa Press. 140 pp.

Denicolo, P.; and M.L. Pope. 2001. *Transformative Professional Practice: Personal Construct Approaches to Education and Research.* Chichester, United Kingdom: John Wiley & Sons.

Fransella, F. (ed.). 2003. *International Handbook of Personal Construct Psychology.* Chichester, United Kingdom: John Wiley & Sons.

Gaines, B. R.; and M.L.G. Shaw. 2004. *Web Grid III.* Cobble Hill, BC, Canada: Centre for Person-Computer Studies. Available online at http://tiger.cpsc.ucalgary.ca/, accessed on August 15, 2007.

Jankowicz, A.D. 2004. *The Easy Guide to Repertory Grids.* Chichester, United Kingdom: John Wiley & Sons.

For a discussion of the Personal Construct Psychology of George Kelly see http://repgrid.com/pcp/, accessed on August 17, 2007.

Social Domain: The Profile of Farming Households in Tobacco Growing Regions of Bangladesh

Key Words

Social Domain, household profiles, Bangladesh, agriculture, economic characteristics, environment, tobacco

Authors and Acknowledgement

D.J. Buckles and F. Akhter. The authors wish to acknowledge the efforts of UBINIG staff and farmer leaders of the Nayakrishi Andolon, who helped to facilitate the assessment, and J.M. Chevalier, who provided useful comments on the report.

Context

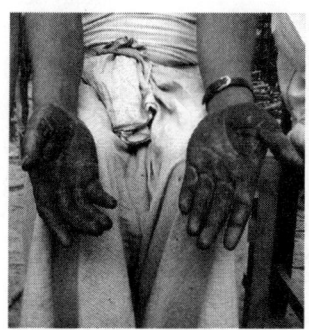

Farmers grow tobacco on some 80,000 acres of agricultural land in Bangladesh, mainly under direct contract with the British American Tobacco Company (BATC). While tobacco is a cash crop for farmers, tobacco farming causes a wide range of environmental, social and health problems in farming communities, including deforestation, soil degradation, indebtedness, and poisoning from the use of pesticides and curing of tobacco leaves. The Government of Bangladesh, as part of its obligations under the World Health Organization's Framework Convention on Tobacco Control, has agreed to reduce the amount of land where tobacco is grown in Bangladesh. One of the main challenges is to find ways to maintain farmers' economic health as they shift away from growing tobacco.

The Bangladesh non-governmental organization UBINIG, in cooperation with Carleton University, Ottawa, Canada, is working with tobacco farmers who have expressed a desire to move away from tobacco into other kinds of farming. A two-year project to organize farmer led experiments with alternatives to tobacco began in 2006. It builds on a long history of collaboration between UBINIG and a national farmer's movement for ecological agriculture (Nayakrishi Andolon) that is active throughout Bangladesh, including the communities where the project is active (Kushtia and Bandarban districts). As they cannot work with all households at the same time, the project needs to form subgroups that can conduct and assess alternatives to tobacco. It wants to do so, based on economic activities, resources and circumstances of households in the villages.

For more information on this project, see Akhter, F. and D. Buckles, 2006, *From Tobacco to Food Production: Assessing Constraints and Transition Strategies in Bangladesh,* First Interim Technical Progress Report to IDRC, 18 pp.

Purpose

To identify household profiles based on similarities and differences meaningful to local people, with a view to forming subgroups that could conduct and assess farmer led experiments with alternatives to tobacco.

Process Summary

UBINIG and the Nayakrishi Andolon convened meetings in seven villages where tobacco farming is common and where farmers had expressed a desire to shift away from growing tobacco. Three villages were in Kusthia district and four in Bandarban district along the Matamuhuri river in the Chittagong Hill Tracts. Local farmer leaders invited villagers to the meetings. The purpose of the meetings was discussed and agreed among participants. The participants in the exercises understood that the results would be used in development of the project, and agreed to share their information.

Ten exercises were conducted—six with men only and four with women only. This was to ensure that women had the opportunity to state their views and raise issues, something that would be difficult for some women in mixed gender groups. The exercises done in the Chittagong Hill Tracts involved some mixed ethnicity groups, including indigenous communities and Bengali settlers as well as some groups made up entirely of people from indigenous communities. The reason for these different groupings was to provide opportunities for differences in cultural perspectives to emerge. Between 12 and 20 people attended each exercise, held in parts of the village with shade and mats for outdoor seating.

Participants were invited to think about (*i*) different kinds of jobs they and immediate family members are engaged in, and (*ii*) the kinds of resources they have at their disposal. They were then asked to think about meaningful differences in these two factors, among them. First, three people at random were asked to identify themselves and stand. They and the remaining participants were then asked to say which two people (and the households they belong to) had some job, activity or resource in common that was different from the third person. The common characteristic was labeled and its opposite was described. A card was prepared with these two opposing features. In some exercises, a drawing or object was used to represent the characteristic. Then, three other people at random stood so that more opposing characteristics could be identified. This proceeded until no new characteristics emerged from the group.

The cards of opposing characteristics were arranged in a column on the ground. Names of participants were written on other cards and arranged in a row to create a table of people and their characteristics. In each exercise, between 8 and 12 people were included in the table.

The extent to which individuals are currently growing tobacco emerged in all exercises and was used by facilitators as a dependent variable. The characteristic was scored first, using a value of 1 for people in the group growing little or no tobacco and rising to 6 for people with large tobacco fields. Seeds such as corn and pulses were used to do the scoring instead of numbers. Once the scoring was complete, the columns (people) were rearranged from the lowest level of tobacco growing to the highest. Other opposing characteristics were then scored by the group for each person, using a scale of 1 to 6. Once the table was complete, participants reviewed the result on the ground, looking for rows and columns with similar scores. As the columns were organized from lowest to highest on the dependent variable (extent of tobacco) the group was able to explore why some farmers grow more tobacco than others. The major findings regarding different kinds of households were discussed and actions defined.

The same process was followed in all exercises, which took about 3 hours each to complete. Participants understood that their information would be used in reports, and agreed to share it with others. The authors later compared results from the different exercises using RepGrid software.

Analysis

The analysis by each group focused on identifying different types of households in the village, why some households grow more tobacco than others, and which kind of household should be involved in conducting or assessing farmer led experiments with tobacco alternatives. Participants in each exercise identified between four and six opposite characteristics they considered to be meaningful distinctions within their group (Table 1). The extent to which people grow tobacco, farm size and the extent to which people grow food crops were characteristics identified by participants in all exercises. Age, frequency of wage work, frequency of tobacco trade, and livestock ownership were characteristics identified by many but not all of the groups. Less common features were fishing, use of a skilled trade (tailoring), share-cropping, and various forms of forestry (collection of firewood and non-timber forest products and *jhum* cultivation, a form of forest-based agriculture). Overall, the features reflect different resources available to households (land, livestock), different activities they engage in (farming, wage work, fishing, forestry), and different stages in life (younger and older people).

Table 1: Characteristics Identified during 10 Exercises in Kushtia and Bandarban, Bangladesh

Group characteristics	Kushtia					Bandarban				
	Kachua women	Bhera-ma men	Chaitan men	Manikpur women	Manikpur men	Sabek men	Sabek settler women	Sabek ethnic women	Dardari men	Maijk men
1 little or no tobacco 6 large tobacco fields	x	x	x	x	x	x	x	x	x	x
1 little or no farmland 6 big farm	x	x	x	x	x	x	x	x	x	x
1 few food crops 6 many food crops	x	x	x	x	x	x	x	x	x	x
1 rarely do wage work 6 frequently do wage work	x		x	x				x		x
1 young 6 old	x	x	x							
1 few or no livestock 6 many livestock					x			x	x	
1 rare tobacco trade 6 frequent tobacco trade		x			x	x				
1 rarely fish 6 frequently fish							x			x
1 rare tailoring 7 frequent tailoring	x									
1 rarely sharecrop 6 frequently sharecrop									x	
1 little or no forestry 6 much forestry								x		x

Table 2 shows five features and related ratings from a men's group in Bherama village, Kushtia. The exercise rated 11 participants on the degree to which they are involved in growing tobacco, ranging from 1 for people with little or no tobacco, to 6 for people with large tobacco fields. They also rated the size of each person's farm, ranging from 1 for people with little or no farmland, to 6 for people with a big farm. For each participant, the group rated the extent of food production (1 for few or no food crops and up to 6 for many food crops), the frequency of work as tobacco traders (1 for rarely trade in tobacco and up to 6 for those who often trade tobacco), and age (ranging from 1 for young to 6 for old).

Table 2: Characteristics and Ratings made by Men in Bherama, Kushtia

Characteristics	Aminul	Hakim	Razzak	Azizul	Nazmul	Alim	Abu Taleb	Huq	Salam
1 little or no tobacco 6 large tobacco fields	1	2	2	2	2	2	3	3	6
1 little or no farmland 6 big farm	6	4	1	2	6	4	2	3	6
1 few food crops 6 many food crops	5	3	4	4	5	2	2	4	3
1 rare tobacco trade 6 frequent tobacco trade	1	1	5	4	2	1	1	6	6
1 young 6 old	3	6	4	2	4	6	5	4	2

Row and column comparisons by the participants pointed to similar profiles among some of the men and their households. For example, it was clear to the group that Salam has a very different profile from the rest. He is a relatively young man with a big farm that mostly produces tobacco. He also engages in the tobacco trade. Nazmul and Aminul also have big farms but they choose to focus on food crops rather than tobacco. By contrast, Huq, Azizul, and Razzak are mainly tobacco traders, dedicating their relatively small farms to a mix of tobacco and food crops. Hakim, Abu Taleb and Alim are older farmers; they combine small amounts of tobacco and food crops on their mid to small-sized farms.

While other relationships in the data could not be easily seen by the participants, group discussion based on their observations noted that age was an important distinguishing factor: participants noted that the BATC directs its promotional campaigns and incentives in Kushtia toward younger farmers. They also pointed out that older farmers often transfer land to their children, and therefore lose control over the way the land is used. Participants concluded that the group was made up of households with one of four profiles: young tobacco farmers; older farmers with small areas of tobacco and food crops; tobacco traders with limited tobacco production of their own; and older, land-rich farmers with the flexibility to avoid tobacco farming. Figure 1 confirms and summarizes this pattern, based on an analysis of the data from Table 2 using RepGrid.

Figure 1: Group Profiles from the Point of View of Men in Bheramara, Kushtia*

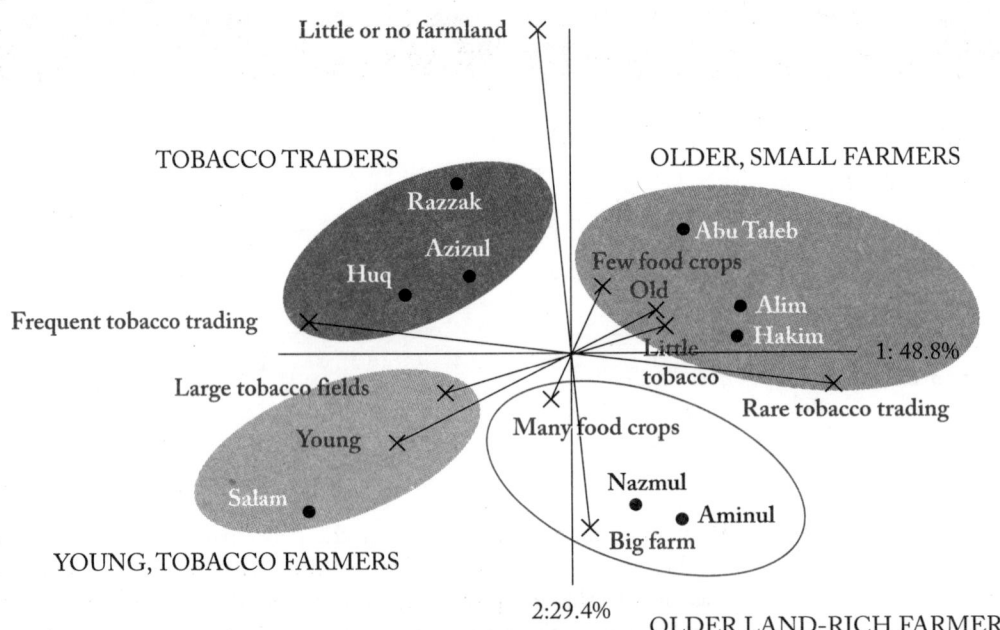

Note: * The statistical technique used to create this figure is called principal component analysis. It simplifies a data set by reducing the multi-dimensional relationships among observed variables to a cross-shaped, two-dimensional representation. In the figure, the scores assigned to people and characteristics (the observed variables) are mapped in relation to two fictive variables. The horizontal line (first component) represents a fictive variable that accounts for 48.8 percent of the total variance in the data (pattern of relationships among dots and crosses). The vertical line (second component) represents a fictive variable that accounts for another 29.4 percent of the total variance. Together, the two principal components account for 78.2 percent of the total variance.

Figure 1 also suggests that being involved in the tobacco trade is particularly important to land-poor farmers such as Razzak, Azizul and Huq. This activity makes them different from other land-poor farmers, giving them a distinct profile that should be taken into account when evaluating alternatives to tobacco production.

Similar profiles were found in other villages, with two notable exceptions. First, half of the exercises raised frequency of wage work as a distinguishing characteristic (Table 1). Some people in the groups rarely do wage work while others do it more often. Wage work in these communities often involves working in tobacco fields or in kilns where tobacco is dried. Three of the four women's groups (Kachua, Manikpur, and Sabek) observed this difference within their groups, as did two of the men's groups (one in Kushtia and another in Bandarban). This observation points to another economic profile relevant to forming groups that will evaluate alternatives to tobacco: wage workers.

Second, regional differences emerged (Table 1). Age was not a distinguishing characteristic in Bandarban but was in Kushtia. Also, the lists of meaningful differences within most of the groups in Bandarban included activities not directly related to farming, such as livestock, fishing, and forestry. These kinds of livelihoods were not mentioned in any of the Kushtia exercises.

Analysis by one of the groups in Bandarban (ethnic women in Sabek) suggests that being involved in forestry is relevant when forming groups that will evaluate alternatives to tobacco growing. Table 3 shows the six characteristics and ratings for individuals in their group. They rated five people on the degree to which they are involved in tobacco production, ranging from 1 for people with little or no tobacco, to 6 for people with large tobacco fields. They also rated how involved people are in forestry work (ranging from 1 for little forestry work, to 6 for frequent forestry work). Forestry work referred mainly to collecting firewood but also included collecting and selling non-timber forest products for medicinal and other uses. The group identified other meaningful differences within their group: the size of each person's farm (ranging from 1 for people with little or no farmland, to 6 for people with a big farm), the extent of vegetable production (1 for few or no vegetable crops, to 6 for many vegetable crops), the frequency of wage work (1 for rarely do wage work, to 6 for frequently do wage work), and the number of livestock they have (ranging from 1 for few or no livestock, to 6 for many livestock).

Table 3: Characteristics and Ratings by Ethnic Women in Sabek, Bandarban

Features	Holachaim	Memasing	Samasing	Dhungmo	Mrakhainu
1 little or no tobacco 6 large tobacco fields	1	6	1	1	1
1 little forestry work 6 frequent forestry work	5	1	6	4	4
1 little wage work 6 frequent wage work	1	1	1	6	4
1 few vegetable crops 6 many vegetable crops	1	6	4	1	1
1 few or no livestock 6 many livestock	2	6	5	1	2
1 little or no farmland 6 big farm	1	6	4	1	1

When participants compared rows and columns and discussed the findings, they concluded that their group had three profiles: established farmers (some of whom grow tobacco); forest workers who collect firewood and other resources from forests; and wage workers (mainly in tobacco production). Figure 2, based on an analysis by the authors using RepGrid, confirms and summarizes this pattern.

Figure 2: Group Profiles from the Point of View of Ethnic Women in Sabek, Bandarban

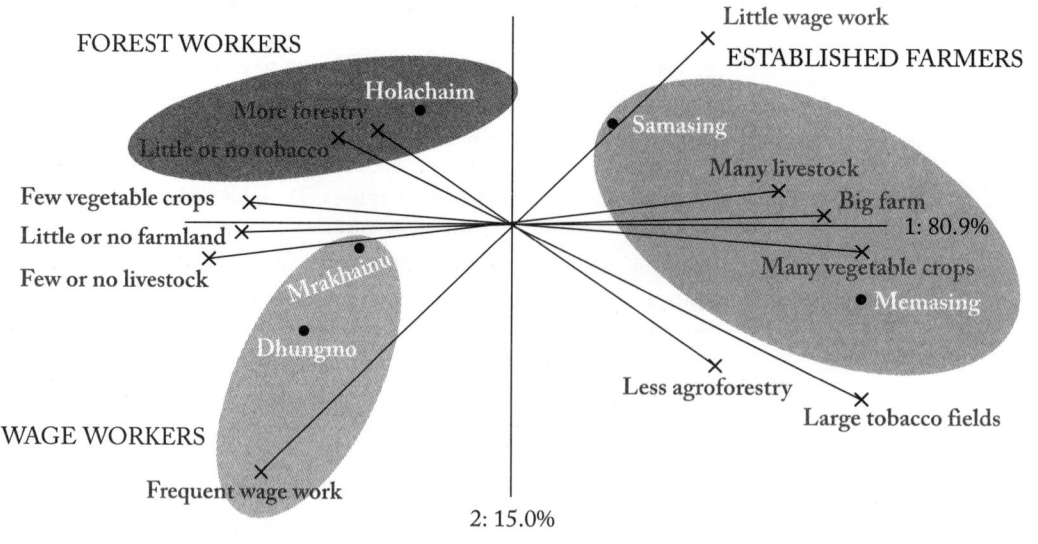

S A S²

Interpretation

Participants interpreted findings only within their own communities. The various discussions converged, however, around a common theme. In general, profiles include households composed of established tobacco farmers, wage workers, land-poor farmers that grow small amounts of tobacco, and tobacco traders. Age tends to separate the farmers focused on tobacco production from those that adopt a mixed strategy or avoid tobacco, at least in Kushtia. Amount of land is also a factor determining the extent to which farmers engage in tobacco production. Owning a big farm gives flexibility: in some communities, farmers with big farms have stayed out of tobacco production by focusing on food crops, livestock and even trade in tobacco. Growing tobacco is the only option for older small farmers.

In comparing all the exercises, the authors saw one important regional difference. In Bandarban, people seem to have access to many ways to earn a living, including fishing, livestock, and forestry. As a result, their profiles are less tightly structured and more diverse compared to Kushtia (Table 1, and Figures 1 and 2). This regional difference stems mostly from the different histories of tobacco in the two regions and access to different sets of resources. Kushtia, once an important food growing region, has been dominated by tobacco production for more than 25 years. Other ways to earn a living have withered, as have resources such as forests and water to support those other options. By contrast, growing tobacco is still relatively new to Bandarban and as a result people and their household profiles are less sharply defined by their relationship to tobacco. This is because extensive forests are nearby and water is abundant in the Matamuhuri watershed, two features that provide alternative livelihoods. The distinct agroforestry practices of the ethnic communities in the region also distinguish them from tobacco-dominated economies.

Action

Participants, the Nayakrishi Andolon and UBINIG decided, as a result of the exercises, to form two different groups in each village: (*i*) farmers leading experiments with alternatives to tobacco, and (*ii*) households (including non-farming households) that would be affected by a widespread shift out of tobacco and whose views need to be taken into account when assessing the gains and losses associated with the alternatives.

In each village, a group of farmers was formed to do experiments with alternatives to tobacco. The group included established tobacco farmers (mainly young men) as well as older, land-poor farmers that had grown tobacco in the previous year. A second group made up of a wider set of household profiles was formed in each village to evaluate the gains and losses associated with the tobacco alternatives. In Kushtia, this group included wage workers and tobacco traders along with the established tobacco farmers and the older land-poor farmers in the first group. In Bandarban, a fifth category of people was incorporated into the assessment group: people who use forest resources, both for tobacco and other purposes.

While the exercises did not reveal significant differences in household characteristics identified by men and women, all parties felt that it was important to continue meeting in gender groups. This would help to ensure that gender differences in economic assessment criteria would be included when considering alternatives to growing tobacco.

Observations on the Process

The process of identifying different household characteristics stimulated a great deal of discussion among participants about the problems of tobacco farming and the need for alternatives. Many were keen to contribute to the exercise even though the method of group formation was new to them. They understood the need to have different types of households evaluate experiments with alternatives to growing tobacco, and recognized the relevance of the characteristics and profiles identified by them for this purpose. While no comparisons could be made across groups until all of the exercises were completed, the results of individual exercises were considered by participants to be useful to the task of group formation and true to the different economic circumstances of households in the village.

V.I.P. (Values, Interests, Positions)

Author	J.M. Chevalier
Purpose	*V.I.P. (Values, Interests, Positions)* helps you compare the positions that stakeholders take on a problem or action with their actual interests and the moral values they hold.

Guiding Principles

1. When you adopt a **position** on a core problem or action, you may make rigid demands or major concessions that do not reflect your actual **interests** or the **moral values** you hold. Negotiations based on this win-lose approach may produce poor results. They leave no room for compromise and lead to solutions that may not last.

2. **Interest-based discussions** may be more effective because they encourage you to think of the various interests you have, including interests that others may share and that you can satisfy in different ways.

3. **Value-based discussions** may also be more effective because they encourage you to speak openly about the moral values and rules of conduct you support. These include rules that others may share and that you may have applied in other situations with positive results.

4. The **usefulness** of an interest-based or a value-based approach to negotiations depends on each situation.

Process

1. Identify an action or situation where the **position or response** you adopt doesn't satisfy you (such as "We don't like it, but we have to use force to stop hunting in the park"). Choose an action or situation that has already occurred, is still going on, or may come about. Define the situation or action as clearly as possible so that the participants can identify the positions, the values, and the interests at stake.

2. Clarify all key ideas used in this technique (values, interests, positions) and replace them with other terms that participants

prefer, if necessary. Make sure that participants do not confuse the idea of "value" with the price that something is worth on the market, or the idea of "acting in one's interest" with "taking an interest in something".

3. Create a diagram by drawing a vertical line that crosses a horizontal line. This gives you a cross within a square. Write 0 where the lines cross. Write your position or response (identified in Step 1) above the diagram using key words or a short sentence.

4. Use the vertical line to rate **how morally acceptable** your position or response is on the whole. Write the highest positive and the lowest negative rating numbers, such as +10 and −10, at opposite ends of this line. Use +10 to represent a position or response that perfectly expresses your values, and −10 to represent one that is contrary to your values. If you want to be more precise, use **indicators** to define the meaning of each number on the scale. If you are the facilitator, do not express positive or negative comments or judgments when you are talking about stakeholder values. See *Active Listening* tips in Part 1.

5. Use the horizontal line to rate the **net gains or losses** that result from your position or response; indicate if these results are expected or observed. Write the highest positive and the lowest negative rating numbers, such as +10 and −10, at opposite ends of this line. Use +10 to represent a position or response that brings you high gains, and −10 to represent a position or response that brings you high losses. If you want to be more precise, identify **indicators** that define the meaning of each number on the scale.

6. In each corner of the diagram, write (or draw) the **scenario** that you obtain when you combine the possible outcomes. To better understand the diagram, you may identify a well-known character or historical figure to represent each of the four scenarios. For instance, monks might represent high moral acceptability combined with high losses (sacrifices); good doctors might represent high moral acceptability combined with high gains (in status and income); drug dealers might represent low moral acceptability combined with high gains (in wealth); and criminals in prison might represent low moral acceptability combined with high losses (in freedom). See example in Step 7.

7. Decide where to locate your position or response (identified in Step 1) on the *horizontal line* representing your actual or expected gains or losses. Then use the *vertical line* to locate your position

or response in relation to the moral values you hold. Draw a line from each location and use the letter "x" to mark the place where the two lines intersect.

Here's an example of a *V.I.P.* diagram (see summary in Step 8):

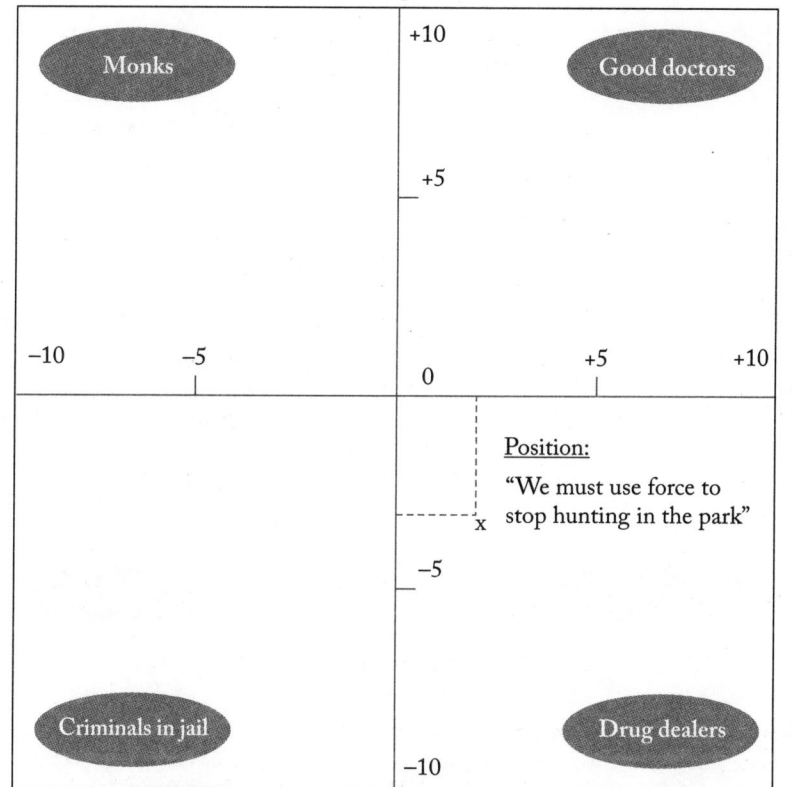

Moral Acceptability
High

Monks

Good doctors

+10

+5

High Losses
(Expected)

−10   −5   0   +5   +10   High Gains
(Expected)

Position:
"We must use force to
stop hunting in the park"

−5

Criminals in jail

Drug dealers

−10

Moral Acceptability
Low

8. Use another "x" mark to locate your best possible position or response, one that would reflect your interests and the moral values you hold. Draw an arrow from the first "x" mark to the second "x" mark. This arrow indicates the direction of **a desired shift, from your actual position to your best possible response**. (You may also use this technique to compare two options for action.)

Here's an example of a complete *V.I.P.* diagram:

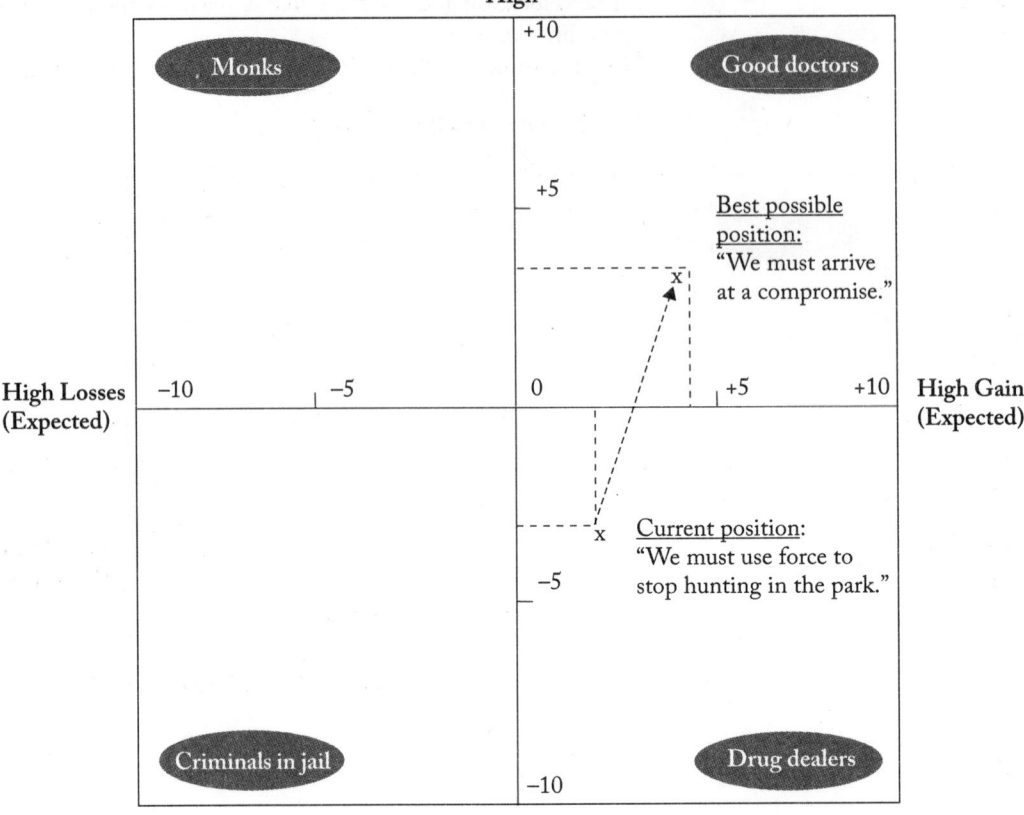

Summary of this example: As forest guards we must use force to stop local people from hunting in the park. But we do not like doing this because we know the people, and we want peace. We recognize that hunting has always been an important part of their traditional livelihood. We also have to admit that force does not work. There may be less hunting in the park but people still hunt a lot, and there is too much violence. Tourists know this and are not coming to the area. Arriving at a compromise would be better for all parties concerned.

Another way to use this diagram is to ask each participant to place its two marks in the diagram (using a different color for each mark). If using this method, decide which question to ask: (*i*) how each participant views its own individual position or response, or (*ii*) how each participant views the position or response adopted by the whole group.

9. Identify which factor—increasing your gains (interests), acting in ways that reflect your moral values—is important to you when

defining your best possible position or response. From the following list, select the scenario that best describes your *V.I.P.* analysis. For instance, the diagram presented in Step 8 suggests a P2 scenario.

P1 P2 P3 (diagram)	Since your initial response *fails to satisfy your interests and your values*, you will shift to a position that satisfies **P1**: …your values mostly **P2**: …your values and interests **P3**: …your interests mostly
P4 P5 (diagram)	Since your initial response *fails to satisfy your interests*, you will shift to a position that satisfies your interests **P4**: …and your values **P5**: …but not your values
P7 P6 (diagram)	Since your initial response *fails to satisfy your values*, you will shift to a position that satisfies your values **P6**: …and your interests **P7**: …but not your interests

Combining V.I.P. and Social Analysis CLIP

10. Discuss what you can do (or could have done) to implement your best possible position or response.

11. Create a table. Write above the table the action or situation identified in Step 1. Insert the list of stakeholders in Column 1. Use results from your *Social Analysis CLIP* to list and rank the stakeholders in Column 1 based on the factors of power, interests, and legitimacy. See example in Step 17, and software (www.sas2.net).

12. Describe each stakeholder's position or response in Column 2 using key words or a short sentence.

13. In the top row insert a scale of five scores: − − (very negative), − (moderately negative), 0 (low/neutral), + (moderately positive), ++ (very positive).

14. For each stakeholder insert the **letter P** (for Position) in the column that reflects the stakeholder's position or response to the action or

situation identified in Step 1. Use the scale appearing in the top row to indicate a neutral position (0), a level of opposition (– or – –), or a level of support (+ or ++) for this action or situation.

15. For each stakeholder insert the **letter I** (for Interests) in the column that reflects the stakeholder's gains or losses resulting from the action or situation (the location of the letter I should match the results of your *Social Analysis CLIP* table). Use the scale in the top row to indicate neutral interests (0), a level of loss (– or – –), or a level of gain (+ or ++) that result from this action or situation.

16. For each stakeholder insert the **letter V** (for Values) in the column that reflects the stakeholder's level of moral satisfaction with its own position or response to the action or situation. Use the scale in the top row to indicate the level of moral satisfaction (–, – –; 0, +, ++) associated with this position or response.

17. Draw a first arrow going from the letter P to the letter I in each stakeholder row. Draw a second arrow going from the letter I to the letter V. These arrows indicate the **degree and the direction of change** that might occur for each party if negotiations better reflected their interests or values.

Here's an example of a *V.I.P.* analysis combined with a *Social Analysis CLIP* table involving two stakeholders only:

Action: Enforcing Conservation Laws in the Forest Park

Stakeholders & categories	Stakeholder position or response	V: Values I: Interests P: Position				
		Negative		Low/Neutral	Positive	
		– –	–	0	+	++
Dominant: Forest guards	Use force		V ←		I ←	P
Marginalized: Hunters	Break law		P → I			
	Burn office		V			

Summary of this example: Local residents are hunting in the park despite laws that prohibit this. Forest guards respond by using force and putting hunters in prison when caught in the act. Forest guards do not like doing this; it goes against what they think forest guards and the Forest Department should be doing. They would prefer to find a peaceful solution that would protect both fauna and local livelihoods at the same time. As for the hunters, they argue that laws forbidding them to hunt in the park threaten their livelihood and way of life. They feel justified in breaking the law and are angry because some hunters have been put in jail. They have decided to set fire to the forest park director's house. But many hunters oppose this action. Many agree that some kind of law is needed to protect local forest animals from extinction and to protect the hunters' livelihood in the long term. Room should be made on both sides for a compromise based on common stakeholder interests and values.

S A S²

18. Identify **alternative positions or options** that could better reflect the interests and values of the parties concerned.

Scaling Up or Down

For Simpler Versions

1. Limit the number of *V.I.P.* diagrams to one or two parties only.

2. Do the *V.I.P.* diagram (Steps 1 to 10) but not the *V.I.P.* diagram combined with *Social Analysis CLIP* (Steps 11 to 18).

3. Do not ask the stakeholders to do the diagrams or tables; instead, use these tools to guide the interview or group facilitation process and to organize your findings.

For More Advanced Versions

1. Take more time to gather the information you need to complete the exercise.

2. During the exercise, discuss and record the views that participants express.

3. Write a description for each stakeholder position and each set of interests and values.

4. Use indicators to define degrees of moral satisfaction and levels of gains and losses.

5. Use *V.I.P.* to compare stakeholder values, interests and positions associated with several responses to a problem or situation.

Reading and Links

Cohen, R. 1991. *Negotiating Across Cultures.* Washington, D.C., USA: United States Institute of Peace Press.

Fisher, R.; and W. Ury. 1981. *Getting to Yes,* 2nd Edition. London, United Kingdom: Penguin Books.

Harass, C.L. 1993. *Give and Take: The Complete Guide to Negotiating Strategies and Techniques.* New York, USA: HarperCollins Publisher.

King, S. 2001. *The Use of Interest Based Negotiation Techniques to Enhance Labor-Management Cooperation.* APEC Human Resources & Development (HRD) Symposium Interactive Session. Mexico City, Mexico. Available online at http://www.fmcs.gov/gnzlz/IBB.htm, accessed on August 17, 2007.

Means, K.; C. Josayma; E. Nielsen; and V. Viriyasakultorn. 2002. *Community-Based Forest Resource Conflict Management: Training Package,* Volume 1, Section 3.3 and Volume 2, Activity 17. Rome, Italy: FAO. Available online at http://www.fao.org/DOCREP/005/Y4300E/Y4300E00.HTM, accessed on August 15, 2007.

Ury, W. 1991. *Getting Past No: Negotiating Your Way from Confrontation to Cooperation.* New York, NY, USA: Bantam Books.

Walsh, E. 1996. *The Negotiator.* New York, USA: The New Yorker.

V.I.P.: Conflict over the Control of Timber in a Municipality in Chiquitania, Bolivia

Key Words

V.I.P. (*Values, Interests, Positions*), conflict management, development projects, forestry, municipalities, Chiquitania, Bolivia

Authors and Acknowledgement

J. Téllez and D.J. Buckles. This report is part of a larger study on forestry issues in Chiquitania, Bolivia supported by Centro Boliviano de Estudios Multidisciplinarios (CEBEM, www.cebem.org). The authors wish to acknowledge the efforts of Pedro Dorado who helped to facilitate the assessment, and J.M. Chevalier who provided useful comments on the report.

Context

Timber in the Chiquitania region of Bolivia includes many precious woods of great value. Currently, timber buyers acquire timber from people and communities at a very low price. They do so by advancing money for basic needs in exchange for commitments to deliver timber at a fixed price. Since many local people have very low incomes and benefit from this method, much of the better wood is captured in this way. Trees are cut in a random way and most timber leaves the area unprocessed.

The Municipal Government has a legal responsibility to help communities develop forest management plans and to ensure that timber is cut legally and according to these plans. It monitors and controls the process by approving timber cutting agreements between buyers and sellers. With help from the Spanish Government, a Municipal Government in the region has set up a project to purchase and partly process timber locally so that communities can realize more of the potential value of the forests. It has opened a small mill, a drying facility and a carpentry shop open for community use. Making sure that the mill has enough high value timber has been difficult because timber buyers are buying timber that was promised to the Municipal Forestry Project by communities. The system of loans and debt forces many people in forest communities to ignore the Project's agreements.

The Forestry Officer employed by the Municipal Government to monitor and authorize all forestry agreements with communities is married to one of the timber buyers in the region. This puts her in a potential conflict of interest. Struggles over the control of high value timber have emerged in at least four communities where her husband is active. The Municipal Government decided that a meeting was needed to develop a strategy to reduce the impact of all timber buyers on the activities of the municipal mill. It invited the lead author, a PhD student undertaking research in the region, to facilitate the discussion.

Purpose

While initially the event purpose was to develop a strategy for dealing with all timber buyers, it shifted during the meeting to a focus on the emerging conflict between the Municipal Forestry Project, the Forestry Officer and a particular timber buyer.

Process Summary

The Mayor of the Municipal Government convened a meeting of elected officials, representatives of the four forest communities, the Director of the Municipal Development Office, the Forestry Officer, the Municipal Legal Counsel, the timber buyer active in the four communities, the Director of the Municipal Forestry Project, and a facilitator (the lead author of this report).

After the Mayor stated the purpose of the meeting, the facilitator began a profile of forestry stakeholders using the SAS[2] technique *Social Analysis CLIP*. The assessment was interrupted when several people accused the Forestry Officer of ignoring what her husband had been doing, namely buying timber that had been committed to the Municipal Forestry Project. They called on the Municipal Government to immediately fire the Forestry Officer. The discussion began to falter. The timber buyer left the group and did not return. The facilitator then asked the group to shift its focus to a discussion of the moral values and interests at stake. This led to an assessment of possible ways to resolve the conflict concerning the Forestry Officer and the timber buyer (her husband) while at the same time meeting the broader goals of the Municipal Forest Project and forest communities.

The assessment continued with participants who represented the four forest communities and the Municipal Forest Project. The Forestry Officer remained to defend herself, but did not participate in the rating exercise. Four possible actions in response to the conflict were discussed and the position of the group on each of these actions assessed in terms of their moral acceptability and the gains and losses (interests) associated with them. A scale of −10 to +10 was used to rate the positions of the group on each action. The meeting ended with the group describing in detail a proposed agreement it felt could be the basis for negotiation with the Forestry Officer and the timber buyer. The participants in the exercise understood that the results would be part of the PhD study by the facilitator, and agreed to share their information so long as the communities and individuals remained anonymous.

Analysis

The group began the exercise by assessing the current situation where the timber buyer pays forest communities very low prices for high-value timber and diverts timber away from the Municipal Forest Project, with the unspoken approval of the Forestry Officer. People argued that allowing the Forestry Officer to ignore the actions of her husband was morally unacceptable to them and would bring very few benefits to the forest communities (due to low sale prices). They gave a value of −5 to the moral acceptability of the current situation and a value of +1 to gains they now have from the sale of timber. This resulted in Position 1 in Figure 1.

Firing the Forestry Officer was an action proposed by a number of participants. The group assessed this as the right thing to do because government officials should not be allowed to favor their own family members when they hold public office. This action received a value of +5 in terms of its moral acceptability. They were aware, however, that doing so would throw the Municipal Forestry Project and all forest communities into an even deeper crisis since the many agreements set up by the Forestry Officer might not go ahead at all. This would affect more than the four communities where the Forestry Officer's husband is active. They also noted that this action would have a political cost for the Municipal Government. It would be embarrassed because the harvesting agreements had failed and because it had fired one of its officials. On balance, the action would result in losses, rated by the group as −8. This assessment resulted in Position 2 in Figure 1.

During the discussion, the Forestry Officer defended herself by saying that if the Municipal Government tried to fire her, she would organize a petition among all forest communities to oppose the action. She argued that many forest communities are satisfied with the harvest agreements they have with timber buyers, and that she has done nothing wrong. The group assessed this proposed action by the Forestry Officer. It decided that even if most of the forest communities supported her petition, this would still not fully satisfy their concerns about the moral acceptability of the timber buyer's actions and the Forestry Officer (−3 on the scale of moral acceptability). Many of the current agreements in communities might go ahead but the Municipal Forest Project would not be able to meet its needs and the Municipal Government would still be embarrassed (−2 on the scale of gains and losses). The group decided that this action would result in fewer losses than firing the Forestry Officer but that it remained morally unacceptable to them (Position 3, Figure 1).

After a lively discussion of these actions and the positions of the group in relation to these actions, the facilitator asked whether or not they could imagine a compromise that would satisfy their interests and the moral values they hold. The group developed a series of conditions it would be willing to negotiate with the timber buyer and the Forestry Officer.

First, the Forestry Officer would need to commit to active monitoring of all harvest agreements made by timber buyers, including her husband, to ensure that high value timber was not diverted from the community and Municipal Forestry Project agreements. Second, the Forestry Officer would need to cooperate with a representative of the Municipal Government who would monitor her work. Third, the timber buyer would need to direct to the Municipal Forestry Project all of the timber it could handle this season. Fourth, the Municipal Government would promptly approve harvest agreements made by the timber buyer as long as the forest communities agreed and had no other options.

The group assessed this proposed agreement and concluded that it would satisfy their current interests (+6 on the scale of gains and losses) and be morally acceptable to them (+6 on the scale of moral acceptability). Their position, shown by the number 4 in Figure 1, reflected the group's view that while the other actions failed to satisfy their interests and their moral values, the proposed agreement could satisfy both.

Figure 1: Positions of the Representatives of Forest Communities and the Municipal Forestry Project on Proposed Actions

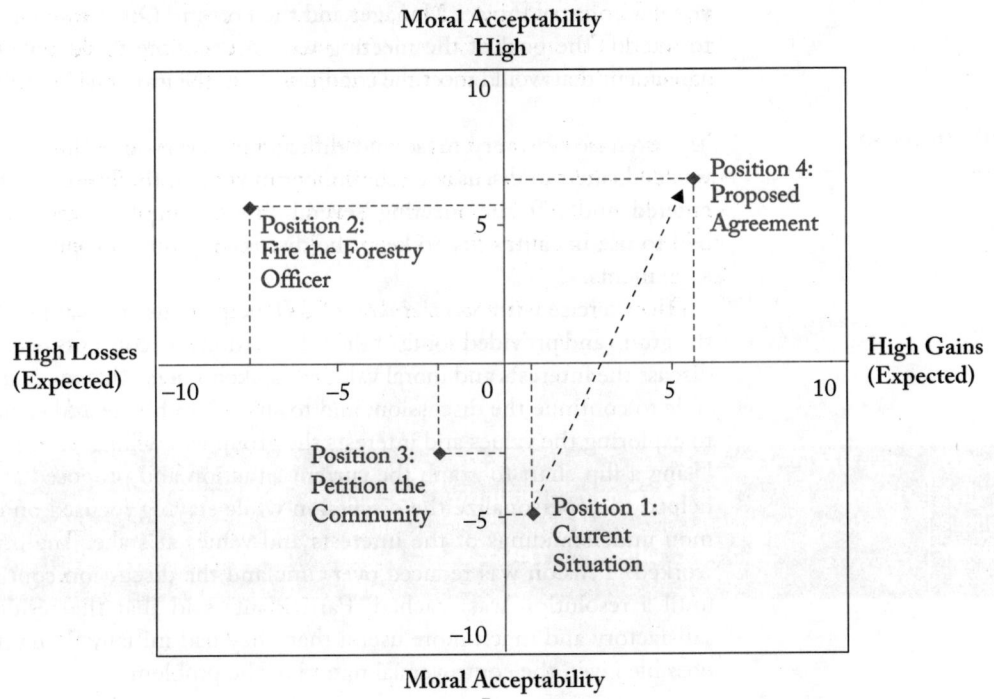

Interpretation	The group was aware that it needed to shift to a position that could satisfy both its interests and moral values while at the same time allowing for compromise. People were willing to negotiate an agreement that would also benefit the timber buyer because the Municipal Forestry Project's capacity to purchase and process timber was limited and the season's harvest would end soon, with the start of the rainy season. Any further delays or complications would reduce the short-term success of the Municipal Forestry Project. This would in turn affect the way forest communities saw its long-term potential and their level of commitment to the project. The group was also aware that some concrete benefits were currently coming to local people, thanks in part to the work of the Forestry Officer. Her conflict of interest could be managed by making it clear to all that favoritism and diverting of wood by timber buyers would not be tolerated by the leaders in the municipality and other stakeholders in the forest sector.
Action	The Forestry Officer made a verbal commitment to the conditions set out in the proposed agreement. The Municipal Government decided to meet the timber buyer in question the next day. The Municipal lawyer, the Forestry Project Manager and the Forestry Officer were invited to attend. The goal of the meeting was to negotiate the details of an agreement that would meet the conditions that the group had developed.
Observations on the Process	The exercise was very tense and difficult for everyone. A lot of time was dedicated to discussion. The timber buyer and the Forestry Officer entered and left the meeting several times. Sometimes the Mayor had to use his authority to keep the discussion going, despite the disagreements.

The exercise with *Social Analysis CLIP* helped raise relevant issues in the group and provided some of the information and concepts needed to discuss the interests and moral values of stakeholders. This made it possible to continue the discussion, and to shift from blame and criticism, to exploring the values and interests the group was willing to negotiate. Using a flip chart to graph the current situation and proposed actions helped to depersonalize the discussion while staying focused on common understandings of the interests and values at stake. The process worked. Tension was reduced over time and the discussion continued until a resolution was reached. Participants said that the result was satisfactory and much more useful than they had initially thought was possible given the controversial nature of the problem.

Post-script: The agreement held until the end of the harvest season. Although the Municipal Forestry Project did not get all of the wood it needed, it got enough to show the Project's potential to the forestry communities. The Forestry Officer was eventually fired and a new person was hired under much clearer working arrangements.

Ideal Scenario

Author

J.M. Chevalier

Acknowledgement

Ideal Scenario is a SAS² adaptation of visioning techniques, some widely used in the field of participatory research (see *Readings and Links*).

Purpose

Ideal Scenario offers several techniques that help you develop visions of an ideal future and take advantage of current strengths and accomplishments while doing so. These techniques include the *Tree of Means and Ends*, a diagram that turns your analysis of a core problem and its causes and effects (using *Problem Tree*) into a statement about your main objective, the ways to achieve it, and the ends that motivate you to pursue it. *I Have a Dream!* starts with a provocative idea and explores its implications. The *Vision Circle* develops a gradual statement about the ideal future, with guided visualization for the group and contributions from individual participants. The *Ideal Scenario Tapestry* brings together a collection of vision drawings using real or imaginary life forms or scenes. Another option is *Two Truths and a Lie*, a game where participants describe three impressive goals they have achieved, one of which is a lie that others must detect.

Guiding Principle

1. It is important that stakeholders communicate their visions for the future when managing a problem or pursuing an objective.

Process

1. Identify **a core problem** or **a main objective** where you need to use *Ideal Scenario*. Define the problem or objective as clearly as possible. Clarify the purpose of this exercise.

2. Create an ideal scenario using one or more of the following techniques. When preparing their scenarios, participants can **appreciate** and incorporate the contributions they can make to their vision for the future based on the strengths (such as shared values, problem solving skills, economic assets, and so on) and accomplishments they already have.

- **The tree of means and ends**: Identify a core problem and its causes and effects using *Problem Tree*. Then, draw a new logical tree by replacing the core **problem** with a main **objective**. Replace the first-level and second-level causes below your core problem with the **means** or ways to achieve your main objective. To help identify these means, ask yourself "What do we need to do or have to achieve our main objective?" Make sure to include all necessary means, but leave out any that you think will have undesirable effects. Record each means on its own card using a short positive sentence. Decide where to place the cards (below the main objective) and draw lines to connect the first-level and the second-level means. Use the same process to replace the first-level and the second-level effects of your core problem with the specific **ends** (or aims) that you believe are important to achieve together with your main objective (see example below).

  You can arrange all the cards in a chronological order and put them in a sequence that shows how to achieve your main objective step by step. After you have done this, you may tell a story that starts with the current situation and describes all the individual and group actions you will need to produce a happy ending.

- **I have a dream**: Create a vision statement that starts with the words "I have a dream", such as "I have a dream! Imagine that cities no longer had cars!" Think about and put into words everything that is positive about your dream, such as the gains that might result, the principles that would make it work, and how individual or group strengths and accomplishments would be part of it.

- **Vision circle**: Invite participants to sit in a circle facing outwards, with their eyes closed. Ask the participants to quietly visualize an ideal scenario, a world "where our children can thrive" that includes individual and group strengths and accomplishments. Invite someone chosen at random to share his or her vision. Others can then join in one at a time (at random or by going around the circle). Each person may repeat the statements already heard and add new elements to the vision. The facilitator may offer images to guide the visualization (such as walking through a natural resource area that people want to preserve). The facilitator should also keep a record of how the dream progresses (especially noting elements that are mentioned by some participants at the beginning of the process but that may be forgotten later).

- **Ideal scenario tapestry**: Invite participants to list the elements of their ideal scenario (including current strengths and accomplishments) and to represent them in a drawing using good quality art paper and crayons (such as pastel), if possible. Participants may use real or imaginary life forms or scenes (such as animals, plants, landscapes, activities) to reflect their vision of the future. Ask participants to explain their drawings to others. Put all the drawings together into a tapestry of ideal scenarios.

- **Two truths and a lie**: Invite participants to prepare three stories of great things they have accomplished in relation to their project or program goals. Two of these stories must be true. The third story must be a convincing lie, something they would like to achieve in the future using their existing strengths. Other participants must find which of the three stories is a lie.

Scaling Up or Down

For Simpler Versions

1. Do not use the *Tree of Means and Ends*.

For More Advanced Versions

1. Take more time to develop your ideal scenario.
2. During the exercise, record the views that participants express. Write a description for each ideal scenario element.

Reading and Links

Borrini-Feyerabend, G.; and M. Brown. 1997. "Social Actors and Stake-holders." in G. Borrini-Feyerabend (ed.). *Beyond Fences: Seeking Social Sustainability in Conservation Gland*. Switzerland: IUCN. Available online at http://www.iucn.org/themes/spg/Files/beyond_fences/bf_section4_1.html, accessed on August 16, 2007.

Cooperrider, D.L.; and S. Srivastva. 1987. "Appreciative Inquiry in Organizational Life" in R. Woodman and W. Pasmore (eds). *Research in Organizational Change and Development*. Volume 1. Greenwich, CT USA: JAI Press. pp. 129–169.

Future Search. 'Future Search Network', Philadelphia, PA, USA. Available online at http://www.futuresearch.net, accessed on August 15, 2007.

Hosking, D.M. nd. 'Relational Constructionism', Utrecht, The Netherlands. Available online at http://www.relational-constructionism.org/, accessed on August 16, 2007.

IISD (International Institute for Sustainable Development). 2002. *Appreciative Inquiry and Community Development.* Winnipeg, MN, Canada: International Institute for Sustainable Development. Available online at http://www.iisd.org/ai, accessed on August 17, 2007.

Informal Working Group on Participatory Approaches and Methods. nd. *Guided Imagery.* Rome, Italy: FAO. Available online at http://www.fao.org/Participation, accessed on August 17, 2007.

Mind Tools. nd. *Provocation.* Wimbledon, London, United Kingdom: Mindtools.com. Available online at http://www.mindtools.com/pages/article/newCT_08.htm, accessed on August 15, 2007.

Storti, Deirdra. *Developing a Community Vision, Conducting a Visioning Process.* (Thesis outline). Rhode Island, USA: Sea Grant College. Available online at http://seagrant.gso.uri.edu/scc/tools/VisionProcess.PDF, accessed on August 15, 2007. (For an overview of the steps of a community vision process.)

Ideal Scenario: The Ideal Scenario of Legal Title in Siddeshwarwadi, Maharashtra, India

Key Words	*Ideal Scenario*, India, tribal population, land tenure, environment
Authors	D.J. Buckles, R. Khedkar, D. Patil, B. Ghevde.
Context	

Siddeshwarwadi is a hamlet of non-literate and very poor tribal people known as the *Katkari*. Most healthy men, women, and children work as bonded labor at brick-making kilns in the region. They move from one place to another, from season to season, to find work, leaving their homes unattended for months at a time. The hamlet is located on parts of three properties owned by people in the nearby caste village (Siddeshwar) some 110 km south-east of Mumbai, Maharashtra. The *Katkari* do not have legal title to the land even though they have lived there for many generations and special clauses in Indian law affirm the rights of tribal people to residential lands (Goathan).

A non-governmental organization (SOBTI) has been working in Siddeshwarwadi and other *Katkari* communities for many years and had conducted an assessment of the problem with residents (using *Problem Tree*, see the present Guide). It had shown that while residents did not feel threatened with immediate eviction from their village they felt strongly that the causes and effects of not having titles to the land touched on matters of more immediate concern. They wanted to do something about it but could not imagine how to inspire other residents to act.

Purpose

To imagine an ideal scenario that residents of Siddeshwarwadi could achieve if they had legal title to residential land.

Process Summary

SOBTI convened an evening meeting in Siddeshwarwadi of the same people who were involved in earlier discussions (see *Problem Tree*). Most attended (seven men and three women) along with several other residents who had not been part of the previous meeting. The core problem (no legal tenure) was discussed and converted into a positive goal shared by the participants (Siddeshwarwadi becomes a legal hamlet). Participants then reviewed the reasons they do not have title to the residential lands (identified during the *Problem Tree* exercise) and converted these causes into positive statements of what they would have to do (means) to secure title. They also reviewed the effects of the problem of not having title (identified using the *Problem Tree*), and converted these into positive statements (ends) of things that could be achieved if they had secure title. The multi-level relationships were displayed in a visual way using cards on a wall and the main findings discussed in detail. The facilitators prepared a draft report on the assessment afterwards. The participants knew that a report would be prepared based on the results, and agreed to share their information.

Analysis

The **ends** and **means** that participants stated during the exercise are presented in Figure 1. The means to achieve the goal (Siddeshwarwadi becomes a legal hamlet) were separated into two categories: those that residents have control over, and those that depend largely on others. Discussion focused on the means within their control, and in particular the fact that all residents would have to take the problem seriously, and collectively demand their rights. Participants also recognized that government would need to act in favor of the hamlet and landowners would need to be convinced to sell or give the land to the hamlet.

If the initial goal was achieved, the *Katkari* could act on many dreams important to them. Government programs that support tribal people could be used to: (*i*) build a school in the hamlet, which would in turn give their children an opportunity to learn and get access to better jobs; (*ii*) build better houses, a road to the village, and a health center, bringing important overall improvements to the quality of life in the village. Presently, these programs were not available to them because of the insecurity of the village land. The participants also said that their incomes would be more stable if they could use their homesteads to raise livestock and grow market vegetables, something not allowed by the current landowners. The dream that generated the most excitement in the group, however, was the idea of building a village stage for cultural events. The *Katkari* have a unique style of music and dance they enjoy immensely. They said that having a stage on which to perform would bring immense benefits to community life and foster unity among residents.

Interpretation

The vision of the future that emerged through the assessment, was inspiring for the participants not only because they saw how the basic amenities of life could improve but also because their dignity and value as individuals and as a distinct community could be affirmed. The possibility of creating a cultural space of their own was particularly important to the participants as they and the *Katkari* in general take particular joy in their own songs, music, and dance. The uncertainty of the participants regarding how to convince other *Katkari* that they should join forces to address the problem was resolved by developing a vision of the future in which they had a cultural life they could enjoy.

Figure 1: Ideal Scenario, Siddeshwarwadi, Maharashtra, India

Ends

Low health costs → Improved health → Better houses → Health facilities → A road and better communication → Basic services available in the village

Unity in hamlet → A better life → Celebrations and cultural events → A stage for cultural events

Stable livelihoods → Children get good jobs → Children educated → School for children in hamlet

Sense of belonging → Privacy and security → Each family has its own house

Stable livelihoods → Various job options → Adequate space to grow vegetables and keep livestock

Siddesharwadi is a legal hamlet

People are serious about the problem → Enhanced awareness / People know legal rights

Land owners have agreed to give/sell the land to the hamlet

Government is forced to act in favor of hamlet

People demand legal title → People attend village Gram Sabha / People are organized and mobilized / People are not afraid of the landowners

Means

Action

Participants decided to discuss their collective dreams with other members of their community, with a particular focus on the cultural stage. If the response was positive, they would organize a petition to the village authorities for support during an upcoming general assembly (*Gram Sabha*). As a symbol of their resolve, the participants and other residents later raised and anointed a stone pillar marking the entrance to the hamlet. Rituals of this kind had marked the boundaries of *Katkari* communities in the past. They also noted that the gesture could be seen positively by the landowners as an indication of the proposed legal limit of their village, beyond which they would not try to expand. SOBTI decided to support these village actions by facilitating an assessment of the stakeholders involved in the *Gram Sabha*, so residents could know how best to approach them.

Observations on the Process

Initially, participants could not imagine the main goal of having legal title to the hamlet because it seemed beyond the reach of any one person. They also thought that the idea of "dreams" was to be taken literally, as in the dreams people have when they are asleep. The idea of a group dream emerged when someone suggested that they build a stage for cultural events. This captured the imagination of the group and stimulated their thinking about different ways their lives could be improved as a community. They said that they had never before considered what it meant to have a collective dream. The participants indicated that they were moved by the breadth and depth of the picture of their community that emerged from the exercise, something they had not thought possible. They also noted that the means identified during the exercise, and in particular inspiring villagers to take the problem seriously, were very relevant to their circumstances and worth pursuing.

Option Domain

Author

J.M. Chevalier

Acknowledgement

Option Domain is a SAS[2] adaptation and development of the concepts and techniques of Personal Construct Psychology (see in particular the works of Kelly, http://repgrid.com/pcp/; Jankowicz, 2004; and Gaines and Shaw, 2004).

Purpose

Option Domain examines how people view options in a situation using words and characteristics that participants themselves choose and define. It also shows how people negotiate their views of options across social and cultural boundaries. The technique may be used to test people's views against experience, solve problems, and learn in the process.

Guiding Principles

1. People make constant efforts to understand and influence other people's views, beliefs, and expectations in life. They do this through role interaction, communications, and strategic action. People's views and knowledge of reality are thus products of social behavior developed across cultural and social boundaries.

2. Your knowledge and understanding of options in a situation is based on how you create and organize relations between alternative options and their characteristics in a particular topic area. You can thus use *Option Domain* to examine:

   (a) A **domain of action** (such as managing natural resources in a certain area);

   (b) **Options** in a domain of action (such as ways of managing natural resources in a certain region);

   (c) **Characteristics** that you organize into continua from one pole to its opposite and that you apply to existing options (for example, you may describe legal measures as more conflictual than technical measures);

   (d) **Relations** consisting of degrees of similarity or difference between options or characteristics (for example, you may describe legal measures that are more conflictual as also costing less compared with technical measures).

3. *Option Domain* is an application of Domain Analysis, a general technique that you can also use to analyze stakeholder profiles (see *Social Domain*), problems (see *Problem Domain*), value systems (see *Value Domain*), and elements in Nature (*Domain Analysis*).

4. Your views of existing options and their characteristics may be logical and coherent. At the same time your views may be flexible and may change according to context. These levels of **coherence** and **flexibility** will vary from one topic or situation to another.

5. You can test your knowledge and views against your experience of reality and develop **new relationships** among existing options and their characteristics. *Option Domain* may thus reveal **learning opportunities** such as overcoming convergence, polarization, fragmentation, vagueness, disagreement, misunderstanding, confusion, instability, resistance to change, and failure to predict.

Process

Mapping Your
Knowledge and Views

1. Identify a **topic area** where you need to use *Option Domain*. Define the topic as clearly as possible, and clarify the purpose of your analysis. For instance, you may focus on ways to manage your local bay fisheries.

2. Identify existing **options for action** within your topic area. Using the same example, you may focus on options to better manage local bay fisheries. These options might include (A) limiting the access to local residents only, (B) applying for state funding, (C) mobilizing political support, (D) obtaining adequate representation and participation, (E) regulating the fisheries, (F) rotating the fisheries, and (G) repopulating some species. These are Options A to G.

   Write (or draw) each option on its own card and describe it on the reverse side of the card. Each option should be clearly defined with the details summarized on a **flipchart**, if necessary. This will help you assess the options.

   The minimum number of options is usually 6 and the maximum is 12. You can **supply** or **negotiate** some or all of these options or simply **ask** the participants to identify them, depending on the purpose of the exercise and your role as facilitator.

3. Create a table. Begin the table by writing **Characteristics** at the top of Column 1. Then, place all the option cards in the top row. Here is an example of a table using the list of options created in Step 2:

Characteristics	Option A Limit access	Option B State funding	Option C Political support	Option D Representation & participation	Option E Regulate	Option F Rotate	Option G Repopulate

4. Choose a **key characteristic** that you can use to rate all the options and that you may want to explain (such as the level of difficulty needed to implement each option). You can supply or negotiate this key characteristic or ask the participants to identify it, depending on the purpose of the exercise and your role as facilitator. If you don't need or can't identify this characteristic, go to Step 7.

   Write down this characteristic on a card, using one or two key words (such as "less difficult"). Give it a score of 1. Add the opposite characteristic (such as "more difficult") on the same card and give it a score of 7. Describe the characteristic and its opposite on the reverse side of the card. If you don't want middle scores that may have ambiguous meanings, use a rating scale with an even number of points (such as 1 to 4 or 1 to 6). Place the card showing these opposite characteristics and scores in the second row (first column; see the table in Step 5).

5. Discuss the **score for each option** until participants reach an agreement. Use the same rating scale that you applied in Step 4, from 1 to 7. You can give the same score to two or several options. Record each score on its own card. To help you interpret the results of this exercise, write the reason given for each score on the reverse side of its card. If the characteristic and its opposite identified in Step 4 do not apply to an option, don't write anything on the card.

   Place each score card in the second row, below the corresponding option, as in the following table:

Characteristics	Option A Limit access	Option B State funding	Option C Political support	Option D Representation & participation	Option E Regulate	Option F Rotate	Option G Repopulate
Less difficult (1) More difficult (7)	7	7	5	4	7	6	3

Do not use **averages** when people have disagreements about scores. Instead discuss the issue until you reach an agreement based on consensus or a majority vote.

If you want this exercise to be more precise, identify **indicators** that define the meaning of each number on the scale. If you don't want to use written numbers when rating the options, use simple **phrases** first and then convert the phrases into measurable objects (from 1 to 7 twigs, stones, noodles or seeds). Another option is to score each option with a scale of 1 to 5 using 5 cards colored white (value 1), light grey (value 2), medium grey (value 3), dark grey (value 4), and black (value 5).

Another rating technique (see *Tree Mapping*) consists in creating a new set of cards for all the options and dividing the cards into two **piles** of any size: one pile that best represents the characteristic, and the other pile that best represents its opposite. Repeat the same exercise with each pile by dividing the options into those that best represent the pile characteristic and those that fall somewhere between the characteristic and its opposite. Do this several times until you have rated all the options along the continuum from one characteristic to its opposite.

6. **Reorganize** all your option cards (row 1) and score cards (row 2), arranging the cards from the highest score to the lowest, as in the following table. This will help you interpret the table and explain the key characteristic you identified in Step 4 (such as the fact that some options are more difficult to implement than others). This step is optional.

Characteristics	Option A Limit access	Option B State funding	Option E Regulate	Option F Rotate	Option C Political support	Option D Representation & participation	Option G Repopulate
Less difficult (1) More difficult (7)	7	7	7	6	5	4	3

7. Choose three option cards from the top row at random. Identify two of them (a pair) that are the same in some way, and different from the third. Then, identify what it is these two have in common, something that is *relevant to your topic and the purpose of your exercise*. Write down the characteristic they share (such as both are "short-term options") on a new card and give the characteristic a score of 1. Place the card in the first column, below the second row.

Then, identify what makes the **third option different from the pair**. Write down this opposite characteristic (such as this is a "long-term option") on the same card that you used to write the pair characteristic, and give it a score of 7. If you don't want middle scores that may have ambiguous meanings, use a rating scale with an even number of points (such as 1 to 4 or 1 to 6). Write down a clear definition of the characteristic and its opposite on the reverse side of the card.

Here are some tips to help you identify a characteristic and its opposite:

(a) You can **supply** or **negotiate** each characteristic and its opposite or **ask** the participants to identify them.

(b) The characteristics you identify should be **relevant** to your topic area. They should also be **focused** and **clear**, consisting of **concrete** nouns, actions or verbs ending in "-ing" rather than abstract terms, qualities or ideas.

(c) If the characteristics are vague or sound like clichés, use the *Laddering Down* technique to make them more meaningful and detailed. Ask "What do you mean by this?", "Can you give an example of this?", "How can you tell this?", or "In what way is this true?" (for instance, "In what way is this option more difficult to implement compared with the others?").

(d) When identifying the opposite of a characteristic, don't use **negative phrases**, such as "not local" to describe the opposite of "local". Negative phrases tend to be vague and meaningless. Use *Laddering Down* questions (such as "What do you mean by this?") to get a precise expression of an opposite which may vary according to the situation or topic. For instance, the opposite of "local" could be either "regional" or "national", depending on the context.

(e) When using characteristics to describe each option, do not interpret the descriptions as statements of facts that are either right or wrong. *Option Domain* statements should be **accurate** only in the sense of truly reflecting people's views and knowledge of reality.

(f) If a characteristic and its opposite **do not apply** to several options, try rewording them or eliminate the characteristic and its opposite.

(g) For other means to identify characteristics and their opposites, see Step 9.

8. Use the characteristic and it opposite created in Step 7 to **rate all the options** again, from 1 to 7. Discuss the score for each option until participants reach an agreement (do not use averages when people have disagreements about scores). Identify **indicators** that define the meaning of each number on the scale, if necessary. You can give the same score to two or several options. Record each score on its own card. To help you interpret the results at the end of this exercise, write the reason given for a score on the reverse side of its card. If the characteristic and its opposite do not apply to an option, do not write anything on the card. If the scores are nearly the same for all options, redefine the characteristic and its opposite or eliminate them.

Place each score card in the third row, below the corresponding option. Here is an example of a table that has two characteristics and their opposites:

Characteristics	Option A Limit access	Option B State funding	Option E Regulate	Option F Rotate	Option C Political support	Option D Representation & participation	Option G Repopulate
Less difficult (1) More difficult (7)	7	7	7	6	5	4	3
Costs less (1) Costs more (7)	2	2	7	6	1	5	6

9. Repeat the process described in Steps 7 to identify **other characteristics and their opposites**.

You cannot use a characteristic together with its opposite more than once, but you can use a characteristic *or* its opposite separately more than once (such as "new" as opposed to "old" in one case, and then "new" as opposed to "recurrent" in the other case).

If the participants cannot identify what it is that two options have in common or what makes the third option different from the pair, ask the question in another way, apply the *Laddering Down* technique (see Step 7), choose another three option cards at random, choose two cards at random or choose two cards instead of three. You can also use one of the techniques described next.

You can use other participatory techniques to identify characteristics and their opposites, without comparing option cards chosen at random. A simple technique consists in asking the **catch-all question**: "Can you think of some new, different characteristic and its opposite?" Another option is the **full context** procedure where you look at all options and find out two that are the most similar and why, and then the option that is the most different from these and ask again why. You can also use **description and storytelling** to explore your topic area (such as describing an ideal scenario where natural resources are well managed), and then use this information to identify the options and their characteristics, with the help of the *Laddering Down* technique (see Step 7).

To identify several characteristics and their opposites in a **short time**, divide all participants into groups of two or three. Ask each group to choose three option cards at random and to identify a relevant characteristic and its opposite (using the process described in Step 7). Collect these new characteristics and their opposites, discuss and clarify their meaning, and group together those that are the same.

10. Repeat the process described in Step 8 to rate all the options again using the new characteristics and their opposites. Add a new row for each characteristic and its opposite and record each score and the reason given for it on the corresponding card. Place each score card in its row, below the corresponding option.

When placing characteristics and their opposites in the first column of your table, you may organize them in order of importance. This will help you interpret the table at the end of the exercise.

To do the ratings in a **shorter time**, divide all participants into smaller groups. Then, ask each group to choose a different characteristic and its opposite, and to use these to rate all the options. Use this technique only if the participants do not need to be involved in all the ratings.

Here is an example of a table involving five new characteristics and their opposites:

Characteristics		Option A Limit access	Option B State funding	Option E Regulate	Option F Rotate	Option C Political support	Option D Representation & participation	Option G Repopulate
Less difficult	(1)	5	7	7	6	5	4	3
More difficult	(7)							
Costs less	(1)	2	2	7	6	1	5	5
Costs more	(7)							
Depends on us	(1)	5	7	5	2	1	3	2
Depends on others	(7)							
Short term	(1)	5	4	6	4	4	2	5
Long term	(7)							
Less conflictive	(1)	4	1	3	2	3	1	2
More conflictive	(7)							
Legally more viable	(1)	6	1	1	1	1	2	1
Legally less viable	(7)							
Situation good	(1)	2	5	6	7	3	3	7
Situation bad	(7)							

11. You can **add up the scores for each column** only if all the rows involve negative and positive characteristics placed at the same poles of each continuum (as in the table shown in Step 10). The total column score gives you the overall evaluation of each corresponding option.

12. If you have many characteristics, you can group them into the appropriate **categories** supplied by the facilitator or created and defined by the participants (such as characteristics that concern the economic aspects of an option, those that concern the political aspects, and so on; see *Sorting*). You can rank the characteristics and their opposites within each category by order of importance. This will help you interpret the table at the end of the exercise.

Interpreting the Results

13. To interpret your *Option Domain* analysis, start with a **review** of the **process** itself, including the way that participants interacted and reached decisions at each step of the process. You can also review the **substance** of the exercise, including the topic that participants selected, their purpose in doing the exercise, the options and the characteristics they identified, the kind of information or

knowledge they used to rate the options, and so on. Summarize all the main points of your review.

14. To interpret the final table (see Step 10), start with a **snapshot** discussion of column scores that describe the options. Look for things that are obvious about the **options**, such as: the way each of them is characterized; whether the scores tend to be in the middle or closer to the poles; if some options have the same scores as others or come close, and so on.

You can then look at row ratings to see if there is anything obvious about the **characteristics**, such as: the fact that some characteristics have scores that vary little and others a lot; some characteristics are more meaningful compared with others that are repetitive or descriptive; the ratings for one row coincide with the ratings for another row (or for the key characteristic identified in Step 5) or they are nearly the opposite; and so on.

Summarize all the main points of your snapshot discussion.

15. To interpret the column scores in greater detail, look for the **options that are similar** and summarize the characteristics they share. You can **group together** these similar options by moving the columns around and placing them side by side (use masking tape to stick the column cards together). You will know that two or more options are alike when they have similar row scores for most characteristics, including the most important ones. In the table shown in Step 10, options involving technical measures such as rotation and repopulation (Options F and G) are very much alike. These measures will be costly and take some time but they are legally viable, they will not cause conflict, and they depend mostly on the fishers.

To help people participate in the analysis, prepare and distribute copies of your option cards among the participants. Leave the original cards in the table. Ask each participant to identify other options with row scores that are identical or similar to theirs. Give special attention to similarities in the first rows, those that describe the most important characteristics (see Step 10). Each group formed around similar cards should then prepare and present a brief description of what their options have *in common*. When a group presents its option cards, other groups may come closer to the group if they feel their cards are similar in significant ways or distance themselves if the differences are more important than the similarities. Following this, all participants should discuss the *main differences* observed between groups.

S A S²

To calculate the level of difference between two columns, calculate the sum of differences (SD) between same-row scores (leave out rows that have empty squares). You then calculate the total maximum difference for all scores (this is MS, the maximum score, minus 1, multiplied by C, the number of row characteristics that got ratings). The level of difference between two options is SD divided by the total maximum difference for all scores, multiplied by 100. To turn this level of difference into a percentage similarity score, subtract it from 100. In other words:

$$100 - \frac{SD \times 100}{(MS - 1) \times C}$$

Define the points where you consider levels of similarities between options to be high or low.

Using the table created in Step 10 as an example, the sum of differences (SD) between the recorded scores for options F and G is 5 and the total maximum difference is 42 [(7 − 1) × 7]. This results in a difference of 12 percent (5/42 × 100). Looking at it another way, the two options are similar at a level of 88 percent.

When comparing several options, you can focus on those row characteristics that are more important or interesting. If you focus on **two characteristics** only, you can create a diagram by drawing a vertical line that crosses a horizontal line. This creates a cross inside a square. If your scale is 1 to 7, write 1 and 7 at opposite ends of both the horizontal line and the vertical line; indicate what these minimum and maximum scores actually mean. Write 4 where the two lines cross. Place each option in the diagram by locating its score on the horizontal line and then its score on the vertical line. Connect the marks from the two lines, using the letter "x" to mark the place where they meet. The closer two options are in the diagram, the more similar they are. Here is an example of this cross-shaped diagram:

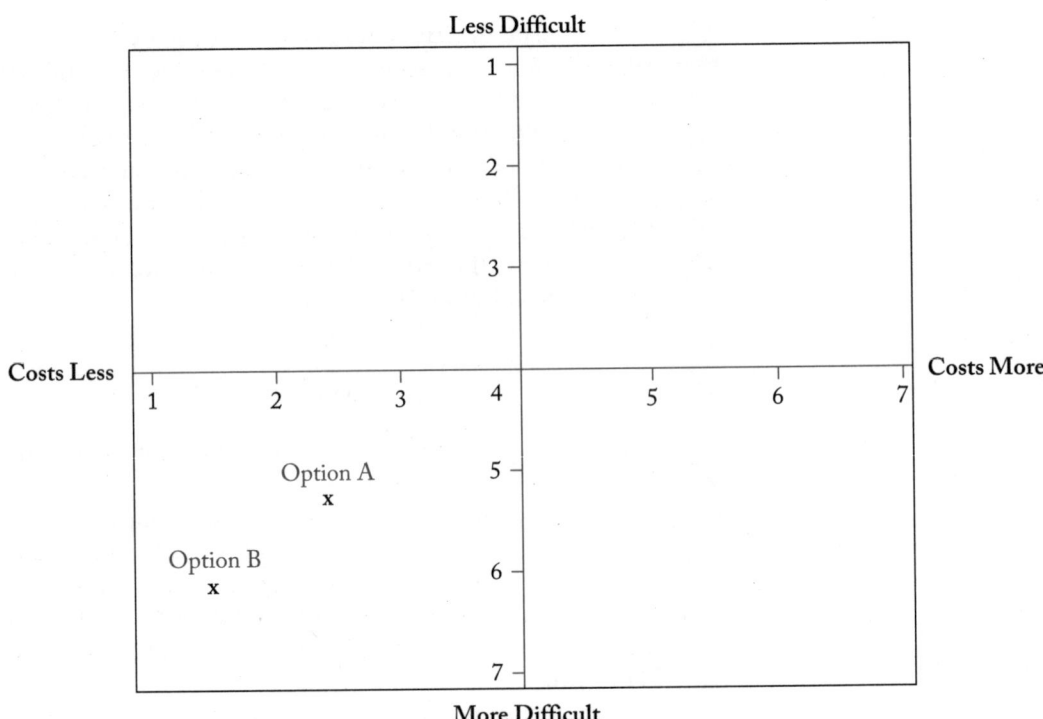

Less Difficult

Costs Less   **Costs More**

Option A
x

Option B
x

More Difficult

16. Now that you have identified similar options, you can interpret the row characteristics in greater detail and look for **matching characteristics**. You can **group together** these matching characteristics by moving the rows around and placing them side by side (use masking tape to stick the row cards together). You will know that there is a **match** between two or more characteristics when you realize that "if participants say score x in one row then they tend to say score y in the other row". Characteristics with scores that match your key characteristic (identified in Step 4) can help you explain important aspects of your topic area (such as why certain options are more difficult to implement than others). For instance, the final table created in Step 10 shows that difficult options tend to take more time and to depend on others for their implementation.

To help people participate in the analysis, divide the participants into smaller groups, and ask each group to choose a different characteristic and its opposite. Then, each group should find other row characteristics with scores that are very similar or that are nearly the opposite (see explanation on the next page).

To calculate the level of difference between two row characteristics, calculate the sum of differences (SD) between same-column scores (leave out columns that have empty squares). You then calculate the total maximum difference for all scores (this is MS, the maximum score, minus 1, multiplied by E, the number of options that got ratings). The level of difference between two characteristics is SD divided by the total maximum difference for all scores, multiplied by 100. To turn this level of difference into a percentage similarity score, subtract it from 100. In other words:

$$100 - \frac{SD \times 100}{(MS - 1) \times E}$$

For instance, the table created in Step 10 shows that the first and third characteristics ("Less difficult" versus "More difficult", "Depends on us" versus "Depends on others") are very similar. The sum of differences between the recorded scores is 12 and the total maximum difference is 42 [(7 − 1) × 7]. The level of difference is therefore 28 percent (12/42 × 100) and the level of similarity, 72 percent.

If the level of similarity is very low, this indicates an inverse relationship between two sets of row scores. This means that "if participants choose a characteristic at one end of the continuum in one row then they tend to choose the characteristic at the opposite end in the other row". When this happens you can turn the inverse relationship into a positive one by reversing all the scores in one row (from 2 to 6 or from 7 to 1, in a scale from 1 to 7, for instance). Positive relationships are easier to interpret. For instance, the following table reverses the scores for the fifth row of the table created in Step 10. Using these reverse scores, the level of similarity between the first and fifth rows ("Less difficult" versus "More difficult", "Less conflictive" versus "More conflictive") is 79 percent.

Characteristics	Option A Limit access	Option B State funding	Option E Regulate	Option F Rotate	Option C Political support	Option D Representation & participation	Option G Repopulate
Less difficult (1) More difficult (7)	5	7	7	6	5	4	3
Less conflictive (1) now 7 More conflictive (7) now 1	(4) now 4	(1) now 7	(3) now 5	(2) now 6	(3) now 5	(1) now 7	(2) now 6

Define the points where you consider levels of similarities between characteristics to be high or low. Where you find high matches between row scores, discuss whether these characteristics and their opposites have the same **meaning** or the same cause, or if some are **examples** or **causes** of others.

When looking for matching characteristics, focus on those characteristics and relationships that are of interest to the participants, and no more. Do not over interpret these relationships, and let the participants play an active role in the analysis.

17. You can look at similarities and differences between some options and their characteristics during the rating process (Step 10), before the table is completed. At the end of the exercise you can enter your options, your characteristics, and your ratings in RepGrid (http://repgrid.com/SAS/) and use the Focus and PrinGrid commands to perform the calculations described in Steps 15 and 16. The Focus command creates a table where options that have the most similar ratings are placed side by side. Characteristics that have the most similar ratings also appear side by side, with negative matches converted into positive relationships. A diagram with lines meeting at various points (outside the table) indicates the levels of similarity between options and between characteristics. This is called **cluster analysis**.

The PrinGrid command creates a graph with calculations based on **principal component analysis**. The graph shows the location of each option in relation to other options (dots). It also shows the location of options in relation to a number of straight lines representing the characteristics (the longer the line is, the more the characteristic varies in its ratings). Closer distances reflect closer relationships between options (dots), between characteristics (lines), and between options and their characteristics. To interpret the graph, focus on the characteristics that are grouped near two imaginary lines, one vertical and the other horizontal; these principal components show percentage figures that indicate the extent to which each component explains all relationships (see example below).

Rethinking Your Analysis

18. You can rename, delete, or add to your options, your characteristics and opposites, and your scores at any time during the process.

You can modify the **details of some of your options** (see Step 2) and then change the way you rate these options using the same characteristics and opposites.

You may want to look for an **extra characteristic** and opposite if you need to split two options that are closely matched. To do this, find the difference between the two options that are almost the same (such as options F and G in the table created in Step 10). Use the new characteristic and its opposite to rate all the options and record your scores in a new row.

You may want to look for an **extra option** if you need to split two characteristics that are closely matched. To do this, find an option that brings together the characteristics that are rarely matched (for instance, in the table created in Step 10, a "less difficult option" that "costs less" to implement). Insert the extra option in a new column and rate it for each characteristic and its opposite.

Learning from Your Analysis

19. *Option Domain* can help you identify **learning opportunities** that are structural (such as convergence, polarization, fragmentation, or vagueness), communicational (such as disagreement, misunderstanding, or confusion), temporal (such as instability or resistance to change) or adaptive (such as the failure to predict).

Structural Learning Opportunities

Convergence

You know there is convergence in your table when the row scores you recorded are closely matched. It will be quite clear that you can regroup most characteristics into two categories that are opposite each other, with the options falling somewhere along the continuum from one set of opposites to another. For instance, the more difficult it is to implement the option, the less it costs, the less time it takes, the less conflict it creates, the more it depends on the local actors, and the more viable it is from a legal perspective.

If convergence is a problem, search for other options that may combine the characteristics in new ways. Give special attention to new ways of combining your options with the key characteristic identified in Step 4 (such as exploring an option that depends on external actors and is not difficult to implement).

Polarization

You know there is polarization in your table when you can regroup most options into two categories that are opposite each other. One group of options has one set of characteristics, and the other group is opposite in all respects. For instance, the options scored in Step 10 would fall into two groups. One group would consist of options that are less difficult to implement, cost less, take less time, cause less conflict, depend more on the local actors, and are more viable legally. The other group would be the opposite in all respects.

If polarization is a problem, search for options that may combine the characteristics in new ways. Give special attention to new ways of combining your options with the key characteristic identified in Step 4 (such as exploring an option that depends on external actors and is not difficult to implement).

Fragmentation

You know there is fragmentation in your table when few options and few characteristics are closely matched. There is no pattern in the system. Each option is entirely different. For instance, the options may be so different from each other that no explanation can be found as to why some are more difficut to implement than others.

If fragmentation is a problem, search for other options or characteristics that may reveal some meaningful pattern in the system.

Vagueness

You know there is vagueness in your table when the scores for the options do not vary much. If this is a problem, search for the likely cause. Some likely reasons include: participants have very different views of the options and will negotiate them through average scores; they see mostly the connections between the options, not the differences; they have limited knowledge of the topic area; or the options they chose are too general.

Communicational Learning Opportunities

Disagreement

You know there is disagreement (between the tables that different people make) when people give very different scores to the same options using the same characteristics. To measure levels of agreement and disagreement between two sets of scores, total the differences between same-square scores and divide this number by the total maximum difference between all squares (this is MS, the maximum score, minus 1, multiplied by E, the number of options that got ratings).

Here is an example of a disagreement at a 62 percent level (26/42) between two parties who rate the same options using the same characteristic and its opposite (whether the current situation is good or bad):

Parties	Option A Limit access	Option B State funding	Option E Regulate	Option F Rotate	Option C Political support	Option D Representation & participation	Option G Repopulate
Party 1	2	1	4	3	1	1	7
Party 2	6	4	1	1	7	5	3
Difference	4	3	3	2	6	4	4

If disagreement is a problem, identify the key area(s) of disagreement (such as Option C in the table shown above) and discuss the scores until they reflect a common assessment of the situation.

There may be cases where you want to *compare many characteristics and tables* representing the views of different individuals or groups. To do this, reorder the row characteristics in each table from top to bottom, with *those at the top matching the ratings of the key characteristic* identified in Step 4. These top matching characteristics represent what each individual or group has in mind when thinking about important aspects of the topic. Then, look for top matching characteristics that participants agree or disagree with across your sample. If the tables contain many characteristics, you can group them into categories (see Step 12), reorder the characteristics from top to bottom within each category, and then look for top match agreements and disagreements across your sample within each category.

Misunderstanding

You know there is misunderstanding when a party (such as men) fails to predict how the other party (such as women) will rate certain options. To measure levels of misunderstanding, each party must try to guess how the other party will rate the same options using the same characteristic(s). Then, total the differences between the original scores and the scores each group predicted for the other. Divide this number by the total maximum difference for all squares (this is the maximum score minus 1, multiplied by the number of options). As an example, the following table shows a high level of misunderstanding between two parties. Although both think that they share similar views about their preferred options, they do not.

Characteristic and Its Opposite: The Current Situation, Good (1) of Bad (7)

Parties	Option A Limit access	Option B State funding	Option E Regulate	Option F Rotate	Option C Political support	Option D Representation & participation	Option G Repopulate
Party 1	2	1	4	3	1	1	7
Party 1 viewed by party 2	5	3	1	6	5	5	3
Difference	3	2	3	3	4	4	4
Party 2	5	4	1	7	7	5	4
Party 2 viewed by party 1	2	1	3	4	2	2	7
Difference	3	3	2	3	5	3	3

If misunderstanding is a problem, identify the key area(s) and the likely causes of misunderstanding (such as Option C in the table shown above). Compare and discuss your scores until you gain a better understanding of each other's views.

Levels of agreement may be combined with levels of understanding to produce *six possible scenarios*:

	Misunderstanding		Understanding
Agreement	Scenario 1 The parties agree but do not know it	Scenario 2 The parties agree but one does not know it	Scenario 3 The parties agree and both know it
Disagreement	Scenario 4 The parties disagree but do not know it	Scenario 5 The parties disagree but one does not know it	Scenario 6 The parties disagree and both know it

Confusion

You know there is confusion (between the tables that different people do) when the parties use different options or characteristics to describe the same situation. If confusion is a problem, search for common options or shared characteristics to create some basis for mutual understanding and agreement.

Temporal Learning Opportunities

Instability

You know there is instability (in the same table over time) when the way that you view a topic and characterize options changes quickly or frequently over time, without any clear justification.

If instability is a problem, identify the factors that may explain this (see techniques in the *Problems* module). You can look for characteristics and options that are more meaningful. You can also take more time to discuss the ratings or to gather the information you need to complete the exercise.

Resistance to Change

You know there is resistance to change (in the same table over time) when you are aware of learning opportunities and prefer to maintain the existing problems of convergence, polarization, fragmentation, vagueness, disagreement, misunderstanding, confusion, instability, or failure to predict. If resistance to change is a problem, identify the factors that may explain this (see techniques in the *Problems* module) or take more time to discuss the topic, the options, and their characteristics. Note that characteristics and options (which reflect *how* people think) are generally more difficult to change compared with option ratings (which reflect *what* people think).

*Adaptive Learning
Opportunities*

Failure to Predict

You know there is a failure to predict when real events do not confirm the characteristics and the ratings you applied to the options in your analysis. To assess the predictive value of your analysis, select key characteristics and their opposites, and then identify outcome indicators that define the meaning of each number on your rating scale (involving levels of difficulty in implementing each option, for instance). Collect reliable information on these indicators in relation to each option to see if the characteristics are relevant and the ratings are confirmed. If the failure to predict is a problem, change your ratings or look for characteristics that have better predictive value.

Scaling Up or Down

For Simpler Versions

1. Work with one or two people or with small groups of people who have many common characteristics.
2. Use no more than six options and six characteristics. Reduce the number of options by eliminating some, or through the *Freelisting* technique.
3. Use drawings or pictures to represent each option and each characteristic.

4. Do not group the characteristics into categories (Step 12).

5. Rate the options with a simple scale (using + or – signs, scores from 1 to 3, or simple phrases).

6. To calculate the level of similarity between two sets of scores, divide the number of SAME scores (include scores that are identical or only one point apart) by the TOTAL number of scores (SAME + DIFFERENT).

7. Do the qualitative interpretation described in Steps 13 and 14 and leave out all mathematical calculations and comparisons.

8. Do not discuss the learning opportunities described in Step 19.

For More Advanced Versions

1. Take more time to gather the information you need to complete the exercise.

2. During the exercise, discuss and record the views that participants express.

3. Work with a greater number of people or groups.

4. Use more than six options and six characteristics.

5. If the options are about natural resources, locate each option on a map of the area.

6. Use surveys to find out how people characterize and rate the options in a topic area.

7. Rate the options using a scale of 1 to 7 or 1 to 9.

8. Write a detailed description for each opion and for each characteristic.

9. Identify indicators to justify each rating exercise.

10. Do advanced calculations and graphics using RepGrid (http://repgrid.com/SAS/). Do a Focus Analysis to measure the level of similarity between options and between characteristics. Do a Principal Component Analysis to identify the main connections within an *Option Domain* table or a "Socio Analysis" to measure the similarities between two or more tables.

11. Use *Causal Dynamics* or *Activity Dynamics* to understand the interaction between options.

Readings and Links

Blowers, G.H.; and K.P. O'Connor. 1996. *Personal Construct Psychology in the Clinical Context*. Ottawa, ON, Canada: University of Ottawa Press. 140 pp.

Denicolo, P.; and M.L. Pope. 2001. *Transformative Professional Practice: Personal Construct Approaches to Education and Research*. Chichester, United Kingdom: John Wiley & Sons.

Fransella, F. (ed.). 2003. *International Handbook of Personal Construct Psychology*. Chichester, United Kingdom: John Wiley & Sons.

Gaines, B.R.; and M.L.G. Shaw. 2004. *Web Grid III*. Cobble Hill, BC, Canada: Centre for Person-Computer Studies. Available online at http://tiger.cpsc. ucalgary.ca/, accessed on August 15, 2007.

Jankowicz, A.D. 2004. *The Easy Guide to Repertory Grids*. Chichester, United Kingdom: John Wiley & Sons.

For a discussion of the Personal Construct Psychology of George Kelly, see http://repgrid.com/pcp/, accessed on August 17, 2007.

Option Domain: Towards a Management Plan for the Common Fishery Zone of Ancud, Chile

Key Words	*Option Domain*, Chile, fisheries, management plans
Authors	J.M. Chevalier, C. Tapia, D. J. Buckles.
Context	About 2,000 artisanal fishers currently exploit shellfish in the Common Fishery Zone of Ancud in central coastal Chile. The kinds of species fishers seek include crabs and clams (*Venus antiqua, Gari solida, Ensis macha*). In 1991, the Chilean Fisheries and Aquaculture Act set up formal fishing zones known as AMERBs. The Act thus provided new ways to manage fisheries in the Bay of Ancud by giving organizations that represent artisanal fishers the right to request segments of seabed that were then to be managed jointly with the Undersecretary of Fisheries. The Act, however, offered no clear way to assign territorial use and rights that include historical claims to the fishery. As a result, two problems have emerged in the Zone of Ancud: (*i*) many fishers from other zones have entered the fishery, and (*ii*) several well-informed and connected organizations have claimed parts of the zone, leaving out other local fishers and organizations. This conflict was resolved in June 2003, with the help of the Archbishop of Ancud and regional authorities. Even so, concerns about resource depletion and conflicts between fishers from outside and those living in the zone have continued.

Purpose	To assess and fully develop plans to set up territorial use rights and better management of the Common Fishery Zone of Ancud.
Process Summary	The Fund for Fisheries Research, as part of the Undersecretary of Fisheries, held a one-day meeting of people from various artisanal fishers' organizations in the Zone of Ancud. Some 57 people attended. Most of them were male fishers and leaders of fishing organizations. A few women also took part. Five fisheries officials and scientists attended, along with several people from the Fund for Fisheries Research. Participants decided that the meeting would focus on the priorities and perspectives of the fisher representatives, and that the officials and scientists would act as their consultants throughout the meeting, as needed. Fishers then wrote on cards their ideas about how to improve territorial access and management of the fishery. They formed 13 piles from the same ideas and labeled each pile as a distinct line of action. They then rated the proposed actions on the basis of urgency, and chose

the seven most urgent for further discussion. Details of the selected actions were discussed and posted on flipcharts throughout the room.

The group was then asked to describe the factors (criteria) it would use to evaluate the proposed actions. Each proposed action was then rated and rating cards were placed on a grid on the floor, with participants forming a semicircle around the grid. During a break, the ratings were entered into the RepGrid software and displayed on a wall. This supported a discussion of the profiles of proposed actions, and allowed participants to identify problems they might encounter during implementation. The group then talked about ways to change the proposed actions to avoid these problems. The details of these suggestions were noted on the flipcharts where each proposed action was displayed. Information gaps (questions) that might require follow-up research and other problems not yet discussed were also listed. Two of the authors were involved in facilitation of the event. The participants understood that the results would be used to prepare reports, and agreed to share their information.

Analysis

The participants identified 13 ways to improve the way the fishery is managed. They rated them based on urgency, using a scale of 1 to 7 where 7 is very urgent (Table 1). Seven proposed actions received the highest score for urgency and were chosen by the group for further discussion and planning.

Table 1: Proposed Actions for the Management of the Common Fishery Zone of Ancud

Proposed Actions	Urgency (1 = low, 7 = high)
Restrict access	7
Form representative bodies	7
Create effective enforcement	7
Raise government funding	7
Mobilize support for implementation	7
Restock	7
Rotate fishing effort	7
Open access	6
Establish seasonal bans	6
Subdivide the fishery into separate zones	5
Train fishers and officials	5
Study markets	5
Support aquiculture	3

The following are details that participants offered for each priority action.

Restrict Access

All fishers who are current members of the Ancud Commune should be allowed equal access to the fishery. This includes both registered and non-registered fishers. New fishers and fishers from outside the area should not be allowed to use the fishery.

Form Representative Bodies

A body should be set up to represent all fishers in the Ancud Commune, with an Administrative Council and equal voice for all members. A Technical Roundtable to bring together all stakeholders in the fishery (including scientists and government officials) should also be formed. The current Communal Fisheries Roundtable does not provide equal representation or voice and does not include all stakeholders.

Create Effective Enforcement

More effective enforcement is needed. The main government body that governs the fishery (SERNAPESCA) needs to show greater willingness to enforce rules and regulations and seek more operating resources. As well, fishers need to be involved in setting the rules and regulations for the fishery, speaking out against violations, and monitoring its use. Immediate measures must be taken to enforce minimum fish size restrictions, fishing bans, and a division of the fishery into sectors.

Raise Government Funding

Higher levels of government funding are needed if a fisheries management plan is to be set up. Needs include resources for administration, enforcement, training, restocking, and so on. Core budget costs are the most difficult to finance. The task is a complex one due to financial rules set by the Chilean government's bureaucracy.

Mobilize Support for Implementation

Eight government bodies play a central role in managing the fishery: the Municipality of Ancud, the Undersecretary of Fisheries, the Fisheries Zone Council, the National Fisheries Service, the Port Authority (governed by the Chilean navy), the Provincial Government, the Prefect of the Xth Region, and the Regional Secretariat of the Ministry of the Economy. Gaining the goodwill and active support of all of these bodies is important. The Municipality of Ancud should play an active role in directing the management plan.

Restocking

Because some fishery stocks have declined due to overfishing, restocking is needed. Based on restocking experiences elsewhere in Chile, efforts should focus on a few of the most affected species. This includes pilot measures scaled to the capacity of the organizations to produce seed material for restocking.

Rotate Fishing Effort

Fishing should happen in many parts of the Bay. This would spread pressure on the fish stocks and allow them time to recover.

Participants then identified seven **criteria** that could be used to evaluate the proposed actions. The criteria included (*i*) the degree of conflict the proposed action is likely to generate when it is being implemented; (*ii*) how easy it will be to implement; (*iii*) cost of the action; (*iv*) the legal feasibility of the action; (*v*) whether the action can be completed in the short or long term; (*vi*) to what extent the action depends on the fishers themselves; and (*vii*) whether current efforts along the same lines are going well or badly. For each of these seven criteria, participants assigned a value of 1 to the positive side of the criteria and a value of 7 to the negative side of the criteria.

Table 2 presents the results of this rating exercise. Totals at the bottom show how proposed actions were rated compared to each other. The actions with higher total scores (create effective enforcement, restrict access) have more problems associated with them while those with lower total scores (mobilize support for implementation, form representative bodies) have fewer constraints. Participants decided to focus further discussion on the most problematic, namely those with the higher total scores.

Table 2: Ratings of Proposed Management Actions for the Common Fishery Zone of Ancud

Criteria/Actions	Restrict access	Form representative bodies	Create effective enforcement	Raise government funding	Mobilize support for implementation	Restock	Rotate fishing effort
1 Conflict low 7 Conflict high	4	1	3	1	3	2	2
1 Easy 7 Hard	5	4	7	7	5	3	5
1 Less costly 2 More costly	2	5	7	2	1	5	6
1 More feasible legally 7 Less feasible legally	6	2	1	1	1	1	1
1 Short term 7 Longer term	5	2	6	4	4	5	4
1 Depends more on fishers 7 Depends less on fishers	5	3	5	7	1	2	2
1 Things going well 7 Things going badly	2	3	6	5	3	7	7
Totals	29	20	35	27	18	25	27

The overall profile of proposed actions are shown in Figures 1 and 2. Figure 1 shows the clusters of actions that have similar ratings (rotate fishing effort and restock are similar at a 95 percent level). It also shows the clusters of characteristics that tend to go together (actions less feasible legally also tend to involve more conflict). Figure 2 highlights the more problematic actions. Restricting access is less feasible legally and will generate some conflict, at least at the beginning. It is, however, less costly and initial efforts to restrict access are going well. By contrast, creating effective enforcement is more feasible legally and creates less conflict because it is an accepted norm. It is going badly, however, and is a costly solution that will take considerably more time. It also depends less on the fishers themselves compared to most other actions. This assessment by participants led to a second discussion on ways to address the more problematic features of these priority actions.

Figure 1: Proposed Management Actions for the Common Fishery Zone of Ancud

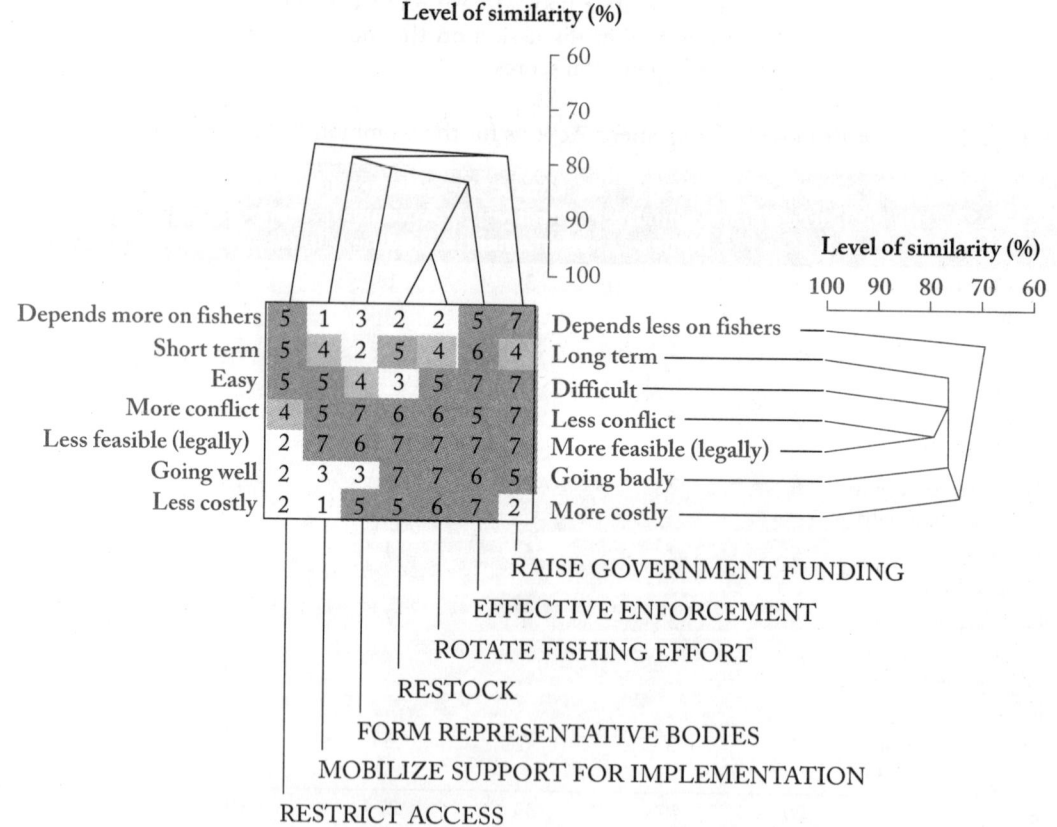

Figure 2: Proposed Management Actions for the Common Fishery Zone of Ancud

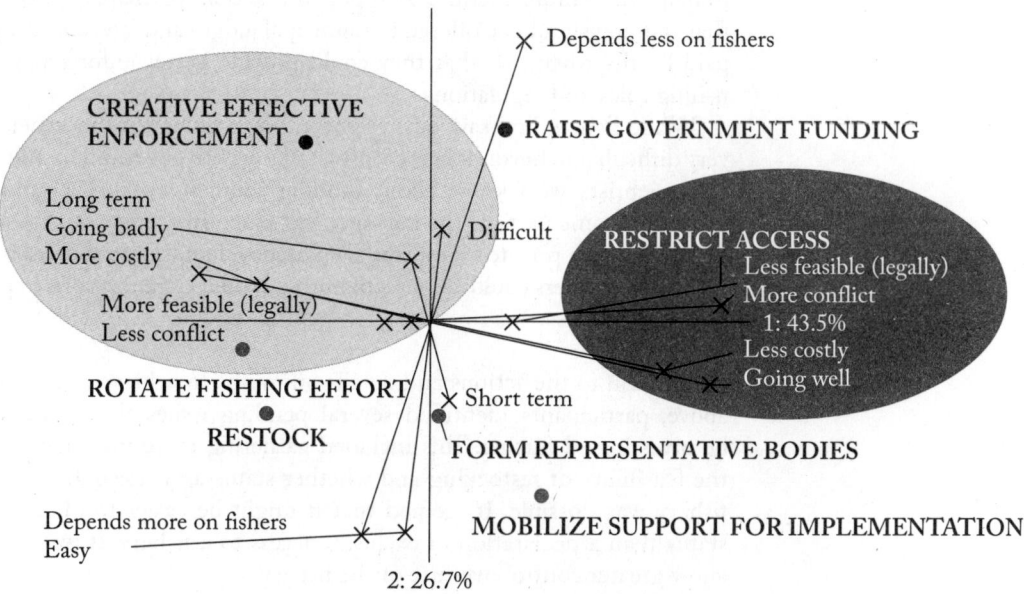

Interpretation

Participants looked very closely at why restricting access to the fishery might generate more conflict. They noted that some fishers are formally registered in fishing unions and organizations, while others are not. This could become the basis for a conflict between those included and those excluded from the fishery. Many of the unregistered fishers are older and less educated men with long-standing and legitimate claims to the fishery. The group talked about ways to register these fishers in organizations so that their right to access the fishery could be upheld and protected. Participants were aware but left unresolved the fact that some fishers would remain unregistered because they have criminal records; they would not be accepted into any organization.

Restricting access to the fishery would still be a problem because the Chilean legal system does not recognize a figure or body that can declare exclusive access to a fishery. Participants decided to seek administrative solutions that could be supported, over time, with the passage of new laws.

Everyone agreed that creating better enforcement was a critical but very costly line of action. When the group talked about how to reduce costs, a possible enforcement role for the municipal government arose. The proposal involved the municipality raising funds through fines and the sale of seized fishing gear. They noted, too, that the municipality had already expressed its desire to assist, by offering the use of a boat to help with enforcement. To support this action, participants decided that training should be offered to municipal judges and lawyers (already paid by the town), so that they could provide better enforcement of fishing rules and regulations.

While fishers first saw raising government funds for the fishery as very difficult and beyond their control, talking with government officials and scientists who know about funding sources revealed a funding source for some parts of the management plan. The prospect of raising funds from the private sector was also discussed and some sources were identified. Fishers could act directly through their organizations to pursue these sources.

Action

In addition to the actions and details on means to achieve them noted above, participants identified several pending issues that needed to be investigated further. This included gathering more information on the feasibility of restocking and whether status as a research-oriented fishery was possible. It seemed that it might be easier to obtain this status than a declaration of exclusive access to a fishery. It would still allow greater control over use of the fishery.

Observations on the Process

A first exercise that involved rating actions as either good or excellent was dropped because the scores did not vary. The remaining 7 rating criteria were considered by participants to be both relevant and sufficient for their purpose. Participants said they were very satisfied with the result and the level of participation of different actors during the process. The contribution of officials acting as consultants was appreciated, without undermining the leadership of fishers directly involved in the situation. The level of agreement or consensus on the various actions identified was very high, an achievement, participants said, they had not thought was possible given the diversity of perspectives among stakeholders.

Competing Goals

Author J.M. Chevalier

Purpose *Competing Goals* helps you rank stakeholders' goals (objectives, or values) in order of importance, and understand disagreements or misunderstandings that people may have in relation to these goals.

Guiding Principles

1. Goals are the objectives that people want to achieve or the values they hold.

2. People generally organize their goals in a hierarchy, from the most important to the least important.

3. People often try to combine different goals and adjust them to the needs of each situation.

4. People may disagree or misunderstand the goals of other stakeholders.

Process

Identify the **situation** where you need to use *Competing Goals*. Define the situation as clearly as possible so that participants can identify the relevant goals. Clarify the purpose of your analysis.

Ask participants to list the **goals** they have that are relevant to the situation identified in Step 1. These goals may involve specific objectives (such as building a clinic, opening a new school, and so on) or the moral values that people hold (such as peace, justice, and so on). Define these goals as clearly as possible. Use positive terms to describe each goal; if people reject a proposed action because the benefits would be mostly for men, this reflects the value those people place on gender fairness, for instance. If the list of goals is too large, use *Freelisting* to help you focus on key goals.

Divide the participants into stakeholder groups (such as men and women, or agricultural workers and landowners). Ask each group to make a card for each goal, using words or a picture to describe the goal, and then to **rank** these goals in order of importance. The most important goal should be ranked 1. Arrange for each group to gather where they cannot be heard by the other group.

If you have many goals to rank, you can divide all the goals into **3 piles**: those with high rankings, those with middle rankings, and those with low rankings. Repeat the same method with each pile until you obtain a precise ranking for each goal.

Another option consists in doing **paired comparisons**. Start by making a ranking choice between two goals chosen at random. Then, choose one goal at a time and compare it with the most similar goal that you have already ranked. If there are many goals to compare, create a table to help you do the paired comparisons (see *Ranking*).

4. Once the ranking by each group is complete, ask each group to rank the goals as they think the other group would have ranked them. This will produce two lists, one of their own priorities, and another of the ranking they think the other group will have.

5. Come together as a single group to compare rankings. This can be done by showing the order using the cards. Look for similarities and differences.

6. To understand **levels of disagreement** between the rankings of two groups, create a table to record the rankings from each stakeholder group and total the differences between same-goal rankings. Then, divide this number by the maximum difference that could have been generated by the two ranked lists. If values range from 1 to 5, then the maximum difference is 5 minus 1, 4 minus 2, 3 minus 3, 4 minus 2, and 5 minus 1, for a total difference of 12.

Here is an example of two rankings involving a maximum difference of 12 and a ranking difference of 8. The result is a 75 percent level of disagreement.

Goals	Ranking by group 1	Ranking by group 2	Ranking differences
Peace	1	2	1
Development	3	4	1
Equity	2	3	1
Conservation	5	1	4
Identity	4	5	1
Total			8/max. 12 = 0.75

7. To assess **levels of misunderstanding**, compare the ranking that each group predicts with the other group's actual ranking (use the same calculations as in Step 6).

Levels of disagreement may be combined with levels of misunderstanding to produce **six possible scenarios**:

S A S²

	Misunderstanding		Understanding
Agreement	Scenario 1 The parties agree but do not know it	Scenario 2 The parties agree but one does not know it	Scenario 3 The parties agree and both know it
Disagreement	Scenario 4 The parties disagree but do not know it	Scenario 5 The parties disagree but one does not know it	Scenario 6 The parties disagree and both know it

8. Discuss the results of your ranking comparisons, with an emphasis on **where and why** there are major disagreements or misunderstandings (such as the goal of conservation in the table shown in Step 6). If you are working with two or more groups, members of each group may wish to discuss these issues among themselves before sharing their views with other groups.

9. To compare the rankings of more than two groups, identify the **two goals** where people seem to **disagree** the most. Create a diagram by drawing a vertical line that crosses a horizontal line. This creates a cross inside a square. Use the vertical line to represent one goal and the horizontal line to represent the other. Write the lowest and the highest ranking numbers at the opposite ends of each line (such as 1 and 7). Place each group's name into your diagram using the group's rankings for the two goals.

Here is an example of a *Competing Goals* diagram:

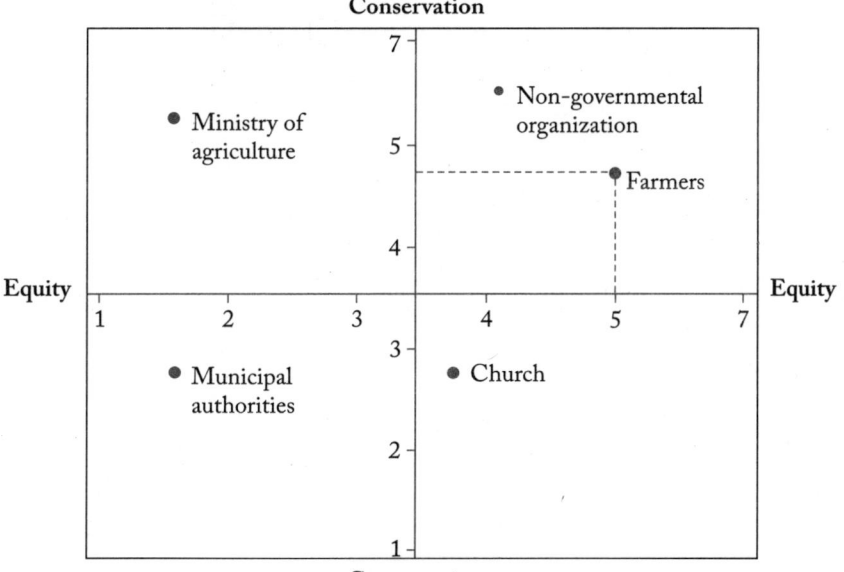

10. Discuss the distribution of groups in the diagram. Identify groups that occupy middle positions in the diagram (closer to the center); they may be able to mediate disagreements over goals.

Scaling Up or Down

For Simpler Versions

1. Limit the number of comparisons by grouping stakeholders who clearly share many characteristics.
2. Do not measure levels of disagreement or misunderstanding (Steps 6 to 10).

For More Advanced Versions

1. Take more time to gather the information you need to complete the exercise.
2. Write a description for each goal and its ranking.
3. During the exercise, discuss, and record the views that participants express when ranking and interpreting results.
4. Do group rankings for a number of stakeholder groups.
5. Use advanced versions of *Ranking*.

Reading and Link

Carney, T.F. 1976. *Mind-Mapping Techniques*, Part 6. Winnipeg, Harbeck: The Natural Resource Institute, University of Manitoba.

Competing Goals: Competing Project Priorities of Men and Women in Mehi, West Bengal

Key Words	*Competing Goals*, priorities, ranking, livelihoods, environment, West Bengal, India
Author and Acknowledgement	D.J. Buckles. The author wishes to acknowledge the efforts of Soma Paul, Niladri Chakraborty, Sujit Mitra and Rajeev Khedkar who helped to design and facilitate the assessment.
Context	Mehi is a village some 336 kilometers from Kolkata in the district of Purulia, West Bengal. The non-governmental organization Development, Research, Communication and Services Centre (DRCSC) is active with two tribal groups in Mehi that are usually not helped by development projects. DRCSC was planning to renew its support for project activities in the village and was also planning to extend these activities to other nearby villages. The activities to continue had not been decided.
Purpose	To assess gender-based differences in project priorities in the village.

Process Summary

DRCSC convened a meeting in the home of one of the villagers in Mehi. About 20 people attended; many were married couples. Before the meeting, DRCSC had made a list of activities to be discussed during the assessment based on its current village program and projects of other organizations in the village. The participants reviewed and ranked these activities from the most beneficial to the least. The ranking was done separately by the men and the women.

In the men's group, participants drew pictures representing each activity and identified from them the one that was most beneficial to them. The selected picture was turned over and the most beneficial activity from the remaining pictures was identified, a process that continued until all pictures were ranked. In the women's group, the activities were ranked by making paired comparisons of pictures drawn by the facilitator to represent each activity. One-to-one ranking choices were made by the women (see Ranking in All-Purpose Techniques on the SAS[2] website, www.sas2.net). The number of times each activity was selected most beneficial was then recorded in a table. The sum of these numbers gave the final rank for each activity. Using two methods to do the ranking reflected the preferences of the two facilitators.

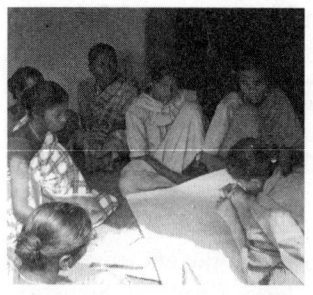

Once both groups had finished ranking the activities they were asked to guess the ranking the other group might have made. The rankings of the two groups were then compared by forming two lines of people (men and women) holding the pictures of the activities in the priority they had indicated. After a discussion of differences, the order was shuffled to show how each group guessed the priorities of the other group. This led to a discussion of differences and misunderstandings between the two groups. DRCSC and the author discussed the consequences of the results for the program in Mehi with the participants. The participants were aware that the result would form part of the reporting and decision making procedures of DRCSC and agreed to share their information.

Analysis

The six activities on the list were: mixed cropping, fisheries, grain bank, road building, children's nursery, and the kitchen garden (Table 1). Road construction and the children's nursery are government projects in the village, while the other four project activities are run by DRCSC. Both kinds of activities had been in place for a number of years.

The way men and women ranked priorities showed a high level of disagreement (8/18 or 45 percent disagreement in priorities), due to major differences in the ranking of three activities. The fisheries project, ranked as most beneficial by the men, was ranked fourth by the women. The children's nursery and the grain bank, ranked highest by the women, received a much lower priority among the men. There was little disagreement on other activities.

The level of misunderstanding was also high for both groups, with men showing a slightly poorer understanding of women's priorities than women did of men's priorities (12/18 or 67 percent level of men's misunderstanding of the women's priorities, and 10/18 or 56 percent level of women's misunderstanding of the men's priorities). The comparison showed the men that they had overestimated the benefits women see in the kitchen garden project and that they had greatly underestimated the benefits women see in the children's nursery project. The fact that the fisheries project was important to the men was clear to the women, but the women had not expected the men's lack of interest in the road building project.

Table 1: Competing Project Priorities of Men and Women in Mehi, West Bengal

Activities	Men	Women	Disagreement	Ranking by women for men	Women's misunder-standing	Ranking by men for women	Men's misunder-standing
Mixed cropping	2	3	1	3	1	5	2
Fisheries	1	4	3	2	1	2	2
Grain bank	4	2	2	4	0	3	1
Road construction*	6	6	0	1	5	6	0
Children's nursery*	3	1	2	5	2	4	3
Kitchen garden	5	5	0	6	1	1	4
All activities			8/18		10/18		12/18

Note: * Projects initiated by government agencies.

Interpretation

The disagreement between men and women regarding priority project activities reflects a gender-based division of labor within the village. Men are active in fisheries while women have greater responsibility for childcare and storing seeds. The high level of misunderstanding when it comes to the priorities of the other gender points to a communication gap between men and women. Men's greater power in the household and the village may have limited discussion of competing priorities in the past.

Action

Several among the men remarked on the communication gap and said they planned to discuss priorities with their wives more often. DRCSC decided to reassess the role of the kitchen garden in the village project, an activity they had assumed was a high priority for women. They also decided to continue support for the grain bank and explore ways to strengthen the children's nursery run by the government. Furthermore, DRCSC decided to convene priority-setting meetings among women and men separately, and to design their program based on negotiated priorities between genders.

Observations on the Process

The use of two different ways of ranking the activities by men and by women was initially confusing for some participants. This was resolved by having people stand up with a picture in hand in the order of priority for their group. This active way of presenting the rankings meant there was no need to create a summary table or list. People were able to see the conclusions right in front of them. The participants said that the different perspectives on priorities made sense to them and that the exercise was very useful to their own discussions not only with DRCSC but also government organizations with programs in the village.

Role Dynamics

Author

J.M. Chevalier

Acknowledgement

Role Dynamics is a SAS[2] adaptation and development of input-output analysis, a well-known technique used in economics and economic policy and planning throughout the world for the past half-century. The author wishes to acknowledge the efforts of Jorge Tellez and Sara Pinzi who helped to design this technique.

Purpose

Role Dynamics helps you assess what stakeholders expect of each other or themselves, as a result of a contract, a promise or a moral responsibility, and how satisfied they are with how stakeholders perform their roles. You can also use the technique to assess the current and ideal levels of interaction between stakeholders or team members (see *Role Dynamics* example).

Guiding Principle

1. When managing a problem or a project, it is important to keep in mind the gaps between the role expectations of key stakeholders and how successful others are in meeting these expectations.

Process

Creating a Table

1. Identify a **situation** where you need to assess what stakeholders expect of each other or of themselves, as a result of a contract, a promise or a moral responsibility, and how successful they are in meeting these expectations. Define the situation as clearly as possible, and clarify the purpose of your analysis.

2. Make a list of the key **stakeholders** with role expectations that are relevant in the situation identified in Step 1. Note that you may include yourself and those who are doing the analysis in your list. You may define the representatives of a group as a stakeholder different from those they represent. Also you may include the community of all stakeholders in your list, as a group with its own

profile. Write (or draw) each stakeholder on two separate cards. See example in Step 9.

3. Create a **table**. Place one set of stakeholder cards in the top row. Then place the other set of cards (showing the same stakeholders in the same order) in the first column. See example in Step 9.

4. Establish a rating scale for **levels of role satisfaction**. The scale could have values from 0 to 5, for instance, with indicators (simple statements) that define the meaning of each number on the scale. Test your scale with the group to make sure that the exercise, the scale(s), and the indicators are clear to everyone.

5. Ask each row stakeholder to describe its expectations in detail and then rate its level of satisfaction with each column stakeholder. Each stakeholder group only does its own rating for its own row. Ask "What do you (stakeholder in row A) expect from stakeholder in column B and how successful is B in meeting these expectations?" If the expectations are too general, ask "What do you mean by this?" or "Can you give an example of this?" Use the scale and the indicators created in Step 4. Write the results on a **separate card** for each stakeholder relationship. To help you interpret the results of this exercise, write the reason given for each score on the reverse side of its card. Place the resulting cards in the appropriate rows and columns. See example in Step 9.

To simplify the analysis, you can focus on the role expectations and levels of satisfaction that exist between **one key stakeholder** and all other stakeholders (the forestry department and all stakeholders receiving services from the department, for instance). Place this key stakeholder in the first row and the first column of your table, and then *complete the first row and the first column only*.

Stakeholders	Stakeholder a	Stakeholder b	Stakeholder c	Stakeholder d
Stakeholder a				
Stakeholder b				
Stakeholder c				
Stakeholder d				

You may insert scores in the squares that **combine a stakeholder with itself** ("Government" by "Government" for instance) if you have stakeholder groups that wish to assess internal role expectations and levels of satisfaction (see example in Step 9).

If you prefer to focus less attention on the table, use a **flipchart** to represent each column stakeholder. Then, place on each flipchart the cards that describe the expectations of other stakeholders and their levels of satisfaction. Each card should indicate who wrote it and to whom it is addressed. Once the flipcharts are completed, use the table created in Step 3 to compile the scores.

If you do not want to use written numbers when rating role performances, use simple **phrases** first (see Step 4) and then convert the phrases into measurable objects (from 0 to 4 twigs, stones, noodles or seeds, for instance). Another option is to score each performance with the help of five cards colored white (value 0), light grey (value 1), medium grey (value 2), dark grey (value 3), and black (value 4).

Since discussions about unsatisfied expectations can create tension, you may encourage participants to include expectations that have been **satisfied** or that express humor.

Note that you can also use this technique to evaluate the extent to which stakeholders are satisfied with their current levels of interaction (see *Role Dynamics* example). If using the technique for this purpose, ask each row stakeholder to describe and rate its current level of contribution to each other column stakeholder, and then the level of contribution it would like to make in each case. Ask "What do you (stakeholder in row A) contribute to stakeholder in column B and what would you like to contribute?" Another option is to ask "What does stakeholder in column B contribute to you (stakeholder in row A) and what would you like that stakeholder to contribute?". Place the two ratings, current and desired, in the same cell of the table. Create a rating scale for **levels of contribution or interaction**. For instance, you may create a scale of 0 to 5 where 0 means that the stakeholder has no obligation in relation to another stakeholder; 1 means that the stakeholder is not obliged to interact with the other; 2 means that the stakeholder is obliged to pass on information to the other; 3 means that the stakeholder must provide analysis and recommendations to the other; 4 means that the stakeholder must assist the other in taking decisions and implementing them; 5 means the stakeholder is expected to direct the other stakeholder's decisions and actions.

6. Calculate how much each stakeholder's expectations are satisfied by all others. To calculate this degree of satisfaction of each stakeholder, total all scores in each row and write the result on a card. Indicate on the same card the maximum total (in parentheses) and the average score for each row (the total score divided by the number of column scores). Create a last column to the right and insert the total and average score card for each row. Write **Satisfaction Level** at the top of the column. See example in Step 9.

7. Calculate how much each stakeholder satisfies the expectations of all other stakeholders. To calculate this degree of role performance of each stakeholder, total all scores in each column and write the result on a card. Indicate on the same card the maximum total (in parentheses) and the average score for each column (the total score divided by the number of row scores). Create a last row at the bottom and insert the role performance card for each column. Write **Performance Level** at the bottom of the first column. See example in Step 9.

8. To calculate the **average level of satisfaction**, total all satisfaction scores you inserted in the *last column* and divide the result by the sum of total maximum scores. To verify these calculations, total all role performance scores you inserted in the *last row* and divide the result by the sum of total maximum scores. This should give you the same percentage figure. Insert the resulting figure at the bottom of the last column.

9. Identify the **scores that contradict** the main tendencies of your table. To do this, compare each score with the average row score to see if they are on the same lower side or upper side of the middle point of your scale (5 in a scale of 0 to 10, for instance). If the score is *not* on the same side as the average row score, compare the score with the average column score to see if they are on the same lower side or upper side of the middle point of your scale. If the score is *not* on the same side again, draw a circle around the score. For instance, in the following table the score for the field officers' level of satisfaction with the financial managers (2) is on the lower side of the middle point (2.5); this contradicts the average row score (3.0) as well as the average column score (3.7), which are on the upper side of the middle point.

Here is an example of a *Role Dynamics* table involving seven stakeholders and a scale for levels of satisfaction ranging from 0 to 5:

Stakeholders	Financial managers	Data managers	Field officers	Project officers	Secretariat	Human resources	General managers	Satisfaction level
Financial Managers	5	4	5	5	5	5	5	34 (35), 4.9
Data Managers	4	5	5	4	5	5	5	33 (35), 4.7
Field Officers	(2)	3	(1)	3	4	5	3	21 (35), 3.0
Project Officers	2	2	1	3	2	2	1	13 (35), 1.9
Secretariat	4	4	(2)	4	5	3	4	26 (35), 3.7
Human Resources	4	5	5	5	4	5	4	32 (35), 4.6
General Managers	5	5	3	5	5	5	5	33 (35), 4.7
Performance Level	26 (35) 3.7	28 (35) 4.0	22 (35) 3.1	29 (35) 4.1	30 (35) 4.3	30 (35) 4.3	27 (35) 3.9	192 (245) 78.4%

Legend (last column and last row): column or row total, with maximum row or column total in parentheses (35), followed by average column or row scores.

10. Create a **diagram** by drawing a vertical line that crosses a horizontal line. This creates a cross within a square. Write the situation identified in Step 1 above the diagram using key words or a drawing. See example in Step 16.

11. Write the number that represents your **middle score** where the lines cross. To calculate the middle score, total the maximum scores in a row and divide the result by two. In the table shown in Step 9, the total maximum row score is 35; the middle score is therefore 17.5. See example in Step 16.

12. Write the minimum and the maximum total scores (0 and 35 in the table shown in Step 9) at opposite ends of the vertical and horizontal lines. Use the **vertical line** to represent satisfaction levels (using the totals in the last column scores from your table in Step 9). Use the **horizontal line** to represent performance levels (using the totals in the last row scores from your table in Step 9). See example in Step 16.

13. In each corner of the diagram, write (or draw) the **type of stake-holder** that you obtain when you combine the possible outcomes. This gives you four types of stakeholders: those that are more satisfied and perform better (top right); those that are more satisfied and perform less (top left); those that are less satisfied and perform better (bottom right); those that are less satisfied and perform less (bottom left). See example in Step 16.

14. To place each stakeholder in the diagram, mark where the stakeholder is located on both the vertical line (using its score for total satisfaction level) and the horizontal line (using its score for total performance level). Draw a line from each location and use a dot to mark the place where the two lines intersect.

15. Use arrows to indicate relationships that **contradict the main tendencies** of your diagram. To identify these relationships, use the scores encircled in Step 9. Use **continuous arrows** for scores above the middle point of your scale, and **broken arrows** for scores below the middle point. The continuous arrows indicate bottom-side stakeholders that are satisfied by the role performance of stakeholders located on the left side of your diagram. The broken arrows indicate upper-side stakeholders that are *not* satisfied by the role performance of stakeholders located on the right side of your diagram. See example in Step 16.

16. You may include in the diagram **other information** that you find useful for this analysis, such as the level of urgency or difficulty involved in satisfying other stakeholders' expectations. Use your own **code** (such as colors or capital letters) to identify these characteristics. Here's an example of a *Role Dynamics* diagram using the scores from the table shown in Step 9:

Situation: Restructuring a Non-Governmental Organization

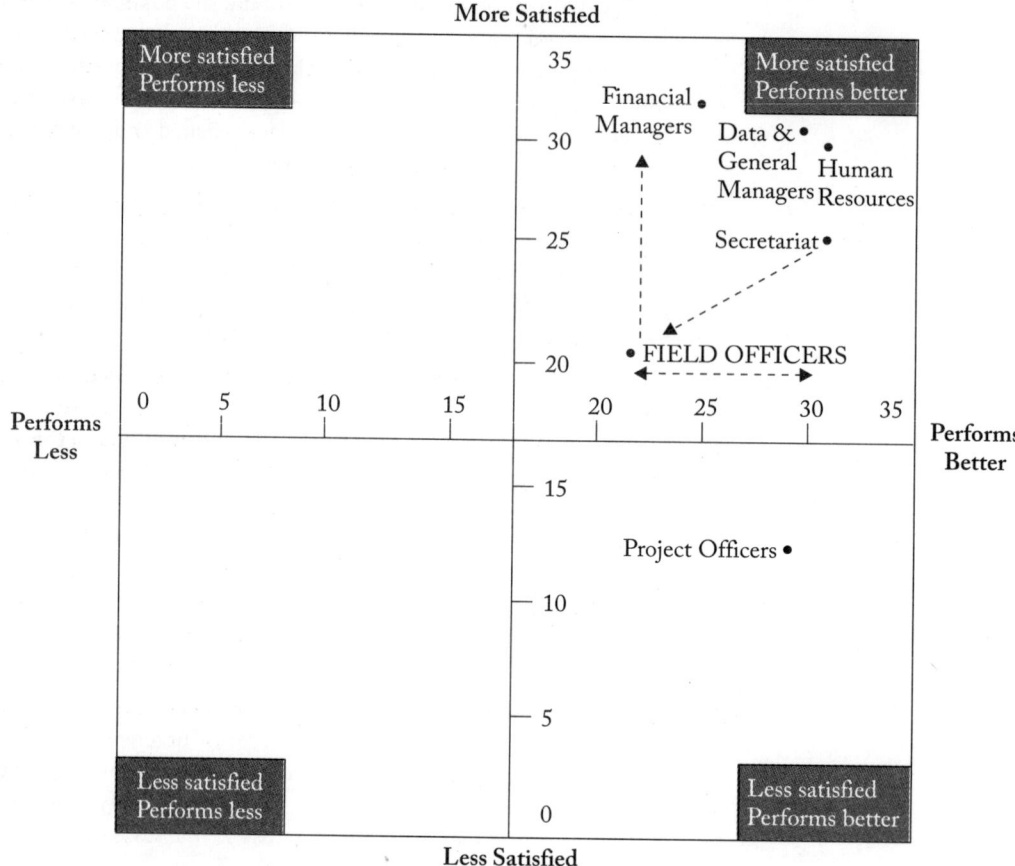

Summary of this example: Restructuring has had a direct impact on the role definitions and activities of seven key groups working within this non-governmental organization. Most groups feel that others are meeting their expectations. Tensions are present, however, in relation to the field officers, noted by the broken arrows. Field officers are dissatisfied with the peroformance of the financial managers and with their own internal interactions. Furthermore, they are not meeting the expectations of the secretariat.

Interpreting the Results

17. To interpret your *Role Dynamics* analysis, start with a **review** of the **process** itself, including the way that participants interacted and reached decisions at each step of the process. You can also review the **substance** of the exercise, including the topic that participants selected, their purpose in doing the exercise, the expectations they

identified, the kind of information or knowledge they used to rate the stakeholders, the contradictions and information added in Steps 15 and 16, and so on. Summarize all the main points of your review.

18. Assess the overall distribution of stakeholders by levels of satisfaction. A *Role Dynamics* analysis can produce three possible results: fulfillment, polarization, or failure. You know there is role **fulfillment** when you have many stakeholders in the top-right section of your diagram. This gives you a high average satisfaction score, usually above 60 percent (calculated in Step 8). Keep in mind that involving a top-right stakeholder may have a *chain effect* on the way you meet the expectations of many other stakeholders and, in turn, meet the expectations of the initial stakeholder.

    You know there is role **polarization** when your diagram shows bottom-right stakeholders that perform well but are dissatisfied with top-left stakeholders that do not perform well. This gives you a middle average satisfaction score, usually between 40 percent and 60 percent (calculated in Step 8).

    You know there is role **failure** when you have many stakeholders in the bottom-left section of your diagram. This gives you a low average satisfaction score, usually below 40 percent (calculated in Step 8). Role failure means that involving a bottom-left stakeholder will not have **a chain effect** on the way you meet the expectations of others.

19. Discuss how you can fill gaps between role expectations and performances and improve the situation identified in Step 1. Discussions can be held between all stakeholders or between the parties concerned only (with conclusions or recommendations presented in a general meeting at the end of the process, if necessary).

Scaling Up or Down

For Simpler Versions

1. Work with small groups of people who have many common characteristics.

2. Reduce the number of key stakeholders by eliminating some, or through the *Freelisting* technique.

3. Rate the role performances with a simple scale (using scores from 0 to 3, or simple phrases).

4. Do not use indicators to define the levels of satisfaction or performance.

5. Do not identify relationships that contradict the main tendencies of your table and diagram, and do not use other codes to insert other kinds of information in your diagram (Steps 9, 15, and 16).

6. Use a flipchart to represent each column stakeholder. Place on each flipchart the cards that describe the expectations of other stakeholders and their levels of satisfaction. Then, discuss how you can fill gaps between role expectations and performances.

7. Do not do the calculations and the analysis described in Steps 6 to 19.

For More Advanced Versions

1. Take more time to gather the information you need to complete the exercise.

2. During the exercise, discuss, and record the views that participants express.

3. Work with a greater number of people or groups.

4. Identify a greater number of key stakeholders.

5. Identify criteria to justify the ratings. Write a description for each indicator and each performance score.

6. Use surveys to find out how people assess role expectations and performance in a topic area.

7. Add more information in Step 16.

8. Use *Social Domain* to produce a detailed profile of all stakeholders.

Readings and Links

EVALSED (Evaluation of Socio-Economic Development). 2004. "Input/ Output Analysis." in *The GUIDE, Methods and Techniques*. Brussels, Belgium: European Commission. Available online at http://www.evalsed. info/page.aspx?id=mth112, accessed on August 15, 2007.

Heussen, H.; and D. Jung. 2003. *SINFONIE*. Berlin, Germany: Denkmodell. Available online at http://www.denkmodell de/WebObjects/wwwDenk modell.woa/wa/CMSshow/1063038, accessed on August 15, 2007.

Krumme, G. 2003. *Analysis of Interdependence Structures: Input-Output*. Seattle, WA: University of Washington. Available online at http://faculty. washington.edu/krumme/207/inputoutput.html#ionet, accessed on August 15, 2007.

Leontief, W.W. 1986. *Input-Output Economics*, 2nd edition. NY, USA: Oxford University Press.

Role Dynamics: The Roles and Mutual Expectations of Workgroups in the CUSO Regional Office

Key Words
Role Dynamics, Costa Rica, Canada, organizational development

Author and Acknowledgement
J.M. Chevalier. The author wishes to acknowledge the efforts of D.J. Buckles who helped to analyze the information and write the report.

Context

CUSO is a Canadian non-governmental organization that supports international development by placing Canadian volunteers in partner organizations around the world. After recent changes in organizational structure and workgroups, CUSO's regional office for Latin America and the Caribbean convened a meeting at its regional office in San Jose, Costa Rica to review how the office works in that region. Staff from its offices in Latin America, Canada, and the Caribbean attended several days of discussion. The meeting used a series of SAS[2] techniques to review goals, values, and roles guiding the organization.

Purpose

To assess the level of role expectations and role satisfaction of workgroups in one of CUSO's regional operations.

Process Summary

The participants organized themselves into workgroups sharing common roles in the organization. All workgroups collectively developed a scale of 5 indicators of possible contributions of each workgroup to other workgroups. Using the scale, each workgroup assessed on its own the level of contribution it would like to make to other workgroups (**role expectation**) and the level of contribution it felt it was actually making (**role satisfaction**). They also rated the level of contribution (actual and expected) among members *within* the workgroup. The results were compiled in a large table and role expectations discussed. Workgroups then identified other workgroups that were not satisfied with their actual level of contribution and sought them to discuss and negotiate how they could work differently to meet their expectations. This step was called a "negotiation fair". Agreements reached between workgroups were put in writing and then shared in a plenary meeting at the end of the exercise. The report, prepared by the facilitator/author, was later circulated among the participants for comment. CUSO agreed to publish the results of this analysis.

Analysis

The scale of possible levels of contribution developed by the participants was: 1 = little direct involvement; 2 = provides information; 3 = involved in analysis and planning; 4 = influences implementation; and 5 = direct

---

involvement in decisions. This was used to generate the ratings row-wise for each of the workgroups listed in Table 1.

The workgroups are: Financial Systems, Information Systems, Program Operations, Planning Special Projects, Office Administration, Human Resources, and Senior Management. The left value in each row is the level of contribution workgroups would like to make. The right value in each row is the level of contribution work-groups feel they are currently making. Gaps between the two values considered particularly significant to the participants are circled.

The last column in the table shows how much each row workgroup expects to contribute (upper-left value) and believes it actually contributes (lower-right value) to all other workgroups. The last row shows the extent to which each column workgroup is expected to depend (upper-left value) and actually depends (lower-right value) on other workgroups. Significant gaps in the extent to which workgroups actually fulfill the expectations of others are marked with a circle.

Table 1: Role Expectations and Role Satisfaction of CUSO Workgroups

Workgroups	Financial Systems	Information Systems	Program Operations	Planning Special Projects	Office Adminis-tration	Human Resources	Senior Man-agement	Contribution Index (total score)
Financial Systems	4 / 4	4 / 3	2 / 2	4 / 4	2 / 2	2 / 2	3 / 3	21 / 20
Information Systems	4 / 3	5 / 4	2 / 1	3 / 2	2 / 1	1 / 1	3 / 3	20 / 15
Program Operations	2 / 2	2 / 2	(4 / 2)	4 / 3	1 / 1	1 / 1	3 / 3	17 / 14
Planning Special Projects	3 / 2	(4 / 2)	5 / 5	3 / 3	2 / 2	2 / 1	5 / 4	24 / 19
Office Administration	1 / 1	1 / 1	(3 / 1)	(3 / 1)	3 / 2	2 / 1	3 / 2	16 / 9
Human Resources	3 / 2	1 / 1	1 / 1	1 / 1	3 / 2	3 / 2	5 / 5	17 / 14
Senior Management	5 / 5	3 / 2	5 / 5	5 / 5	3 / 3	3 / 3	5 / 5	29 / 28
Dependency Index (total score)	22 / 19	20 / 15	22 / 17	23 / 19	16 / 13	14 / 11	27 / 25	144 / 119

Graph 1 shows the desired shifts from actual to expected contributions and dependency for each workgroup. The level of overall interaction among workgroups currently is relatively low, with all but Senior Management contributing little to other groups and depending little on them. This suggests that most workgroups actually work quite independently of other workgroups. The graph also shows that there are some gaps between this currently low level of interaction and role expectations: all workgroups want to shift both horizontally and vertically. The biggest expected shifts are for Information Systems, Program Operations, Planning Special Projects, and Office Administration. By contrast, Senior Management, Financial Systems and Human Resources are operating close to expectations.

Discussion of gaps during the "negotiation fair" led to the following agreements (see circled relationships in Table 1):

Graph 1: The Interaction of Contributions and Dependency for Role Expectations and Actual Role Satisfaction among CUSO Workgroups

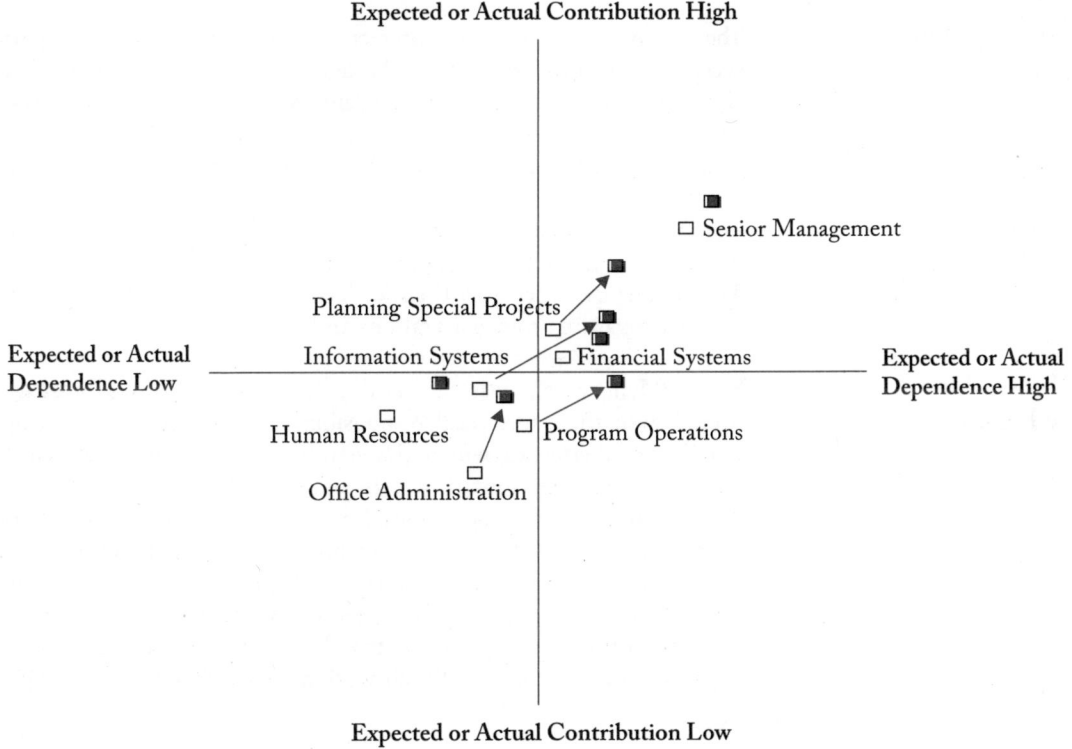

1. The Information Systems workgroup should play a stronger role in helping to structure and improve the flow of information needed by the Planning and Special Programs workgroup and by Senior Management.

2. The Program Operations workgroup needs to apply and share information on procedures more uniformly within the workgroup both in Costa Rica and in Canada. Better flows of information about these procedures with the Office Administration workgroup would also improve the performance of the system.

3. The Office Administration workgroup needs to share information from planning meetings more uniformly within the group. The Planning and Special Programs workgroup and Senior Management agreed to ensure that both office staff and executive assistants are present in future planning meetings.

4. The Financial Systems and Human Resources workgroups need to work more closely together to analyze and plan the financial aspects of personnel benefits.

Interpretation

The relatively low level of interaction among workgroups is partly acceptable to most workgroups because roles and responsibilities are clearly defined and staff communicate well among themselves. Some improvements are needed because of recent changes in the way the organization is structured, and the hiring of new staff.

Action

The group decided to follow up on selected improvements in role definitions identified during the assessment. It also conveyed to Senior Management the need for their leadership in scheduling periodic discussions regarding role expectations and role satisfaction.

Observations on the Process

Senior Management was surprised at how satisfied workgroups were overall with their roles and responsibilities. In a secret vote, people ranked the degree to which the new structure of the regional office served their personal interests and personal values. When these scores were displayed, they showed high levels of satisfaction for both factors. This upheld the positive picture that emerged from the *Role Dynamics* assessment. The participants said they also found the exercise useful as a process for building greater understanding and appreciation of the work of colleagues. It reduced the anxiety some had felt regarding the perceptions of their work held by other groups.

Levels of Support

Author	J.M. Chevalier
Acknowledgement	*Levels of Support* is a SAS[2] adaptation of a technique developed by S. Kaner et al. (see *Readings and Links*).
Purpose	*Levels of Support* is a technique that helps you choose the decision method and level of support that are appropriate to particular activities and options for action.

Guiding Principle

1. The level of support from stakeholders needed for a decision to be implemented successfully varies according to the situation.

2. Decision methods based on a majority of either yes or no votes are poor indicators of level of stakeholder support.

3. Levels of support are easier to understand when we use terms that are chosen and negotiated by the parties themselves.

Process

Defining the Level of Support Needed

1. Select a precise **option** for action that a group is seriously considering. Define the option as clearly as possible, and clarify the purpose of this exercise.

2. List the **reasons or factors** that are needed for actions to require **high levels of support** (such as "A proposed action requires a high level of support if ... there is a lot at stake for all parties concerned").

3. Assess each reason or factor in relation to your option for action. **Rate** each factor using a scale from 1 to 10. The maximum score 10 means that the factor "applies perfectly well" to the proposed action. If you want to be more precise, identify **indicators** that define the meaning of each number on the scale.

4. If you consider certain factors to be less important, you may use a different **scale** (1 to 8, or 1 to 5, for example). If you decide to do this, write (in parentheses) the maximum score possible with the scale. Here is an example of a list of reasons and scores using a variable scale:

Proposed action: Renovating the School

Suggested scale: 1 = False (does not apply at all) ⟶ 10 = True (applies perfectly well)

This proposed action requires a high level of support because...

There is a lot a stake for all parties concerned	score 9 (maximum 10)
We will not be able to change the decision once it is made	score 3 (maximum 10)
We need everyone's active involvement	score 6 (maximum 10)
We will need to work hard to achieve our goal	score 3 (maximum 8)
This is going to cost a lot	score 5 (maximum 5)
Total	score 26 (maximum 43)
Percentage score	26 / 43 = 60%

---

5. To convert the total score into a percentage, total the scores and divide this number by the maximum total. Results that are closer to 100 percent suggest you need higher levels of support for a decision to be implemented successfully.

Support Levels and Polling

6. Before polling participants, talk about and develop the precise wording or pictures you will use in your support scale. The support scale should consist of nine or so statements or pictures, ranging from the most positive to the most negative, or from the highest level of commitment to the lowest. Remind participants that the polling exercise is not a final decision.

Use words or images to express levels of support, not numbers. Be sure to use expressions of support and commitment that clearly indicate what participants may expect from each other. Avoid expressions that are too vague or too extreme for the option you are discussing.

Here is an example of a set of nine statements that express support and lack of support.

S A S²

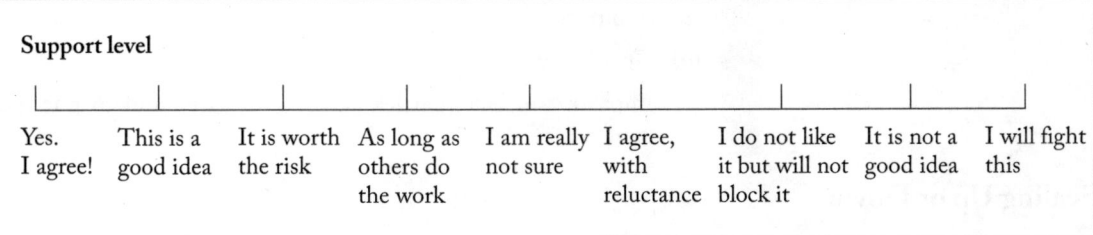

Support level

Yes. I agree!	This is a good idea	It is worth the risk	As long as others do the work	I am really not sure	I agree, with reluctance	I do not like it but will not block it	It is not a good idea	I will fight this

7. Discuss whether participants should express their levels of support openly (by raising their hands, displaying cards or marking their responses on the whiteboard or flipchart) or through secret ballots. Be aware that participants may prefer to express their level of support by consensus.

8. Ask each participant or group to choose the support level that suits them best. Collect the responses using the method chosen in Step 7.

9. Map out the responses on the support scale (using X marks). For a clearer view of differences between group responses, use a separate row for each group.

10. Discuss the results, and compare them with the level of support that participants are aiming for.

11. If the level of support is not as high as the group wants it to be or if key stakeholders reject the proposal, participants may wish to continue the discussion and modify the proposal. If the exercise is done with secret ballots and the non-supporters are anonymous, the facilitator may invite all participants to speak out as if they were the ones who opposed the proposal. Role playing allows the group to continue the discussion at the same time as it preserves anonymity.

Reaching a Decision

12. Before reaching a final decision, discuss the ways the group can decide. Choose one of the following decision methods (see Attachment A):

    (a) Majority rule (50 % + 1 or 2/3 support);

    (b) Minority rule (designated expert, appropriate authority, executive committee, forceful action);

    (c) Mutual agreement (achieved through bargaining or mediation);

(d) Arbitration;

(e) Unanimity;

(f) Impasse and exit (parties agree to disagree and to put the issue aside).

Scaling Up or Down

For Simpler Versions

1. Do not define the level of support needed.
2. Use the same rating scale for all factors (such as 1 to 10).
3. Do not use precise indicators when assessing reasons or factors that are needed for actions, to require high levels of support (Step 3).

For More Advanced Versions

1. Use the technique to assess and compare two or more options for action.
2. Repeat this polling exercise at a later date (such as one month later).
3. During the exercise, discuss and record the views that parties express.
4. Take more time to gather the information you need to complete the exercise.
5. Write a description for each reason or factor that seems to favor high levels of support; do the same for statements that express support and lack of support.

Readings and Links

Accurate Democracy. nd. *Principles in Voting Rules*. Available online at http://accuratedemocracy.com/a_primer.htm#nine, accessed on August 16, 2007.

CRC (Conflict Research Consortium). nd. *Dealing Constructively with Intractable Conflicts*. Boulder, CO, USA: CRC, University of Colorado. Available online at http://www.beyondintractability.org, accessed on August 15, 2007.

Kaner, S.; L. Lind; C. Toldi; S. Fisk; and D. Berger. 1996. *Facilitator's Guide to Participatory Decision-Making*, 255 pp. Gabriola Island, BC, Canada: New Society Publishers.

http://www.colorado.edu/conflict/peace/treatment/majority.htm, accessed on August 15, 2007 (for majority rule processes).

http://www.colorado.edu/conflict/peace/treatment/consenpr.htm, accessed on August 15, 2007 (for consensus rule processes).

Attachment A: The Pros and Cons of Various Decision-making Rules

Rules	Pros	Cons
Majority Rule	Quick and efficient	Minorities may feel left out
	Practical when working with large groups	Quality of decisions may be questionable
Minority Rule Designated expert or authority Executive committee Forceful people within the group	Saves time Clear and efficient One part of the group may be more informed and committed	Expertise may be hard to determine No group input Members may compete for attention and to impress authority Weak commitment to decision
Unanimity Rule Consensus	Quality decisions Commitment Satisfaction	Time consuming Difficult May create tension

Source: Lynn Meade, nd. *Group Discussion: Effective Decision Making and Problem Solving* (edited version), Chapter Seven. Available online at http://lynn_meade.tripod.com/id183.htm, accessed on August 16, 2007.

Levels of Support: Levels of Support for Community Woodlots in Kajla, West Bengal, India

Key Words

Levels of Support, India, West Bengal, common property resources, environment, natural resource management

Author and Acknowledgement

S. Panda. The author wishes to acknowledge the efforts of N. Panda, P. Sahoo, N. Pariali, and K. Bhattacharya of DRCSC, who helped to design and facilitate the assessment, and D.J. Buckles (Carleton University) who helped to write the report.

Context

Kajla is a village in the Purba Medinipur district of West Bengal, India. About 10 percent of the people who live here are landless. The men from the village migrate seasonally for work in other areas, leaving their families without support for long periods of time. The Development, Research, Communication and Services Centre (DRCSC), a non-governmental organization based in Kolkata, has international funding to support the development of community woodlots in Kajla for use by landless households. DRCSC has worked jointly with a community-based organization in Kajla for 15 years (Kajla Jana Kalyan Samity, KJKS). Support from KJKS staff, from a majority of landless families, and from local authorities (known as the Panchayat), is vital for the project to succeed. Support from the irrigation department of the state government is also needed, since it controls some of the land in the village that might be used for woodlots.

Purpose

To assess the level of support for community woodlots among stakeholders in the village.

Process Summary

KJKS and DRCSC convened a meeting at the Kajla Primary School. Those invited to the meeting were: landless households, other village households, representatives of the Panchayat, and members of the irrigation department. Some 38 people attended, including 16 landless households, six KJKS staff, several members of the Irrigation Department, and people from the village and Panchayat. A proposal to establish community woodlots was described in detail, including plans to plant trees on the roadside, canal banks, and fallow areas. The potential benefits of the plan were also described by KJKS, noting in particular improved access by landless households to fuel, food, and fodder. Participants stated their views and concerns about the proposal, which were noted on cards. Similar opinions were then piled together and a simple

phrase was chosen from among them to represent that category. Nine phrases, accompanied by pictures, were lined up on the ground, with the most positive at one end and the most negative at the other. Participants then indicated their position on the proposal by placing a piece of brick beside the opinion he or she most strongly agreed with. The level of support vital to success of the proposal, possible revisions to the proposal and the overall result were discussed. The facilitator later prepared a report. Planned use of the report was understood by the participants, who agreed to share their information.

Analysis

The level of support for community woodlots is presented in Table 1. While only four participants gave their support to *all* aspects of the proposal, 15 people (almost half the group) gave full support for community woodlots on the roadside and indicated that they were willing to provide their time and effort to this aspect of the proposal. A few recognized the risk of loss of their time but said they would help to get it done. Two smaller groups, adding up to eight individuals, agreed that the community woodlot proposal was important but they would not be willing to assist directly. Very low levels of support and opposition to the proposal were expressed by four individuals. The concerns they expressed were the amount of effort needed to prepare the land properly, and whether or not the trees could be protected. When discussed further, it became evident that from the point of view of the people with concerns about the proposal, a community woodlot might also hamper cattle grazing. These concerns were raised by villagers who had land of their own and little to gain directly from the initiative.

Table 1: Levels of Support for Community Woodlots in Kajla, West Bengal, India

							XXX	
							XXXX	
							XXXX	
XX	X	X		XXXX	XXXX	XX	XXXX	XXXX
Tree planting not possible	Trees cannot be protected	Land needs to be prepared	All group members will not spare time	Tree planting is necessary	Tree planting is essential	Though risk of loss, must be done	We will plant on roadside	We will fully support woodlots

Interpretation

People without land of their own are willing to give time and effort to create community woodlots because the project meets their needs, and outside help or resources for landless families is rare. The participants observed that the high level of support for putting woodlots on the roadside is because this land is state property and has few other uses. Those with concerns about the proposal are not directly involved in the proposed activity and are not in a position to block uses of public lands by landless groups.

Action

The participants, including the various organizations involved in the proposal, agreed to create community woodlots on only part of the roadside, covering an area 2.5 km in length. Woodlots on other lands would be considered once the project could be shown to be valuable to all community members and concerns about impacts on cattle grazing were discussed further. KJKS decided to identify the steps needed to ensure that group members contribute time equally, to prepare the land properly, and to protect the trees.

Observations on the Process

The specific reasons for opposition to the project by some participants did not come out initially. The facilitators talked privately with them during a break and determined that they were concerned about the impact of a woodlot on cattle grazing on village lands. They agreed to discuss these concerns openly with the other participants, who recognized the legitimacy of the concern and the need to discuss it further, prior to widespeard implementation of the project. The majority felt confident, however, that there was sufficient support in the village to proceed with the revised proposal focusing on the roadside. Several participants said that they appreciated how the exercise had led to modification of the proposal rather than a simple approval or rejection that might have resulted from a standard voting procedure.

The Wheel

Author J.M. Chevalier

Acknowledgement *The Wheel* is a SAS[2] adaptation and development of a rating technique used in the field of participatory research (see in particular D. Howlett et al., 2000).

Purpose *The Wheel* helps you visualize and compare multiple ratings (see *Rating*). The technique is useful when you need to organize information, compare the views of different parties, assess the same element or situation at different points in time, identify priorities or expectations, and evaluate the process of learning over time.

Guiding Principles

1. People have different ways of rating elements in a list. This may be the source of disagreement or misunderstanding within groups.

2. New knowledge and learning may affect how you look back at the past and the way you would rate the same elements if you were to do it again.

Process

Wheel Mapping

1. Identify a **topic area** where you need to use *The Wheel*. Define the topic as clearly as possible, and clarify the purpose of your exercise.

2. Establish a list of the **elements** that you need to rate (such as actors or community projects). Write (or draw) each element on its own card. Describe each element on the reverse side of its card.

   You may include an ideal element (the ideal self or community project, for instance) in your list. If the elements are actors, you may define the representatives of a group as an actor, different from those they represent. Also you may include the community of all actors in your list, as a group with its own profile.

3. Identify several **rating criteria** using positive terms (such as competencies when assessing actors; or gender equity, sustainability, stakeholder support, cost effectiveness, and time availability when assessing community projects).

   The elements and the criteria should be concrete, clearly defined, and relevant to the topic. If the elements or the rating criteria are vague, use the *Laddering Down* technique to make them more meaningful and detailed. Ask "What do you mean by this?", "Can you give an example of this?", "How can you tell this?", or "In what way is this true?" (for instance, "In what way are some actors more knowledgeable compared with others?" or "In what way are some commmunity projects more complex compared with others?").

   A simple technique to identify several rating criteria consists in asking the **catch-all question**: "Can you think of some new, different rating criteria?" Another option is the **full context** procedure where you look at all elements and find out two that have a positive characteristic in common, and then the element that is the most different from these and ask why. You can also use **description and storytelling** to explore your topic area (such as describing various skills or community projects), and then use this information to identify the rating criteria.

   You can **supply** or **negotiate** some or all of the elements and the rating criteria or you can **ask** the participants to identify them, depending on the purpose of the exercise and your role as facilitator.

4. Establish a **rating scale** (with values from 0 to 10, for instance). If you want this exercise to be more precise, identify **indicators** that define the meaning of each number on the scale. For instance, you may decide that a score of 8 out of 10 for sustainability means that the impact is expected to last for at least eight years.

   If you do not want to use written numbers when rating the elements, use simple **phrases** first and then convert the phrases into measurable objects (from 1 to 5 twigs, stones, noodles, or seeds). Another option is to score each element with the help of five cards colored white (value 1), light grey (value 2), medium grey (value 3), dark grey (value 4), and black (value 5).

5. Draw **one circle or wheel for each element** (in a list of actors or community projects, for instance). Insert lines that extend from the center to the border of the circle. Each line represents a different rating criterion. Identify each criterion by placing a label at

the end of each line, outside the circle (see example in Step 8). You may also insert brief descriptions of each criterion between the lines inside the wheel.

Make sure that all wheels are the same size and that the lines and criteria are located in the same places. Leave part of the wheel empty, in case participants decide to add new criteria.

6. **Test** your wheel with the group to ensure that the elements, the rating criteria, the rating scale, and the indicators are clear to everyone.

7. Use each line or criterion to **rate each element** in a range from 0 to 10, where the lowest value (0, negative) is located at the center and where the highest (10, positive) is located at the circle's border. You can give the same score to two or several elements. Record each score by placing a mark along the corresponding line inside the wheel.

There are several methods you can use to rate the elements: (*i*) You can ask individuals or groups to rate the elements they know best. Use this method if individuals or groups are assessing their own characteristics or assets (resources, competencies, and so on). (*ii*) You can divide all participants into smaller groups and ask each group to select a few criteria and to use these to rate all the elements. Use this technique only if the participants do not need to be involved in all the ratings. (*iii*) Another option is to discuss the scores for each element until participants reach an agreement based on consensus or a majority vote. (*iv*) Or you can ask each participant to rate each element using one criterion at a time, and then calculate the average rating for each element (such as land management options). To calculate an average rating, multiply each rating value by the number of times it is assigned to the element, total the results, and divide the total by the number of people responding.

8. To obtain the profile of each element, draw **straight lines between the marks** you have made on each line. Here is an example of a wheel using 5 rating criteria:

Option 1: Project to Repair the School

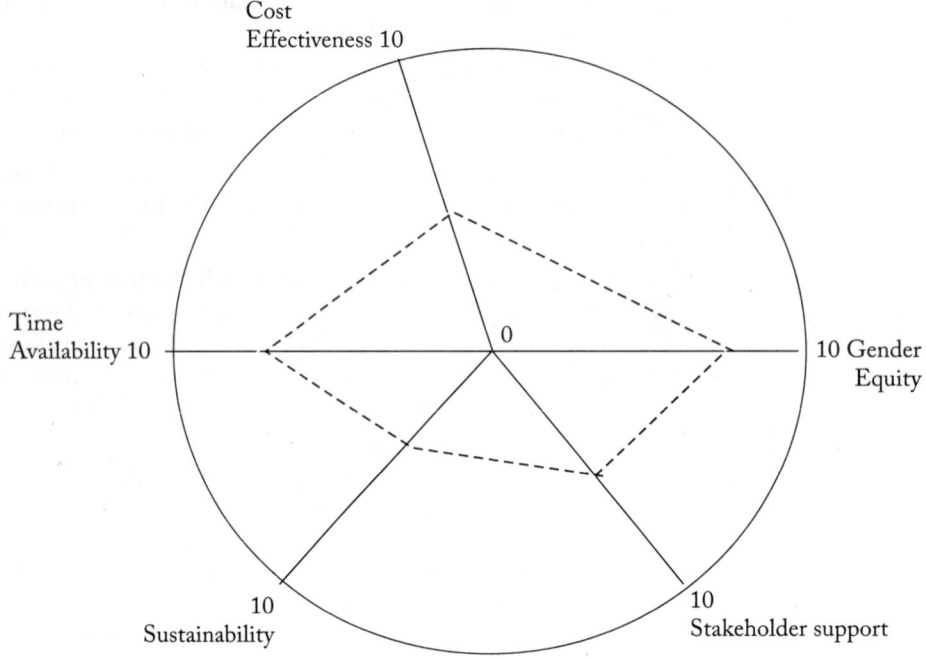

Comparing Wheels

9. To **compare** two wheels, superimpose one on the other. By superimposing one wheel on another you can see the **similarities and differences** between two elements (the profiles of two different actors or community projects, for instance). Or you can see how different parties view the same element (a particular community project, for instance); this will tell you if there is a **disagreement** between the parties (such as men and women), and also the areas of disagreement. For calculations of levels of difference or disagreement, see *Rating*.

10. To assess levels of **understanding** between parties (such as men and women), rate the elements as you think the other party would rate them. Then, compare the rating you predict with the other party's actual ratings. Superimpose the two wheels to do the comparison. For calculations of levels of misunderstanding, see *Rating*.

11. Levels of agreements may be combined with levels of understanding to produce **six possible scenarios**:

	Misunderstanding		Understanding
Agreement	Scenario 1 The parties agree but do not know it	Scenario 2 The parties agree but one does not know it	Scenario 3 The parties agree and both know it
Disagreement	Scenario 4 The parties disagree but do not know it	Scenario 5 The parties disagree but one does not know it	Scenario 6 The parties disagree and both know it

12. Discuss the results of your wheel comparisons, with an emphasis on **where and why** there are major differences, disagreements, or misunderstandings. If you are working with two or more groups, members of each group may wish to discuss these issues among themselves before sharing their views with other groups.

13. Come together as a single group to discuss the wheel exercise and to explore how it has affected the views or priorities of individuals or subgroups.

Expectations, Results, and Socratic Learning

14. You can use *The Wheel* to compare the ratings of the same element at **different points in time**. You can also compare the **actual** and the **expected** ratings for the same element (an actor's competencies or an ongoing project, for instance). To compare elements over time, you need three ratings for each line or criterion inside you wheel. You need (*i*) the current rating of the element, (*ii*) the rating you are expecting or hoping for, within a certain time limit, and (*iii*) the final rating obtained once the time limit is reached.

Record these three ratings for each criterion by placing marks along the corresponding lines inside the wheel. Draw straight lines (*i*) between the marks that describe the current ratings, (*ii*) between the marks that describe the expected ratings, and then (*iii*) between the marks that represent the final ratings.

Here is an example of a wheel with five lines representing different competencies. The diagram describes an actor's own assesment of his initial level of competency for each line, his learning expectations, and the final results achieved after a year.

Actor 1: Competency Profile

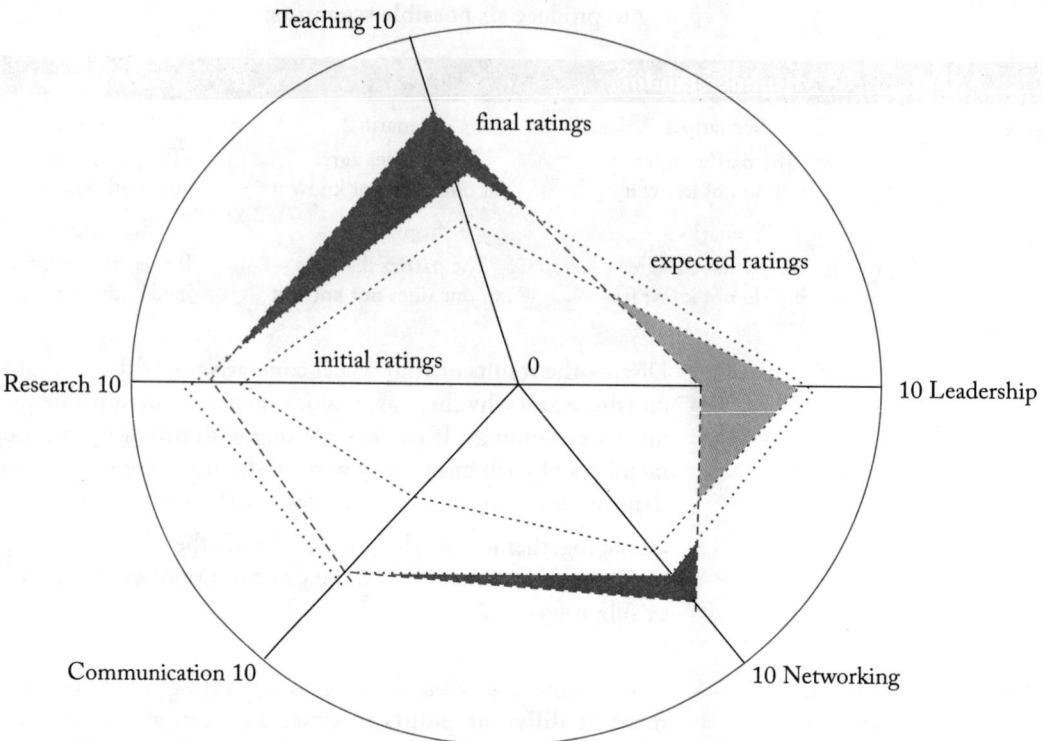

Summary of this example: This actor improved his *communication* skills at the level he was aiming for. He also managed to get better at *networking* and *teaching*, beyond his expectations. When he looks back at the initial rating he gave himself for his *teaching* skills, he realizes that his skills were better than he thought, which is encouraging. On the negative side of things, he did not improve his leadership skills as much as he had hoped for. But he is not necessarily disappointed by this. The training in leadership he took was very stimulating. He realizes now that he knew very little about what leadership means and hopes to learn a lot more.

15. You can also add a fourth set of ratings: the **initial ratings revised**. This is the way you would rate the same element if you were to do it again (in the past). To evaluate the real results achieved over time (column D – C, of the following table), compare your "initial ratings revised" with the final ratings (see columns C and D, again of the same table):

Rating criteria	Initial rating A	Expected rating B	Expected result B – A	Initial rating revised C	Final rating D	Real result D – C

16. Discuss and interpret the results of your analysis. Be aware of two effects of **Socratic learning** that may occur. Participants may discover that what they knew or achieved in the past was more than what they thought they knew or achieved, and might view this as a positive finding ("Now I know that I knew!"). Or they might discover that they now know or achieved less than what they thought they knew or achieved in the past, and might also consider this to be positive ("Now I know that I do not know!"). For an example of Socratic learning, see Step 14.

Scaling Up or Down

For Simpler Versions

1. Reduce the number of elements by eliminating some, or through the *Freelisting* technique.

2. Use only 3 or 4 rating criteria.

3. Do not use indicators when rating the elements.

4. Identify the areas where there are differences, disagreements, or misunderstandings, but not the level of disagreement or misunderstanding (Steps 9 and 10).

5. Do not compare current ratings of the element with the expected and the final ratings (Steps 14 to 16).

For More Advanced Versions

1. During the exercise, discuss and record the views that parties express.

2. Take more time to gather the information you need to complete your wheel.

3. Write a description for each element of your list and for each criterion.

4. Take note of the reason given for each score.

5. Increase the number of elements and rating criteria.

6. Use precise indicators to justify your ratings.

Reading and Link

Howlett, D.; R. Bond; P. Woodhouse; and D. Rigby. 2000. *Stakeholder Analysis and Local Identification of Indicators of the Success and Sustainability of Farming Based Livelihood Systems.* Working Paper No. 5. Manchester, United Kingdom: Centre for Agricultural Food and Resource Economics, University of Manchester. Available online at http://les.man.ac.uk/ses/research/CAFRE/indicators/wpaper5.htm, accessed on August 16, 2007.

The Wheel: Impacts on Knowledge and Skills among Participants in a Youth Exchange Program

Key Words

The Wheel, Cuba, Benin, Thailand, Ukraine, Canada, impact assessment, skills

Authors and Acknowledgements

J.M. Chevalier and D.J. Buckles. The authors wish to acknowledge Paul Turcot, Kate McLaren, and Helen Patterson, who contributed to the source reports.

Context

Canada World Youth (CWY) is a Canadian non-governmental organization focused on youth programming in Canada and abroad. Previous assessments of CWY programs suggested that knowledge and skills is an important impact area from the point of view of past participants and future program design. In 2006 it undertook a new assessment of the impact the Youth Exchange Program had on participants and communities in five countries, including Canada, Cuba, the Ukraine, Benin, and Thailand. One-day workshops for past participants in the Youth Exchange Program were organized in each country, covering six impact areas identified in previous CWY assessments: (*i*) values and attitudes; (*ii*) knowledge; (*iii*) skills; (*iv*) occupational gains; (*v*) interpersonal relationships; and (*vi*) civic engagement (local or global). Half-day workshops were also organized with representatives of participating communities and an on-line survey was conducted with a sample of Canadian past participants and representatives of communities. CWY staff at various levels were engaged in comparing and analyzing results from different countries. The evaluation team included CWY staff in each country as well as external consultants. They selected, tested, adapted, and sequenced various SAS[2] techniques for the purpose of assessing how and to what extent the Youth Exchange Program contributed to the mission of CWY.

For more information on the assessment see the following reports on the SAS[2] website: South House Exchange, SAS[2] Learning Systems, and Canada World Youth, 2006, Canada World Youth Impact Assessment Guide, Montréal: Canada World Youth, Social Analysis Systems[2] Plans and Protocol Report #1, 58 pp; South House Exchange, SAS[2] Learning Systems, and Canada World Youth, 2006, Canada World Youth Impact Assessment: Synthesis Report, Montréal: Canada World Youth, 84 pp.

Purpose	To assess the impact of the Youth Exchange Program on past participants.

Process Summary

The evaluation team convened one-day workshops in 17 different locations involving a total of 289 past participants in the Youth Exchange Program between 1995 and 2002. The participation rates for overseas participants ranged from 60 percent of all past participants in Benin, to approximately 25 percent of all past participants in Thailand and Ukraine. Canadian participation rates were lower given that the number of Canadians involved between 1993 and 2003 was over 5,000. The participants were fairly representative of their country programs with respect to gender balance and rural/urban balance. There were one or more representatives from every year under review in all countries.

During the workshops, a series of assessments were conducted on various impact areas using different SAS[2] techniques. After discussing the knowledge and skill impact areas during the workshop, and the purpose of this part of the assessment, each participant scored the impact of the Youth Exchange Program on five knowledge and skills areas, using a scale of zero to five. Participants were reminded by the facilitators that skills were understood to mean a concrete ability to do something, rather than something like being open-minded, which is an attitude. Individuals charted their scores on a wheel and noted details explaining their scores. Participants then looked for others with similar scores marked on their wheels, and formed groups with similar impact profiles. The members of each group discussed what they had in common and chose an image or symbol that represented the set of knowledge or skills, the group had most developed or strengthened through the CWY experience. Similarities and differences between groups were discussed, along with the reasons why the program had more impact in some areas and less impact in others. The results were integrated into workshop, national, and summary reports by the evaluation team. Participants understood that the results would be used in reports on the program, and agreed to share their information.

Analysis

Participants rated five specific impact areas identified by CWY: (*i*) knowledge; (*ii*) organizational skills; (*iii*) communication skills; (*iv*) learning skills; and (*v*) technical skills. Examples provided of knowledge impacts included the increase among participants in their knowledge of history, culture, geography, politics, development issues, aid, or any other related knowledge area. Organizational skill impacts referred to improvements in team work, leadership, facilitation, mediation, planning, or any other related ability. Communication skill impacts referred to abilities in language, cross-cultural communications, non-verbal communications, listening, interviewing, speaking in public or any other related ability. Examples of learning skill impacts were, increase in analysis, data collection, capacity to adapt, creative thinking, and other related abilities. Technical skill impacts referred to farming, computer use, teaching or any other ability requiring technical know-how.

The rating scale used by the participants was:

0 = No impact
1 = Very small impact
2 = Small impact
3 = Moderate impact
4 = Important impact
5 = Very important impact

The average of all scores on all impact areas is four, indicating an "important impact" of the Youth Exchange Program from the point of view of past participants. The average of individual scores for each country also shows a consistent pattern of high impacts on the knowledge and skills of past participants (Table 1). The top two skill areas indicated by these national averages are **communication skills** and **organization skills**. These two received the highest rating in every country except in Thailand where communication skills were rated lower than organization and learning skills.

The impact areas, with the highest variability between the countries are knowledge and learning skills, scoring higher on average in some countries and lower in others. For example, participants in Benin rated knowledge at 3.1, their lowest rating among all of the impact areas in this exercise. Participants in Cuba rated this impact area at 4.3. Impact on learning skills received ratings from as low as 3.5 (Canada) to a high of 4.2 (Cuba). It is interesting to note that while the Cuban rating was the highest for this impact area, learning skills received a relatively low score compared to other impact areas. This may be explained by the fact that the Cuban participants are all teachers by profession and view themselves as expert learners. The skill area receiving the lowest rating in every country (except Benin) is technical skills.

Table 1: Average of Individual Scores for Knowledge and Skills, by Country

Country	Number of participants	Communi- cation skills	Organization skills	Learning skills	Knowledge	Technical skills	Av. Score
		Average of Individual Scores*					
Cuba	61	**4.5**	**4.5**	4.2	4.3	4.0	4.3
Ukraine	28	**4.5**	4.3	3.9	4.0	3.3	4.0
Canada	64	**4.3**	3.9	3.5	4.0	2.4	3.6
Benin	74	**4.0**	**4.0**	3.7	3.1	3.4	3.6
Thailand	62	3.8	**4.1**	**4.1**	3.8	3.6	3.9
Weighted average for all 289		4.2	4.1	3.9	3.8	3.3	3.9

Note: * The highest scores per country are in bold. The maximum possible score is 5.

Within each country, there are some variations among workshops. However, the highest and lowest rated areas remain the same. The small group averages also tend to reflect the tendencies of the workshop averages.

The individual and small group observations on the scores are consistent with the general pattern. Participants typically make references to high impacts in many areas, as in the following case:

> The impact it had on my life was very significant because it developed in me organizational skills such as team work, leadership—because a teacher must be a leader par excellence, mediation, organization, and planning work, among other skills. As for knowledge, I learnt about history, culture, geography, social and political problems in another country, in addition to mine. We spoke so much about sustainable development and environmental protection that I developed an ecological awareness. Seven years later, knowing that I have grown more mature, I now realize that CWY was the force, the principal source of motivation to learn and take decisions, to grow as an independent person, and to maintain my equilibrium. (Authors' translation)

The key words used by individuals and small groups to describe these impacts show up with different frequencies. Among the key **communication skills**, language and knowing how to listen are frequently mentioned. Speaking in public and non-verbal communication is mentioned less frequently. References to impacts on key **organizational skills** frequently include leadership, team work, and facilitation. Being organized and planning skills are also mentioned, though less often. Although the average impact on **knowledge** varies from country to country, there are many references in individual notes to learning about the culture and history of the host countries and their own countries as they struggled to share their knowledge with others. The ability to adapt was the **learning skill** most frequently mentioned in notes by the participants. A word count for "adaptability" found 20 out of 64 participants in Canada making reference to this skill. Other learning skills, such as analytic skills, data or information management, and creative thinking, are mentioned by participants in other countries, although much less often. A few references are also made to critical thinking and knowing how to carry out research. **Technical skills** developed through the program involve mostly the use of computer and the internet. Manual skills (agriculture, carpentry) are mentioned rarely. Some participants noted that the program offers them few opportunities to develop new technical skills, something they would have liked to see built into the program design. Others, like the Canadian and some of the Ukrainian participants, noted that they already had computer skills when they joined the program.

Interpretation

The CWY program had an important impact on the development of all knowledge and skill areas (Graph 1 and Table 1). Many discovered and developed skills, they did not think they had or needed to strengthen, pointing to the Socratic discovery of latent learning. These results reflect the theory that the impact areas are interrelated and that the CWY experience is holistic. It is also consistent with the CWY mission "to foster the acquisition of knowledge, skills, attitudes and values necessary for active community involvement."

Graph 1: Average of Individual Scores for Knowledge and Skills, by Country

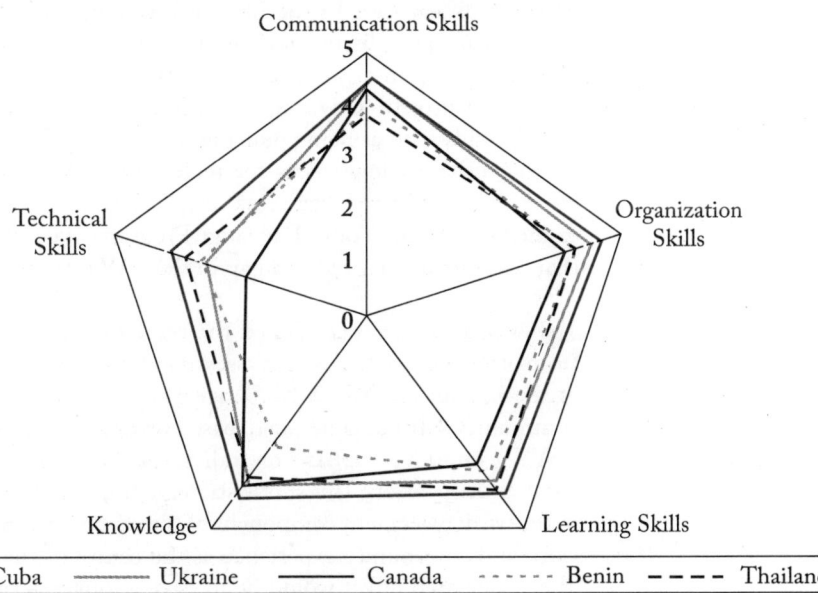

The skills that consistently benefited the most from the Youth Exchange Program are communication and organizational skills. This confirms the centrality of impacts on interpersonal relationships flagged in other parts of the impact assessment. This category of skills is targeted in various program activities and are strengthened through educational activity days, group activities, and in the interaction between counterparts and their host families and work placements.

Better **communication skills** reflect the strengthening of English language skills that are part and parcel of the CWY experience, but also the opportunity to live and work across cultural and linguistic divides. Being able to express oneself well, listen and understand, pick up non-verbal cues and to be comfortable speaking in groups or in public, are clear effects of the situation participants found themselves in, during the exchange.

The high scores given for **organizational skills**, such as teamwork, leadership, facilitation, planning, and mediation, reflect the emphasis that CWY places on working collaboratively in groups, on building leadership capacities and on taking responsibility for one's work and commitments. It also reflects the fact that participation in the program involves a "constant need to plan and organize activities with one's counterpart or the group. Mastering these skills became essential for the good functioning of the program" (Thai Report). To work in a team, each individual needs to deal with a range of human behaviors, needs and expectations, and to understand and mediate cultural and personal differences. In the intense learning process of the program, some participants discovered skills they did not know they had, like the "leaders" group in a workshop in Ukraine. Through work placements, group and project activities, participants learnt other important job-related skills such as being punctual and personally well organized.

The relatively low scores for **technical** skills stand apart from the other skill and knowledge areas since building technical skill is not an explicit goal of the Youth Exchange Program. It is, however, a skill area that participants flagged as a gap in the CWY experience.

Action

The evaluation team combined the results of the exercise with results from other parts of the impact assessment, towards an overall assessment of the impact the Youth Exchange Program had on participants and communities. It recommended, based on the broader set of results, that CWY ground its emphasis on individual learning objectives in specific community projects. This subtle strategic shift would imply adjustments to the work placement component of the exchange program, to put both work and community experience at the centre of the learning agenda. The anticipated effect would be to have a longer-term impact on host communities while at the same time building relevant individual technical or professional skills, in addition to communication, learning, and organizational skills.

Observations on the Process

Participants initially thought that low scores would imply that a participant feels the program did a poor job of skill transfer. This concern was managed by workshop facilitators who emphasized that a low score could be given if the participant thought they had these skills before coming to the program.

The results of individual exercises were strongly endorsed by the participants, many of whom noted that the visual display of the scores made it easy to appreciate the overall impact of the program on skills. While comparisons between groups were made after the individual exercises were complete, a thorough review of the final report by members of the Board of CWY, staff, and representatives of the various national exchange programs confirmed the relevance and usefulness of both the individual and the compiled results.

Conclusions and Acknowledgements

The guiding idea of this book, and the broader initiative in which it is embedded, is that the current era must become an era of dialogue and social engagement in the use and creation of knowledge. It is a matter of survival. Humanity can no longer rely on solutions engineered by experts and private interests alone. Social issues must be addressed socially and fully integrated into processes of learning and decision-making that broaden and deepen understanding and inspire action. This requires that we acknowledge and value more than ever the rich knowledge embodied in the lives of people from all corners of the world. Building on the living character of knowledge creates the possibility of immediate application, and the synergy needed to free us from rigid forms of higher learning and inquiry that are no longer adapted to our world. Whether the inquiry involves selecting economic crops for next season or developing a strategy to assert land rights, the concepts and tools outlined in this book are a modest contribution to this pressing endeavor.

A key message of this Guide concerns the skillful means to make good on the opportunities and promise of people-based and evidence-based thinking. While many people would agree with this goal, the means to realize its potential remains largely unexplored. Conventional methods such as surveys, questionnaires, and focus groups offer little scope for imagination or originality in search for solutions to issues, that are meaningful and relevant to the people involved. SAS² provides guidance on how to walk-the-talk both in the form of specific tools for assessing problems, actors and options and in the concepts and guidelines for the design of processes and events that can support dialogue and social innovation. Together they make a novel contribution to conventional notions of public engagement and expert research.

SAS² itself is a particular expression of living knowledge that is evolving in different places through the efforts of many people. It is the result of collaboration between people with a common purpose: to create fertile ground for group thinking and action that will achieve the common good. Many people have contributed towards this work. The various institutional partners listed in the introduction have been particularly helpful and creative in their applications and adaptations of SAS² to their own contexts. Canada World Youth and CUSO in both Ottawa and Latin America supported several assessments that were key turning points in our understanding of the implications of SAS² concepts for monitoring and evaluation and for organizational development. The financial support of the International Development Research Centre, and encouragement from Merle Faminow, Giséle Morin-Labatut, Raul Zelaya, and other IDRC staff, made it possible to engage with partners around the world and enhance the scope of the SAS² initiative. This Guide is greatly enriched by the examples of SAS² applications provided by Laura Suazo-Gallardo of IDRC in Honduras, Rajeev Khedkar, Dnyaneshwar Patil, and Bansi Ghevde of ADS in India, Diwakar Poudel and Tek Sapkota of LIBIRD in Nepal,

Farida Akhter of UBINIG in Bangladesh, Jorge Téllez of CEBEM in Bolivia, Carlos Tapia of the University de la Serena in Chile, and Shyamel Panda of the Development, Research, Communication and Service Centre in India. Michelle Bourassa of the University of Ottawa contributed significantly to developing some of the key concepts and techniques presented in this Guide. Debra Huron helped us enormously by editing the Guide, and encouraging us to pay careful attention to clear language, the active voice and the salient points. Bill Carman of IDRC and Richa Raj of SAGE Publications were very helpful and patient throughout the publication process. While we take full responsibility for the opinions expressed and any factual errors that remain, the Guide owes a great deal to the insights, feedback, and direct assistance provided by these individuals. More generally, the SAS[2] initiative is, and will always remain, a work-in-progress that all people interested in furthering "social thinking" can contribute to and learn from.

The approach described in this book is direct and systematic, but it is not always easy. It is not enough to simply think that dialogue and social engagement is a good idea. There are many concepts to be appropriated and adapted as well as skills to be learned, with patience and incrementally. We encourage readers who decide to travel along this path to meet and work with others to design and implement real-life events and processes using SAS[2] and other methods at your disposal, and share your experiences and learning in communities of practice you create or join. Learning to learn differently might change our respective worlds, while also helping us change the world we all share. To succeed in this endeavor, what we require above all is the commitment to engage in bold new ways. In the words of Goethe, "Whatever you can do, or dream you can, begin it. Boldness has genius, power, and magic in it."

Notes on Contributors

Farida Akhter is the Executive Director of UBINIG (Policy Research for Development Alternative), a non-governmental organization in Bangladesh supporting farmer-based research and policy initiatives on a range of topics. She is also a leading member of many regional and international women's networks such as Feminist International Network of Resistance to Reproductive and Genetic Engineering (FINRAGE), the Asian Women's Human Rights Council (AWHRC), and the United Women's Front in Bangladesh. She began her work as a journalist and completed a Masters Degree in Economics at Chittagong University.

Michelle Bourassa is an Associate Professor at the Faculty of Education, Ottawa University where she teaches the psychological foundations of learning and differentiated teaching. She has published articles on student assessment and special education, edited a special SAS^2 edition of the journal *Éducation et Francophonie* (www.acelf.ca/revue, Vol. XXXV-2, Autumn 2007), and recently published a book on the contribution of the neurosciences to educational and clinical psychology (*Le Cerveau Nomade*, Presses de l'Université d'Ottawa, 2006). She leads the Collectif des Savoirs Apprenants, a SAS^2 Community of Practice involving university researchers and students in the field of education with a common interest in collaborative action-research and systemic change.

Bansi Ghevde is a land-rights activist and member of the Academy of Development Science, a non-governmental organization near Mumbai, India. He has worked for 20 years with Adavasi and small and marginal farmers in Raigad district.

Rajeev Khedkar is a member of the Board of Trustees of the Academy of Development Science (ADS), a non-governmental organization near Mumbai, India. He was the Director of ADS for more than 10 years, and lead the organization's work on traditional medicine and ecological agriculture. The Village Grain Bank program developed by ADS during this time was adopted by the Government of Maharashtra for use in Adavasi communities throughout the state.

Shyamel Panda works with Kajla Jana Kalyan Samity (KJKS), a grassroots organization in the coastal belt of West Bengal, India. He is a farmer and coordinator of action-research activities with small and marginal farmers supported by the non-governmental organization, Development Research, Communication and Services Centre (DRCSC) based in Kolkata.

Dnyaneshwar Patil is the Director of SOBTI, a grassroots organization based in Pali, Maharashtra, India. He is a long-time facilitator of initiatives coming from the *Katkari* Adavasi community in the Pali region.

Diwakar Poudel is an economist with Local Initiatives for Biodiversity Research and Development (LIBIRD), a research-oriented non-governmental organization based in Pokhara, Nepal. He is currently pursuing a PhD in the Department of Economics at the University of Oslo, Norway.

Tek Sapkota is an agronomist with Local Initiatives for Biodiversity Research and Development (LIBIRD), a research-oriented non-governmental organization based in Pokhara, Nepal.

Laura Suazo-Gallardo is a consultant based in Honduras, and the author of *The Human Farm: Transformative Learning among Hillside Honduran Farmers* published in 2002 by Cornell University, Ithaca, New York, and co-author of *Learning from the Past: Lessons on LEIT in the Central Region of Honduras*, published by CIDICCO and ODI in 2005. She coordinated SAS[2] activities in Honduras for IDRC from 2005 to 2007. She began her career as an agronomist and completed a PhD in Education and Development at Cornell University.

Carlos Tapia Jopia is a marine biologist and social psychologist, and is currently at the Department of Psychology of Universidad de La Serena (Chile).

Jorge Téllez is an independent consultant and has recently completed his PhD in Social Forestry at the Universidad de Córdoba, Spain. His work, supported in part by the Centro Boliviano de Estudios Multidisciplinarios (CEBEM), examines the role of dialogue in understanding and negotiating the interests of different groups involved in forestry projects.

About the Authors

Jacques M. Chevalier is Chancellor's Professor in the Department of Sociology and Anthropology and the Institute of Political Economy at Carleton University, Ottawa. He is the author of many scholarly books in fields ranging from Latin American anthropology and development theory (*A Land without Gods: Process Theory, Maldevelopment and the Mexican Nahuas*, co-authored with Daniel J. Buckles, Zed Books, 1995; *Civilization and the Stolen Gift: Capital, Kin and Cult in Eastern Peru*, UTP, 1982) to symbolic analysis and semiotics (*The 3-D Mind*, Volumes 1, 2, and 3, McGill-Queen's University Press, 2002; *The Hot and the Cold: Ills of Humans and Maize in Native Mexico*, co-authored with Andrés Sánchez Bain, UTP, 2002; *A Post-Modern-Revelation: Signs of Astrology and the Apocalypse*, UTP, 1997; and *Semiotics, Romanticism and the Scriptures*, Mouton de Gruyter, 1990).

Daniel J. Buckles is an Adjunct Professor in the Department of Sociology and Anthropology at Carleton University. He is the author of books on indigenous peoples (*A Land without Gods: Process Theory, Maldevelopment and the Mexican Nahuas*, co-authored with Jacques M. Chevalier, Zed Books, 1995), agriculture (*Food Sovereignty and Uncultivated Biodiversity in South Asia*, co-authored with F. Mazhar, P.V. Satheesh, and F. Akhter, Academic Foundation/IDRC, 2007; *Cover Crops in Hillside Agriculture*, co-authored with B. Triomphe and G. Sain, CIMMYT/IDRC, 1998), and conflict management (*Cultivating Peace: Conflict and Collaboration in Natural Resource Management*, World Bank Institute/IDRC, 1999). While a Senior Program Specialist with the International Development Research Centre, he facilitated the development of over 100 research projects in South Asia, Latin America, and Africa. He is an active artist and photographer, and has contributed the photographs included in this volume.